Negotiating the Past in the Past

Negotiating the Past in the Past

Identity, Memory, and Landscape in Archaeological Research

Edited by Norman Yoffee

The University of Arizona Press   Tucson

The University of Arizona Press
© 2007 The Arizona Board of Regents
All rights reserved

Library of Congress Cataloging-in-Publication Data

Negotiating the past in the past : identity, memory, and landscape in archaeological research / edited by Norman Yoffee.
   p. cm.
  Includes bibliographical references and index.
  ISBN 978-0-8165-2670-3 (pbk. : alk. paper)
  1. Social archaeology. 2. Archaeology and history. 3. Archaeology—Research.
4. Civilization, Ancient. 5. Identity (Psychology)—History. 6. Memory—Social aspects—History. 7. Landscape—Social aspects—History. I. Yoffee, Norman.
  CC72.4.N44 2007
  930.1—dc22   2007019334

Manufactured in the United States of America on acid-free, archival-quality paper containing a minimum of 50% post-consumer waste and processed chlorine free.

12 11 10 09 08 07   6 5 4 3 2 1

Contents

1 Peering into the Palimpsest: An Introduction to the Volume   1
Norman Yoffee

2 Collecting, Defacing, Reinscribing (and Otherwise Performing) Memory in the Ancient World   10
Catherine Lyon Crawford

3 Unforgettable Landscapes: Attachments to the Past in Hellenistic Armenia   43
Lori Khatchadourian

4 Mortuary Studies, Memory, and the Mycenaean Polity   76
Seth Button

5 Identity under Construction in Roman Athens   104
Sanjaya Thakur

6 Inscribing the Napatan Landscape: Architecture and Royal Identity   128
Lindsay Ambridge

7 Negotiated Pasts and the Memorialized Present in Ancient India: Chalukyas of Vatapi   155
Hemanth Kadambi

8 Creating, Transforming, Rejecting, and Reinterpreting Ancient Maya Urban Landscapes: Insights from Lagartera and Margarita   183
Laura P. Villamil

9 Back to the Future: From the Past in the Present to the Past in the Past   215
Lynn Meskell

10 Memory Groups and the State: Erasing the Past and Inscribing the Present in the Landscapes of the Mediterranean and Near East   227
Jack L. Davis

About the Editor   257
About the Contributors   259
Index   261

Negotiating the Past in the Past

1 Peering into the Palimpsest
AN INTRODUCTION TO THE VOLUME

Norman Yoffee

The first emperor of China was apparently history's first great book burner. Not content to obliterate the literate record of the past, he also destroyed ancient objects in his zeal to portray himself as the creator of an utterly new form of society, indeed, of history itself. Subsequent historians of the Han dynasty, however, returned to the past (which they molded and created) as the necessary prologue to the present and seamless justification for their own dynasty. The Confucian classics in particular were the key to the idea of the state, and the literati system based on them was integral to its proper functioning.

One might generalize that the present is, among other things, always a battleground about the interpretation of the events and meaning of the past. That is, the present is constructed, in part, by beliefs of how things were, and so how they should or should not be. The past must be subjugated and harnessed in order to create the social order of the present.

Archaeologists know this especially well. In the last decade or so, archaeologists have investigated how we in the present have built our identities by using the past (e.g., Kohl and Fawcett, eds., 1995; Meskell, ed., 1998; and the inspiration for many of those works, Lowenthal 1985). However, archaeologists have only recently recognized and begun to study how the past was used in the past itself, although it seems perfectly obvious to all archaeologists that such must have been the case.

Archaeology and archaeological theory are fast-changing fields. In two relatively recent and excellent books on the history of archaeological theory, by Gordon Willey and Jeremy Sabloff, *A History of American Archaeology* (1980, 2nd edition), and by Bruce Trigger, *A History of Archaeological Thought* (1989), the authors devoted little space to archaeological studies of identity, memory, and landscape (hereafter IML). Of course, in archaeological theory–years, 1980 is eons ago, and 1989 millennia in the past. In a collection of essays published in 2001, *Archaeology at the*

Millennium (but which must have been written at least a year or two earlier—and mainly by American archaeologists), which attempted to gauge old and new directions of archaeological research, the editors, Gary Feinman and Douglas Price, were untroubled by the omission of our IML topics. By 2001, however, archaeological studies of landscape were not rare (e.g., Bender, ed., 1993; Tilley 1994). In Ian Hodder's collection of essays (written mainly by British archaeologists) taking the pulse of archaeological theory, also published in 2001 (but, again, written at least a year earlier), two essays were devoted to identity and landscape. Studies on social memory in archaeology were still to appear in the new millennium.

No course on, or survey of, modern archaeological theory today would exclude IML studies and would certainly include the following works: *Archaeologies of Landscape*, edited by Wendy Ashmore and A. Bernard Knapp (1999); *An Archaeology of Natural Places* and *The Significance of Monuments*, by Richard Bradley (2000 and 1998 respectively); *Archaeologies of the Greek Past: Landscape, Monuments, and Memories*, by Susan Alcock (2002); *The Political Landscape*, by Adam T. Smith (2003); "The Intersection of Politics and Identity" by Lynn Meskell (2002); and *Archaeologies of Memory*, edited by Ruth M. Van Dyke and Susan E. Alcock (2003). Ruggedly progressive journals such as the *Cambridge Archaeological Journal*, *Archaeological Dialogues*, and the *Norwegian Archaeological Review* have in recent issues published literally dozens of articles on IML.

In winter semester 2004 I convened a seminar at the University of Michigan to discuss "Identity, Memory, and Landscape in Archaeological Theory." Participants included classical, Near Eastern, and anthropological archaeologists (to identify them through their formal departmental affiliations). We wanted to examine what these new IML studies were contributing to our understanding of the past and what were the influences of historians like Simon Schama (1996), cultural anthropologists like Keith Basso (1996), and geographers like Edward Soja (2000) on archaeologists who were citing them as inspirations. We also surveyed "neo-canonical" readings about the "invention of tradition" (Hobsbawm and Ranger 1983) and communities that are "imagined" (Anderson 1983).[1] Why have such works led archaeologists increasingly to studies of identity, the cultural meanings of natural and built landscapes, and in general to the use of the past in the past that archaeologists had always to some extent realized but were now focusing on? We quickly observed that most of the studies before us were programmatic, that is, calling for new work, but seldom offering substantive examples from archaeological research. We also wanted to consider the *relations* among issues of identity, memory, and landscape that had mainly been kept separate (with the exception of Susan Alcock's work).

Although the ideal of "holistic" analysis has meant various things to archaeologists, we concluded that it is impossible to study identity, memory, and landscape as if they were separate categories. The chapters in this volume exemplify the interrelations of IML in two ways. First, as stressed in landscape studies, the actions and routines both of everyday life and of high ceremony are structured in space. Space consists, of course, in both natural and constructed terrain as people live among monuments, ruins, and environments all of which are the seats of stories about events and personalities. Landscapes, thus, form the material of "memory communities" (as Alcock, using Maurice Halbwachs's term, puts it), and such communities provide important aspects of people's identities. These identities then "overarch" other, local identities; the landscapes of everyday life are the sites where the various and diverse levels of identity are negotiated.

Memories are also "performed" in space through the use of artifacts, heirlooms, and spolia in new places and in abandoned places. People make choices of which part of the past to accommodate and which to reject and how the past can be, within limits, created. Our authors discuss "strategies of forgetting" and how identities are transformed through the use and modification of certain spaces and of selected objects. They consider how "acts of remembering" are constructed, sometimes as innovations, and how objects are altered in order to accentuate their meaning or give them new meanings. These transformations are especially visible in times of transition, that is, during sociocultural and political change, and such change cannot be understood without reference to how the past was framed in service of the new present.

Second, our authors argue that holistic studies of identity, memory, and landscape *do not* and *should not* represent a new "paradigm" (or theory) in archaeological research. Rather, we see IML studies as a new point-of-entry for archaeological studies, especially as a break from older preoccupations with finding "types" of societies in the archaeological record. (I have spoken for myself on this topic in *Myths of the*

Archaic State: Evolution of the Earliest Cities, States, and Civilizations [2005]). That is, IML studies move investigators away from typological abstractions and toward research into how people lived and understood their lives. IML studies, which focus on the rich data concerning beliefs and experiences, cannot lead in and of themselves to explanations of the causes and effects of all change. Using IML perspectives, however, archaeologists can better probe how and why things changed as they did—as active processes of adoption and/or rejection of ideas, and not as inevitable outcomes of social or environmental circumstances, no matter how powerful they were, that were unmediated by human agency.

Let me present one generalization and then a brief series of examples in order to illustrate these points. First, the construction of memory in the past existed just as it does in the present. It involved creating links to ancestors and antiquity and entailed the (re)interpretation of history, monuments, and landscapes. Especially in times of social change, individuals who belonged to multiple and overlapping groups had to negotiate their economic and social status to the extent possible, as Eric Wolf (1990) suggested (paraphrasing): exploiting the ambiguities of inherited forms, evaluating their options, borrowing ideas from other groups and from their own pasts, and creating new identities to answer to changing circumstances. Although today's globalization studies are (rightly) concerned with how modern, multinational corporations alter or destroy traditional neighborhoods, behaviors, and cultural ways, archaeologists can show how what we think of as "traditional" was formed and reformed over time: no tradition is outside of history.

Saddam Hussein's use of images of Mesopotamian rulers and the restoration of ancient places to link him as the rightful heir to rule in Iraq was only the latest attempt by a ruler of historic Mesopotamia to justify his seizure of power as the fulfillment of divine ordinance and the logic of history. The use of artifacts was critical to the needed symbolism. For example, Hammurabi's code of laws was erected on a stela and written in an archaic script that would have been legible only to the most highly trained of scribes. One audience for the stela was the gods themselves, a most serious audience for ancient kings. When kings carved inscriptions into nearly inaccessible mountainsides, which were barely visible from below (but even this had an effect on the few and distant viewers), or applied texts on paving stones or on statues that then were placed in walls, the only readers were the gods.

When the stelae bearing Hammurabi's code were captured by an Elamite king from Iran about 600 years after Hammurabi's death, in 1750 BC, Elamite scribes set about installing their own inscription on the stelae. Amorite rulers of Mesopotamia (like Hammurabi) wrote only in Sumerian and Akkadian, the traditional languages of Mesopotamia; and Kassites, whose names betray their native, non-Mesopotamian language, revived the venerable Sumerian language for their inscriptions although no one had spoken Sumerian for at least 500 years at the time of their rule in the mid-second millennium BC. In the first millennium BC, Neo-Babylonian rulers such as Nabonidus not only produced inscriptions in the style of Hammurabi but also piously excavated cities and flourished material from his claimed distant ancestors. As Zainab Bahrani (1998) has wittily observed, current exhibitions in the United States and in Europe of Mesopotamian artifacts that were found in Iran carefully and pointedly document the Elamite illegal seizure of Mesopotamian materials and their haughty display in ancient Iran, which glorified the power of Iranian Elamite rulers over Mesopotamia and its ancient culture. Modern American and European curators seem immune to the irony that these materials were also excavated/seized, this time from Iran, and displayed today in Western museums as symbols of the power of Western countries and as testimony to the skills of their archaeological researchers.

Modern archaeologists are not only able to perceive the use of the past in the past but also to be self-critical about their own activities in providing a past for present uses. The days of archaeologists viewing themselves as dispassionate detectives of past lifeways is over for two reasons: archaeologists undertake research inspired by fashionable and fundable academic research agendas and for career advancement, which is abundantly clear. Archaeologists also have responsibilities in monitoring the depiction of an admittedly unstable past, but which is often manipulated by modern politicians and by more or less venal authors and filmmakers, who have little interest in seeing the past in its own terms. The past lives as many lives in the present as it did in the past.

The chapters in this volume concern the archaeologies of the eastern Mediterranean, including Mesopotamia, Iran, Greece, and Rome (by Catherine Lyon Crawford); prehistoric Greece (by Seth Button), Achaemenid and Hellenistic Armenia (by Lori Khatchadourian); Athens in the Roman period (by Sanjaya Thakur); in Nubia and Egypt (by Lindsay Ambridge); in medieval south India (by Hemanth Kadambi); and in northern Maya Qintana Roo (by Laura P. Villamil). Since these chapters are discussed by Lynn Meskell and Jack Davis, archaeologists who have written about identity, memory, and landscape in their own work, I need not provide digests of the chapters here. Main themes include how and why certain versions of the past were promoted while others were (aggressively) forgotten so as to promote innovation. Memories were common threads that held people together in acts of remembrance, but the past of some people could be rejected in order to create ties with the pasts of others, often for political advantage in the creation of new identities. Ancient societies can hardly be understood as "integrated" since there are many social orientations and identities in all societies, and these are often contested, fragile, and transformable. Artifacts have lives after their creation, especially as sites of memory (in museums, galleries, and collections), and memory could be performed to transfer the meaning of objects and monuments to new audiences. Finally, ancient societies cannot be adequately appreciated solely in political and economic terms.

As in any good seminar and volume, the chapters are products of cross-fertilization, and they have been read and critiqued by all the authors, who refer frequently to chapters in this volume.

Finally, there are two subtexts in this book that I want to declare. First, in the diverse chapters that are written by apprentice archaeologists from various university departments, there is a commonality of purpose in the investigations of how the past was negotiated and used in the past. That is, there is no "great tradition versus the great divide," as Colin Renfrew (1980) ruefully articulated in considering distinctions between classical archaeology and anthropological archaeology (Cherry, Margomenou, and Talalay 2005). Anthropological archaeologists, furthermore, are increasingly literate in case studies from the ancient world that employ and evaluate historical texts alongside material culture. These include research in ancient Egypt, the Near East, and China, as well as investigations of the Maya, Aztecs, Incas, Greeks, and Romans (Yoffee and Crowell 2006) and in South Asia (Ray and Sinopoli 2004).

The chapters in this volume are enriched by relevant cross-cultural comparisons in historical archaeology.

Second, we want to be clear that in this book we neither adopt any single thesis nor do we test any model. Furthermore, we do not march under any banner or exemplify any brand of archaeological theory, as I have already noted. Rather, our authors in the volume, using old and new data sets, innovatively examine how people constructed and gave meaning to their natural and built environments, how they privileged aspects of their personas at the expense of other aspects, and why people chose to regard their pasts in the ways they did. They also seek to understand who controlled which landscapes, identities, and memories and how these were or were not contested (or even contestable).

The young chapter authors in this volume not only zestfully signpost new and significant trends in archaeological research, but they also expand the disciplinary boundaries of our field.

Note

1. We read John Fritz's essay (1978) on landscape and ideology at Chaco Canyon as an early classic archaeological article on landscape. I had envisioned using this article, which was ignored and even lampooned by "processual" archaeologists, as part of a discussion on how IML studies fit or did not fit into debates between "processual" and "postprocessual" archaeologists. The seminarians were utterly bored by the idea of this discussion and thought that such allegiance to these self-proclaimed paradigms was of little interest to modern graduate students. Indeed, IML studies, by drawing attention to how the past was accommodated, respected, and creatively altered and forgotten, obviated tedious arguments over the correctness of "schools" of archaeological theory.

Bibliography

Alcock, Susan E. 2002. *Archaeologies of the Greek Past: Landscape, Monuments, and Memories*. Cambridge: Cambridge University Press.

Anderson, Benedict. 1983. *Imagined Communities: Reflections on the Origin and Spread of Nationalism*. London: Verso.

Ashmore, Wendy, and A. Bernard Knapp, eds. 1999. *Archaeologies of Landscape: Comparative Perspectives*. Oxford: Blackwell.

Bahrani, Zainab. 1998. Conjuring Mesopotamia: Imaginative Geography and a World Past. In *Archaeology Under Fire: Nationalism, Politics, and Heritage in the Eastern Mediterranean and the Middle East*, ed. Lynn Meskell, 159–74. London: Routledge.

Basso, Keith. 1996. *Wisdom Sits in Places*. Albuquerque: University of New Mexico Press.

Bender, Barbara, ed. 1993. *Landscape: Politics and Perspectives*. Oxford: Berg.

Bradley, Richard. 1998. *The Significance of Monuments*. London: Routledge.

—— 2000. *An Archaeology of Natural Places*. London: Routledge.

Cherry, John, Despina Margomenou, and Lauren Talalay. 2005. *Prehistorians Round the Pond: Reflections on Aegean Prehistory as a Discipline*. Ann Arbor, Mich.: Kelsey Museum of Archaeology.

Feinman, Gary, and Douglas Price, eds. 2001. *Archaeology at the Millennium: A Sourcebook*. New York: Kluwer Academic/Plenum.

Fritz, John. 1978. Paleopsychology Today: Ideational Systems and Human Adaptation in Prehistory. In *Social Archaeology: Beyond Subsistence and Dating*, eds. Charles Redman et al., 37–59. New York: Academic Press.

Halbwachs, Maurice. 1992. *On Collective Memory*. Ed. and trans. Lewis A. Coser. Chicago: University of Chicago Press.

Hobsbawm, Eric, and Terence Ranger, eds. 1983. *The Invention of Tradition*. Cambridge: Cambridge University Press.

Hodder, Ian, ed. 2001. *Archaeological Theory Today*. Oxford: Polity Press.

Kohl, Philip, and Clare Fawcett, eds. 1995. *Nationalism, Politics, and the Practice of Archaeology*. Cambridge: Cambridge University Press.

Lowenthal, David. 1985. *The Past Is a Foreign Country*. Cambridge: Cambridge University Press.

Meskell, Lynn. 1998. ed., *Archaeology Under Fire: Nationalism, Politics, and Heritage in the Eastern Mediterranean and the Middle East*. London: Routledge.

—— 2002. The Intersection of Politics and Identity. *Annual Review of Anthropology* 31:279–301.

Ray, Himanshu Prabha, and Carla M. Sinopoli, eds. 2004. *Archaeology as History in Early South Asia*. New Delhi: Aryan Books International.

Renfrew, Colin. 1980. The Great Tradition Versus the Great Divide: Archaeology as Anthropology? *American Journal of Archaeology* 84:287–98.

Schama, Simon. 1996. *Landscape and Memory*. New York: Vintage Books.

Smith, Adam T. 2003. *The Political Landscape*. Berkeley: University of California Press.

Soja, Edward W. 2000. *Postmetropolis: Critical Studies of Cities and Regions*. Oxford: Blackwell.

Tilley, Christopher. 1994. *A Phenomenology of Landscape: Places, Paths, and Monuments*. Oxford: Berg.

Trigger, Bruce. 1989. *A History of Archaeological Thought*. Cambridge: Cambridge University Press.

Van Dyke, Ruth M., and Susan E. Alcock, eds. 2003. *Archaeologies of Memory*. Malden, Mass.: Blackwell.

Willey, Gordon, and Jeremy Sabloff. 1980. *A History of American Archaeology*. 2nd ed. San Francisco: W. H. Freeman.

Wolf, Eric. 1990. Facing Power: Old Insights, New Questions. *American Anthropologist* 92:586–96.

Yoffee, Norman. 2005. *Myths of the Archaic State: Evolution of the Earliest Cities, States, and Civilizations*. Cambridge: Cambridge University Press.

Yoffee, Norman, and Bradley L. Crowell, eds. 2006. *Excavating Asian History: Interdisciplinary Studies in Archaeology and History*. Tucson: University of Arizona Press.

2 Collecting, Defacing, Reinscribing (and Otherwise Performing) Memory in the Ancient World

Catherine Lyon Crawford

My first encounter with the Stele of Naram-Sin (fig. 2.1) was in an introductory archaeology class. The class discussed this famous monument primarily through an historical and art historical framework: we learned that the monumental and virile figure of Naram-Sin (reigned 2254–2218 BC), wearing the horned helmet of divine authority, provided a conscious visual cue elevating the status of the ruler to that of a god. Lectures and textbooks provided the historical facts relating to the stele's creation: it was commissioned to celebrate the king's military victory over the Lullubi, and then erected in the central Mesopotamian city of Sippar (fig. 2.2).

It was not until much later that I learned that this monument to Akkadian greatness had actually been excavated in Susa, an Elamite city (in Iran) that thrived nearly a millennium after Naram-Sin's death. A well-preserved inscription of the Elamite king, Shutruk-Nahhunte (reigned 1185–1155 BC) explains this mystery: he brought the stele to Susa after destroying Sippar (Harper 1992, 168). In other words, when excavators found this monument on the Susa acropolis in 1898, it was clearly a piece of war booty. In fact, this was only one of several fine Mesopotamian objects that had been captured and brought to the Elamite capital over the course of Shutruk-Nahhunte's reign.

The circumstances surrounding the removal of this stele to Susa raise several questions that this chapter will investigate. Why did the Elamite king bring this stele back to his homeland? Simply to move the stele itself—a solid stone slab nearly two meters high—the 300 miles from Sippar to Susa would have been a significant undertaking; surely its removal to Susa constituted something more than mere royal whim (Bahrani 2003, 162). What significance did it have in its new context? How was this object handled once captured by the Elamites? Was it damaged, and if so, why? What is the significance of the lengthy Elamite

FIGURE 2.1 Stele of Naram-Sin, from Susa, Louvre, Paris (photo: Lewandowski. Art Resource)

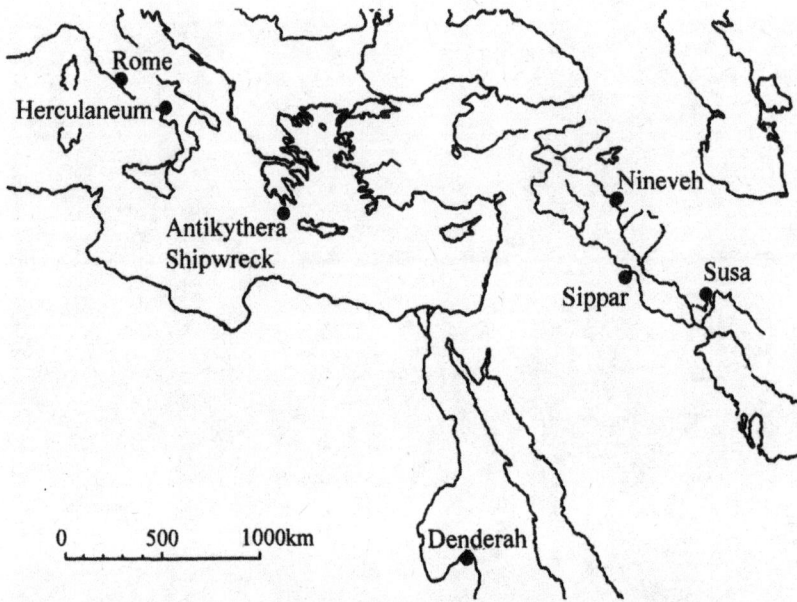

FIGURE 2.2 Map of the Mediterranean and Near Eastern regions

inscription that tells of its capture and rededication to the Elamite god Inshushinak?

The conventional answer to each of these questions would be that the capture and reerection of Naram-Sin's victory monument was an act of legitimization and appropriation: that through such a display of the spoils of a victorious war, Shutruk-Nahhunte conveyed his power both to his own people and to the conquered Babylonians. For the most part, such an analysis seems uncontroversial, but it leaves an important underlying question unanswered: why would such a process of cultural appropriation "legitimize" local power?

I propose that memory (both collective and individual) is integral to this process of legitimization and assimilation. If the basis of legitimized power lies in the minds and attitudes of both ruler and ruled, memory becomes an essential component of legitimization. Material culture provides the ability to manipulate memories. The meaning of a collection such as the Mesopotamian objects from Susa was created again and again in the minds of the royal conquerors, of the defeated Babylonians, and of the Elamite viewers, and these meanings likely had everything to do with the memory of the past and its associations to the present. Despite the close cultural ties and somewhat shared history among these Mesopotamian peoples, the various "memory communities" (Burke 1989; Alcock 2002, 15–16) that they comprised probably had vastly different feelings about the seizure of Naram-Sin's stele. Rather than attempting to unpack these competing sets of memories, however, I will focus only on particular actors and the objects acted upon, since they are the most accessible archaeologically. It is this intersection of actor, object, and memory that forms the basis of this chapter.

Object Biographies and Memory Performances

The physicality of objects allows for their manipulation—both in terms of spatial setting and physical appearance. Objects are central to the human experience; Pearce has suggested that part of our self-recognition as human beings has to do with the physical manipulation of the material world (Pearce 1995, 17). Csikszentmihalyi (1993, 22) likewise proposes that the relationship between humans and objects serves to order and stabilize the mind. Objects thus help us to keep ideas straight, order temporal events, and avoid psychic entropy.

> Artifacts help objectify the self in at least three major ways. They do so first by demonstrating the owner's power, vital erotic energy, and place in the social hierarchy. Second, objects reveal the continuity of the self through time, by providing foci of involvement in the present, mementoes and souvenirs of the past, and signposts to future goals. Third, objects give concrete evidence of one's place in a social network as symbols (literally the joining together) of valued relationships. (Csikszentmihalyi 1993, 23)

While arguably not all objects fulfill all or any of these roles, I draw attention to Csikszentmihalyi's second point—that objects "reveal the continuity of the self through time, by providing foci of involvement in the present, mementoes and souvenirs of the past, and signposts to future goals" (1993, 23). This is the arena in which memory and the object intersect. Through such "foci of involvement," we are able to relate ourselves equally to past, present, and future, and a single meaningful artifact has the potential to simultaneously signify all three periods of time.

Ancient-art historians have long been familiar with the way that ancient peoples manipulated the past in their artistic endeavors, something very much akin to more recent discussions of memory among anthropologists and archaeologists. Images that refer to past events and legends are commonplace in art of most periods. Often such allusions also take on political significance—an iconography of legitimization (Root 1979; Zanker 1988). Generally, however, analyses of ancient art focus on the design and creation of art objects—the desires of patrons and artists, and the original contexts in which those objects were located. The later significance of such objects to an ever-changing audience has received less attention.

For the present set of questions, however, it is precisely these oft-neglected "after-lives" that are vitally important. Recently archaeologists have begun to look to material culture and its uses as entry points for a discussion of memory in the ancient world (Alcock 2002; Van Dyke and Alcock 2003; Joyce 2003; Meskell 2004); the reuse of material in later periods forms an important facet of this scholarship. Object histories provide an avenue for investigating value and meaning within the material record. As Arjun Appadurai states in his influential 1986 article, "We have to follow the things themselves, *for their meanings are inscribed in their forms*, their uses, their trajectories. It is only through the analysis of these trajectories that we can interpret the human transactions and calculations that enliven things," (Appadurai 1986, 5; my emphasis).

Artifacts have meaning, not from some intrinsic quality of craftsmanship or artisanship, but from the palimpsest of past associations and relationships with people, their "object biography" (Kopytoff 1986). The interdependence of humans and their material world forms the core of Lynn Meskell's recent book on objects in Egypt, although she also warns against essentializing these relationships (Meskell 2004, 5). Because objects are "culturally constructed to connote and consolidate the possession of past events associated with their use or ownership" (Rowlands 1993, 44), object life histories and memory are inextricably linked.

Due to this accumulation of different meanings over time, the memories associated with a particular object are mutable and transient. They can change with ownership, audience, time, and place, and with cultural context.

Many of these "life events" are invisible in the archaeological record. Yet there are moments when, due to the physicality of an artifact, archaeology can pinpoint certain moments in its life history. It can be moved, destroyed, mutilated, repaired, collected, inscribed, preserved, reinscribed, and so forth. Such actions imprint the object with a set of meanings and memories. The act of changing the physicality of an object constitutes a "performance of memory," which crystallizes this shifting bed of meaning at a very specific point in time and place. These consecutive and compounded "memory performances" or "memory acts" are thus what create the life history of the object.

Over the millennia, much—even most—of an object's biography will have been long forgotten, but there are glimpses of memory being performed from prehistory through historical time, and from Mesopotamia to Rome. These memory acts provide a methodological avenue for viewing human and social contexts through a process of reversal pinpointed by Appadurai (1986, 5): even though people originally encoded these objects with meaning, it is these very "things-in-motion" that illuminate their cultural significance.

In her 2004 book, Meskell stresses that each performance of memory is unique to its own time and space. To better illustrate both the contrasting and complementary ways that objects serve as foci for the performance of memory in the ancient world, the case studies contained in this chapter cover an enormous expanse of time and space. Though such a structure allows for only a brief overview of each individual object, this is hopefully balanced by the exploration of memory performances in a wide variety of settings. Individual case studies of object biographies and the memories associated with them appear from time to time in the archaeological literature (see especially Langdon 2001; Joyce 2003), but there have been far fewer synthetic studies that examine these issues from a wider perspective. While the following can only be considered a prolegomenon to such studies in the future, I do aim to demonstrate how the motivations and meanings involved in memory performances change—sometimes drastically—with context.

The memory performances presented in this chapter fall naturally into three different groups: collecting and abducting, erasing and defacing, and reinscribing and replacing. Within each area I adduce several examples of artifacts that allow me to develop these themes in slightly different directions. Students and scholars of classical and Near Eastern antiquity will likely be familiar with most of the objects and monuments to be discussed, and they have been selected for this very reason. A reframing of familiar material can shed new light even on those objects that fill the pages of introductory textbooks.

Collecting and Abducting

In speaking of modern collecting practices, Susan Pearce singles out the element of choice. A collection is thus a group of objects that have "been selected out and set apart from the ordinary consuming processes of life," (Pearce 1995, 24). This "separateness" is perhaps the defining characteristic of any collection, indicative of a process that she likens to a passage from the profane to the sacred. In the same selection process, certain objects become valuable for reasons that become clear as one studies the biographies of those objects. "Collections occupy a particular position in the processes by which value is created, because value is, to a considerable extent, a creation of the imagination rather than of need; and in the play of the imagination the objects themselves are powerful actors" (Pearce 1995, 27).

What remains implicit and unexpressed in these characterizations of collections, however, is the element of memory. Memory is often the imaginative element that makes a collection more than the sum of its parts. It is integral to the process of making meaning from objects. Through the act of collecting and gathering, the relationships of objects both to space and person are drastically altered. The act of acquiring objects and creating a collection (in its broadest sense) need not always constitute a performance of memory, but I will look at three examples from the ancient world where this seems to be the case: the library of Assurbanipal at Nineveh, the Mesopotamian plunder from Susa, and Roman collections of classical and Hellenistic Greek art.

Assurbanipal's Library

The library of the Assyrian king Assurbanipal (reigned 668–627 BC) at Nineveh is rightly famous. We are fortunate to have these collections of cuneiform tablets substantially intact after the fire that destroyed the palace in 612 BC. Approximately 30,000 tablets and fragments have been found in the various archives at Nineveh, although it is not certain how many different texts these fragments comprised (Parpola 1983, 6). The vast majority of these tablets are examples of Mesopotamian (especially Babylonian) scientific and religious professional texts and treatises; only a handful of tablets and boards contain what today might be considered literature—stories, myths, epics, and so on (Parpola 1983, 6).

In Parpola's investigation of a series of tablets that record large acquisitions to the library, he shows that texts came to Nineveh in a variety of ways. First were the texts produced and copied within the palace itself; these are easily recognizable by the elaborate colophons at the end of each tablet that give certain details about that particular tablet. Other acquisitions came from private collections, probably donated voluntarily (Assurbanipal's brother is mentioned as one of the contributors), although there is also ample evidence for texts arriving at Nineveh in accordance with a royal demand. This was almost certainly the case in a letter to the governor of Borsippa that orders the confiscation of works from both temple and private libraries for inclusion in the Ninevite archives (Parpola 1983, 11). Finally, the dates of some of these acquisitions correlate to the months following war with Babylonia, and Parpola notes that many of these seem to be Babylonian texts (Parpola 1983, 11). These texts, then, came to Assyria as the spoils of war.

Assurbanipal's library illustrates the multitude of ways that collections in antiquity could have been amassed: war, private production, private donation, and confiscation. It must be noted that libraries and archives were not uncommon in ancient Mesopotamia (Grayson 1991, 227); nor did Assurbanipal initiate the building of the library—there was already a royal archive at Nineveh. What make Assurbanipal's acquisitions unique are their sheer number and his drive to acquire them (Grayson 1991, 228).

What motivated the king to gather these texts from all parts of Assyria and Babylonia? The contents of the library give at least one clue: the majority of these texts—omens, lexical works, religious texts, and scientific texts—represent a huge body of arcane and priestly knowledge. One might well imagine that the king saw a need to organize and preserve this knowledge.

The colophon at the end of each text prepared at Nineveh provides a second clue. Although several standard colophons were in use, the longest type points to religion as a major motivating factor in the collection of these texts.

> Written and collated according to its ancient form. I, Assurbanipal, king of all, king of Assyria. On whom Nabu and Tashmetu [the god of writing and his consort] have bestowed keen intelligence [literally a "broad ear"] and clear eyes to grasp the most precious parts of scribal knowledge, who amongst the kings who preceded me no one understood this matter. I wrote on the tablets the wisdom of Nabu, the pricking in of cuneiform signs as many as there are, and I checked and collated them. I placed them for futurity in the library of the temple of my lord, Nabu, the Great Lord, which is within Nineveh, for my life, for the guarding of my soul, that I might not have illness, and for making firm the foundation of my royal throne. O Nabu, look with gladness, and ever bless my kingship. Whenever I call on you, take my hand. While I walk about in your House, guard my steps continually. When this work is put in your House, and placed in front of you, look on it and remember me with favor. (Saggs 1984, 281)

This colophon presents a unique opportunity to study the impetus behind an ancient collection. Clearly, Assurbanipal hoped for spiritual and temporal blessings from Nabu as a reward for organizing this library. "[The tablets] contained the wisdom of Nabu, and to preserve them and be associated with them brought merit and reward from the god," (Saggs 1984, 281). However, these blessings also seem to stem from the texts themselves, many of which contained powerful knowledge—omens, rituals, incantations, and so on. This knowledge is what the king hoped to preserve. The library was a repository of past learning and wisdom, a potential site of history and memory.

The Stele of Naram-Sin and Mesopotamian Booty in Elam

The Stele of Naram-Sin stems from a rather different sort of collection. Though Assurbanipal's library included tablets taken from a defeated enemy, it seems that no special importance was attached to those that were spoils of war. The opposite is true of the Mesopotamian objects gathered at Susa, where war booty seems to have been prized on a more symbolic level. These objects, unearthed in the French excavations of

1898, included *kudurrus* (boundary stones), stone tablets, the Stele of Naram-Sin, a Kassite monument to which Shutruk-Nahhunte added his own image, and probably the "Law Code" of Hammurabi (Potts 1999, 233). It is clear from the inscriptions on many of these objects that they were brought back to Susa as war booty from Shutruk-Nahhunte's conquests in Babylonia in 1158 BC (Potts 1999, 233; Harper 1992, 159; Bahrani 2003, 156). Some of these objects may have been acquired by later kings (Potts 1999, 234), but what remains important is the tradition of acquiring and reerecting war booty at Susa.

Unfortunately, the exact location of the objects in Susa—a vital piece of information for investigating audience and the politics of display—is not clear. The early excavations indicate only that many of these monuments came from trenches 7 and 7α, which were each ninety meters long and five meters wide. Part of these trenches, however, uncovered an extensive pavement just south of the temple of Inshushinak (Harper 1992, 161), and it is likely that at least some of these objects were associated with the temple grounds. Support for such an argument comes from the final sections of the Elamite inscriptions on several of these monuments: "I have offered it to [placed it before?] Inshushinak, my god" (Harper 1992, 172).

Why were these objects brought to Susa? While Harper (1992, 159) suggested that the Elamites brought these monuments back to Susa unharmed in an effort to "preserve" them, Bahrani's subsequent examination of the objects themselves opens up alternate avenues for investigation. Her close inspection of the overall surface condition led her to propose that the deterioration of the Akkadian inscription of Naram-Sin was the result of intentional erasure at the hands of Shutruk-Nahhunte rather than natural erosion (Bahrani 2003, 156). If so, then clearly this destruction was a purposeful act, and the mutilation of the objects was more than accidental wartime violence (Bahrani 2003, 162). In fact, the common practice of abducting royal statuary was an act of psychological and magical warfare rather than random plunder. As will be discussed in greater detail in the following section, images of gods and kings often stand in for the deity or person him/herself. Thus, "The image replaced the king. Its capture replaced his capture. Therefore, the statue was the king's substitute" (Bahrani 2003, 179).

Part of the importance of this object was almost certainly its association with Naram-Sin, who had ruled an empire the equal of his grandfather,

Sargon, extending from Cyprus to Elam, where Susa now stood (Bahrani 2003, 156). Indeed, a large part of the allure of this monument may have been its association with a past conqueror of the region. The importance of Naram-Sin in the mind-set of subsequent Mesopotamian conquerors (including Shutruk-Nahhunte) probably cannot be understated—Bahrani makes the point that, in its original location in Sippar, the stele was certainly admired "not just for its antiquity but venerated as a monument of a powerful ancestral king" (Bahrani 2003, 156). Thus, in the case of the Stele of Naram-Sin and probably many of the other monuments brought to Susa, it is the memory of the abducted king and the control of his image that makes such memory performances particularly powerful. The reerection of this war booty acted as a "memory transfer," in which the memories, powers, and relationships associated with the former possessor became the property and prerogative of the new one—in this case, the Elamite king, and the gods of Elam.

Roman Collecting

Two examples from the Roman world indicate just how important cultural context is for the assessment of memory performance in the ancient world. Seen together, the group of statues from the shipwreck near Antikythera and the sculptural assemblage from the Villa dei Papiri near Herculaneum tell a complicated story of collection and emulation in the last centuries BC and the first centuries AD. Though collecting plunder for display in sanctuaries (as must have been the case at Susa) had long been part of the greater Mediterranean cultural milieu, the Romans took this practice to a new level.

After the sack of Syracuse in 211 BC and that of Corinth in 146 BC, classical and Hellenistic Greek art flooded into Italy (Pape 1975). We gain a glimpse of this constant flow of art, especially sculpture, from east to west through Republican-period shipwrecks. Perhaps the most famous of these was discovered in 1900 near the island of Antikythera. This wreck provides invaluable evidence for classical and Hellenistic marble and bronze statues. While the bronze statue of an athlete (fig. 2.3) is the most familiar statue from the wreck, it was only one piece of a statue-laden cargo. Bol suggests, in fact, that at least some of the pieces were from a four-horse chariot group, the size and value of

FIGURE 2.3 The "Antikythera Youth," National Museum, Athens (Bol 1972, pl. 6)

which suggest that it may have been removed and transported at the behest of the Roman government (1972, 120).

That the ship was bound for Italy seems clear from its find spot south of the Peloponnesus. Though Bol argues that these statues may have been booty, since the date of the wreck (ca. 80 BC) coincides well with the end of the Mithridatic Wars (1972, 108), the letters of Cicero also provide evidence for the importation and purchase of Greek art at this time. In either case, the Antikythera wreck helps to illustrate the transport of art from east to west on a large scale, probably at the highest levels of society.

In the beginning, the Romans increasingly built public buildings for the display of sculptures, paintings, and other objects captured from the enemy (Strong 1994). Strabo (6.381) comments that after the sack of Corinth, massive quantities of art soon decorated the greatest number and best of the public monuments of Rome. The wealth of material soon extended into the private sphere, and it is important to note that not all Romans reacted to this influx of Greek art in the same way. Republican authors would debate the moral implications of Roman collecting for many years. Some, like Cato the Elder, saw the taste for Greek art as a potential sign of decadence and corruption; others, like Cicero, saw in Greek art a refinement and sophistication that was eminently appealing.

Despite these societal tensions, Greek art became a symbol of wealth, erudition, and leisure that recalled the pinnacle of classical Greek culture (Bartman 1991). While the existence of Roman "art collections" in the modern sense remains debatable (Neudecker 1998, 77), there seems to be little argument that obtaining certain types of artworks accrued status to the owner. In some cases, at least, such acts of acquisition were almost certainly "supplemented by an emotional remembrance of the original places of cult and culture in Greece" (Neudecker 1998, 78). The acquisition of such works performed memory in the broadest sense by associating the new owner with the aura of a past, respected culture.

As the supply of plunder began to be exhausted, the demand for Greek art increased, and collectors found new avenues for expanding their collections. During the late Republican Period, in fact, an "art market" appeared for the first time in Western history (Pollitt 1978, 162). Jerome Pollitt explains this shift from plunder to purchase.

All of this emanated from the fact that upper class Romans who had once been free to seize Greek art were now content to buy it in order to adorn their townhouses and villas. The great private collections of the time apparently drew not only upon the limited reservoir of earlier Greek masterpieces that happened to be available but also on works by contemporary artists. (1978, 162)

Thus was born a tradition of creating Roman artwork in classical and Hellenistic styles, commonly called "Roman copies" (Bieber 1977). To what extent such works were actual copies of earlier artworks or Roman reinterpretations of traditional Hellenic themes, subjects, and forms is still very much under discussion (Perry 2005; Gazda 2002), but it is the practice of looking backward to some cultural conception of "Greece" that is of concern here. Sculptural examples of such Roman mediations of Greek culture are omnipresent in modern museums, and I suggest that these reflect a series of memory acts, which, while initially rooted in the actual movement of objects, ended with self-replicating memory performances that could be divorced from the realm of the object into the realm of the idea.

One well-known collection that illustrates the apparent allure of Greek art from every period is that from the Villa dei Papiri, near Herculaneum (Mattusch 2004; Warden and Romano 1994; Wojcik 1986). This villa, which provided the model for the modern-day Getty Museum in Malibu, California, was buried by the eruption of Vesuvius in AD 79, and contained twenty-four bronze and fifty-one marble pieces of statuary—by far one of the most extensive sculptural assemblages that have so far come to light. Attempts at discerning a programmatic "theme" for this collection have been generally unsuccessful (Bartman 1991), but there is little question that Hellenic influences pervade the artworks. This is not to say, however, that all, or even a single one, of the sculptures from the peristyle of the villa were imported from Greece. In fact, when dealing with a villa assemblage such as this one, the actual locus of creation is all but impossible to identify. Instead, the important facet of this collection is not that it consisted of Greek objects, but that it manages in some way to collect "Greekness" through a variety of sculptural styles.

A visitor to the villa, upon entering the smaller peristyle, would find himself confronted by a series of bronze heads, one of which is a partial

FIGURE 2.4 Apollonios's copy of Polykleitos's *Doryphoros*, from the Villa dei Papiri, Herculaneum, National Archaeological Museum, Naples (photo: Koppermann, Dair, Inst. Neg. 64.1804)

copy of Polykleitos's famous *Doryphoros,* signed by Apollonios (fig. 2.4). Michael Koortbojian's comments on this piece in an essay dealing with the aesthetic uses of Roman "copies" (referring to the history of scholarship surrounding pieces that seem to have been derived from a Greek model) are worth quoting here.

> Roman beholders might have admired, as we do, Apollonios's artistic skill as a worker of bronze. This was, in large measure, what the ancients understood as the artist's role, his ability or *techne,* and it was to this that Apollonios's signature laid claim. . . . Yet the fact that his work represented the Doryphoros was recognizable as well. It is a striking paradox . . . that, in antiquity, when tradition and convention were the cornerstones of statuary production, what made something recognizable as roughly equivalent to our modern notion of a "work of art" was, more often than not, the fact that it was *not* an original invention, but a "copy." (2002, 178–79)

Throughout the villa were more Greek-inspired sculptures, including two pieces designed to look like Archaic statues: a head of Apollo and an impressive archaizing Athena Promachos. "The overall impression clearly aims at introducing the visitor into a cultural environment that is defined as Greek and corresponds to the social and intellectual standing of his host" (Neudecker 1998, 84). The collection of the Villa dei Papiri exemplifies the result of a long tradition of performances of memory that began centuries earlier with the looting and abduction of art from the Greek East and continued with the assimilation of this art into a Roman value system.

What all of these examples of collecting—from Assyria, Elam, and Italy—illustrate, however, is a type of memory act that claims ownership of the past. At the same time, each memory act is intimately tied to unique cultural beliefs about the role of powerful objects in society. Assurbanipal's library seems to have served at least a partially religious purpose, since as the owner of these important texts, the king expected to be rewarded and protected by Nabu. Religion may also have played a role in the display of the monuments at Susa, although the acquisition of these objects would also have served to legitimize the king's rule and show his power over the legendary kings of the past. In the Roman example, the loot that began as a symbol of occupation (Bergmann 1995, 90) soon became incorporated into ideas about wealth, luxury, and aristocracy. In all of these cases, however, the acquisition of these foreign, powerful objects could only have served to enhance the prestige of their new owner, whose performance of memory simultaneously related these collected objects both to the past and the present.

Defacing and Erasing

The destruction of an enemy's sites of memory, especially those of ritual significance, is a well-documented occurrence throughout ancient, and even contemporary, history. David Freedberg devotes a chapter to the phenomenon of iconoclasm in his book on viewership and response. Although the main thrust of his argument is to show that the modern Western world has been reluctant to acknowledge the power that images have to arouse, inspire, and terrify, many of his examples are drawn from the ancient world, where art historians have much more readily recognized the psychological and spiritual effects of the abuse of art. He responds to the objections of "empirical historians" that the removal of political images is never more than "the removal of the symbols of a hated order" (Freedberg 1989, 390); he insists that the currents of response strike a much deeper chord: "Could it be that by assailing the dead images, getting rid of them, one was assailing the very men and women they represented? And if so, were they there in their images, or did the hostile act somehow carry over to the signified by a kind of magical transference or contagion?" (Freedberg 1989, 392). We need only watch television to see modern reenactments of this ancient drama as soldiers and citizens pull down the statues of Saddam Hussein in Iraq.

This concept of an image standing in for an absent person is the basis for much thought about the destruction of images, and one that we have already encountered in the discussion of the Susa collection. If the actions that we perpetrate on a representational image somehow are transferred to the subject of that representation, then the role of objects in the manipulation of memory becomes vital. In each of the following examples, the destruction and defacement of the monuments and objects involved occurred in highly charged political environments of personal and institutional power struggles. Cultural turmoil exposes a host of conflicting and competing attitudes, and memories and representational objects can become significant actors in this strife.

It could be naively assumed, based on Freedberg's image-person correlation, that the destruction of images throughout the ancient world was designed to remove completely an individual from existence. What I attempt to show, however, is that memory acts such as these include both elements of remembrance and forgetting. It appears that the destruction of memory becomes more powerful when traces of this destruction continue to inhabit the visual landscape. I investigate ancient iconoclasm from three different angles: the Roman practice of *damnatio memoriae*, the early Christian defacement of the Temple of Hathor at Denderah, and finally the mutilation of a bronze head from Nineveh.

Damnatio Memoriae and Geta in Third-Century Rome

The (modern) Latin term for the official condemnation of a person's memory—*damnatio memoriae*—suggests that the Romans were aware of a relationship between object and memory act. A ban of remembrance was considered one of the severest penalties under Roman law, and was enacted only against those persons deemed most unworthy of membership in society (Varner 2000, 10). In imperial times, this destruction of memory often targeted emperors—for example, Caligula, Nero, or Domitian—who were disgraced at the time of their deaths. Varner (2000, 11) has suggested that this practice conveys a Roman awareness of the malleability of historical truth and illuminates a Roman preoccupation with posthumous memory and fame. The sanctions against a person who had suffered damnatio memoriae could be quite extensive, including the erasure of the condemned's name from official lists, the outlawing of funeral masks representing the condemned, forfeiture of property rights, annulment of wills, the declaration of the person's birthday as an ill-omened day for the Roman people, the public celebration of the day of their death, and prohibitions against the continued use of the condemned's first name (Varner 2000, 10).

In the material record, however, the practice of damnatio memoriae is best attested through the destruction and transformation of images of the condemned. Especially during the imperial period, portraits of the emperor acted as an ancient form of mass media, and strict laws governed the treatment of such imperial images. Once an emperor suffered damnatio memoriae, however, his images were transformed in a variety of ways. Sculpted portraits of Caligula, for example, were often recarved, either into images of Augustus or Claudius (Varner 2000, 11). Portraits of these disgraced emperors also suffered disfigurement or the removal of their images from the public eye.

Though this practice existed throughout the Roman Empire, some of the most striking visual evidence of damnatio memoriae occurs during the Severan period (AD 193–235). After the death of the emperor Septimius Severus, his two sons, Caracalla and Geta, jointly inherited rule of the empire. It was a situation bound for failure. After only ten months of joint rule, Caracalla murdered Geta and then, "He [Caracalla] exhibited his hatred for his brother by abolishing the observance of his birthday, and he vented his anger upon the stones that had supported his statues, and melted down the coinage that had displayed his features" (Cassius Dio, LXXVIII.12).

Geta's name and image were erased from numerous monuments, including the Arch of the Argentarii, which celebrated the family of Septimius Severus. His portrait was erased from the pilasters of the arch and the honorific inscription was recut to remove any mention of him. Likewise, every image and reference to Geta was also erased from the Arch of Septimius Severus in Rome and the Severan arch at Lepcis Magna in Africa.

Perhaps the most familiar example of this erasure of Geta's image, however, occurs on a painted tondo from Egypt representing Septimius Severus, his wife, Julia Domna, and their sons, Caracalla and Geta (fig. 2.5). The painting was likely displayed in a public or domestic setting associated with the imperial cult (Varner 2000, 19), and was probably created prior to AD 205, based on Caracalla's portrait type. When originally completed, the painting would have served as a visual connection to the imperial family. In its present state, however, the face of Geta has been entirely obliterated, leaving only a blank space in the tondo.

A damnatio memoriae such as this is an extremely powerful performance of memory—it is an act of vengeance and an attempt to rewrite Roman history. It should be noted, however, that this attempt at erasure, if that was the intent, was incomplete. Nearly 2,000 years after his death, we still know Geta's name; there even exist several examples of his imperial portraiture (Budde 1951). On the tondo itself, only Geta's face was erased; his shoulders and bust remain clearly visible. Nor was there any attempt to "smooth over" the names and images of Geta on any of the

FIGURE 2.5 Tondo representing Septimius Severus, Julia Domna, and their sons, Caracalla and Geta, from Egypt, Antikensammlung, Staatliche Museen Zu Berlin, Berlin (photo: Bildarchiv Preussicher Kulturbesitz, Art Resource)

monuments (Flower 2000). Instead, the destruction left obvious scars of this removal, and it might be worth asking whether this itself was partly by design: instead of a seamless visual landscape that leads from Septimius Severus to Caracalla, these voided spaces become reminders of the son and brother who had failed.

Christian Iconoclasm at Denderah

The word *iconoclasm* in modern parlance often carries religious overtones, and this is not without reason. The advent of Christianity in Egypt was at a particularly turbulent time in which iconoclasm was relatively commonplace. The great temples at Luxor, Karnak, and Philae all bear evidence of violent destruction directed at the pagan gods of earlier antiquity (Frankfurter 1998, 265). To the ancient Egyptians, their cult statues were powerful objects, in which the divinity could reside (Assmann 2001, 43). With the advent of Christianity, this belief was subtly transformed: images of pagan gods became repositories for "demons" (Frankfurter 1998). These dangerous denizens of the spirit world were the subject of diatribes from countless early Christian authors; the destruction of the inhabitable images would soon follow. "This kind of iconoclasm bears little connection to biblical stories of overturning altars of Baal. It is a pragmatic, traditional act that recognizes the abiding power in religious images and neutralizes that power for the safety of all" (Frankfurter 1998, 280).

The Temple of Hathor at Denderah, which was begun in 54 BC, provides an ideal locale for demonstrating both the power inherent in objects and images as well as the lengths that people will go to in order to control this power. Representations of Hathor, with the characteristic bovine ears and headdress made from horns and the sun disk, abound throughout the temple. Her head appears as column capitals in the enormous hypostyle hall, and her form occurs on numerous figural reliefs throughout the temple. The most important representation of the goddess, however, was on the exterior south wall, where a huge gilded head of Hathor functioned as a shrine for non-priestly Egyptians to worship the cult statue of the goddess on the other side of the wall (Frankfurter 2004).

At some point, however—probably in the fifth or sixth century, when a new Christian basilica was built within the temple precinct (Grossman 1991, 690–91)—Hathor's features were hacked out wherever her image appeared. The gilded representation on the southern wall, which was accessible only with ladders and scaffolding, was gouged out nearly beyond recognition, leaving a gaping scar in the masonry (fig. 2.6). David Frankfurter has commented on the vehemence of this destruction, arguing that even after several centuries of Christianity in Egypt, Hathor's image was still "hot" (Frankfurter 2004). In reference to the mutilations at Denderah, he discussed the potency of the face and eyes and the possible ritual interaction with the image and the demon that resided inside it. In particular, the assault of Hathor's image on the south wall of the temple seemed to be an indication of fear.

FIGURE 2.6 Defacement of the south wall of the Temple of Hathor at Denderah (Cauville 1990, 86)

This is a clear demonstration of the power that images and objects have, and the destruction of them is probably an attempt to destroy what they signified. What is not generally pointed out, however, is the fact that although the face of Hathor was destroyed throughout the temple complex, the form of her head remained intact, including the bovine ears (fig. 2.7). This small fact would indicate that an interpretation of this memory performance that focuses only on "forgetting" would be incomplete. Hathor's image, like Geta's, did not disappear completely from view; rather, it appeared in a damaged and impotent form. This new, *safe*, representation of the goddess could then stand as a witness to the superior power of the Christian monks and bishops who had likely instigated the violence, as elsewhere in Egypt (Frankfurter 1998). Thus, the force of this memory performance was not aimed at complete forgetfulness, but at a revised memory of the past, that remembered both the power of the goddess and the superior power of those who had neutralized her.

The Mutilated Head of an Akkadian Ruler

This relationship between remembering and forgetting can also be applied to Carl Nylander's careful analysis of the copper head of Sargon (or perhaps Naram-Sin) more than twenty years ago. This head had been mutilated in antiquity, and Nylander showed that this damage was not

FIGURE 2.7 Defacement of the Hathor kiosk at Denderah (Cauville 1990, 66)

the result of random violence: the statue's left eye was gouged out, the bridge and point of its nose were damaged, and both ears were cut off (fig. 2.8). In this instance, the bronze head reflects traditional Median punishments, thus dating the mutilation of the statue to the time of the Median conquest of Nineveh (Nylander 1980, 332). The close relationship between image and reality implies that the mutilations carried symbolic weight. In fact, he says, "the closer the correspondence between the practices of real life and the treatment of the image, the more effective the message of overthrow and humiliation" (Nylander 1980, 331).

FIGURE 2.8 Mutilated head of an Akkadian ruler (perhaps Sargon or Naram-Sin) from Nineveh, Iraq Museum, Baghdad (photo: Scala, Art Resource)

The very survival of this head into modern times to be excavated in Nineveh at the end of the nineteenth century would indicate that the mutilation of the king's image was not aimed at the complete erasure of his memory and existence. Instead, Nylander suggests that this pattern of destruction shows a deliberate act on the part of the Median conquerors not to erase the memory of the earlier king, but to show his eventual humiliation (Nylander 1980, 331). Thus, both memories, that of the king's greatness and also his humiliation at the hands of the Medes, remain intact. There is a dialogue between the two sets of memories, and the life history of the object serves to relate the owner and viewer to both the past and the present.

The preceding examples demonstrate that performances of memory can be complicated, multilayered processes that stress the power of forgetting as much as that of remembering. It perhaps comes as a surprise, however, that those acts of iconoclasm aimed at destroying or erasing the power of an enemy might be dependent on the preservation of certain parts of the affected object to be effective. We can only now imagine the audience for whom these displays of power were intended. At least at Denderah we might guess that the audience was widespread; the same is true for the erasure of Geta's image on large public monuments. With easily portable objects such as the Severan tondo or the head of Sargon, we might suppose a much smaller audience, although there is no way to confirm this. In all of these examples, however, one result of the destruction of an enemy's sites of memory was the accretion of power and legitimacy to the iconoclast.

Reinscribing and Replacing

The final part of this chapter presents object biographies in a realm that is far less well studied than either collecting or defacing. Here I deal with the physical transformation of an object through a process of substitution in which its meaning is utterly changed, although the object remains essentially intact. Such transformations allow objects to simultaneously exist in both the past and the present, as the result of a rather explicit performance of memory. Following, I investigate two well-known transformations and the implications that these would have had on memory.

Alexander, Augustus, Claudius, and the Paintings of Apelles

In every example up to this point, the objects themselves have been the bearers of their biographies. The following example, however, focuses on two objects that have long since been lost to us and are mentioned only by the historian Pliny, writing in the first century AD. This narrative again begins with the Roman conquest of Greece, involving one of the most admired Greek painters, Apelles, who had been court painter to Alexander the Great. Pliny mentions several panels by the painter and comments on the fate of two of them.

> At Samos, there is a Habron by him, that is greatly admired; at Rhodes a Menander, king of Caria, and an Ancæus; at Alexandria, a Gorgosthenes, the Tragedian; and at Rome, a Castor and Pollux, with figures of Victory and Alexander the Great, and an emblematical figure of War with her hands tied behind her, and Alexander seated in a triumphal car; both of which pictures the late Emperor Augustus, with a great degree of moderation and good taste, consecrated in the most frequented parts of his Forum: the Emperor Claudius, however, thought it advisable to efface the head of Alexander in both pictures, and substitute likenesses of his predecessor Augustus. (Pliny 1938, 35.36.93–94)

Pliny's own reactions to the history of these paintings are interesting in themselves. Augustus's actions, which simultaneously preserved the paintings and placed them within the public purview, were admirable in Pliny's opinion, and evidence of moderation. The author does not mention, however, any of the associations that might have surrounded the placement of these panels in the Forum of Augustus. By the time of Augustus, Alexander the Great seems to have become a symbol for a great ruler, and ancient sources suggest that he may have even been a personal role model of Augustus. Suetonius remarks that, for a time, Augustus used Alexander's portrait as his personal seal (Suetonius 1914, 50), and also tells the well-known anecdote of Augustus's visit to Alexander's mortuary shrine in Alexandria. Upon being asked if he would like to also see the tombs of the Ptolemies, Augustus replied, "My wish was to see a king, not corpses" (Suetonius 1914, 18). The equation between Alexander and Augustus made by the placement of these two panels in the Augustan Forum is one that Pollitt expects would not have been lost on any Roman passing by: "By his victories over Antony and the assassins of Caesar, Augustus had been supported by the old gods, like Castor, whose reign he had re-established . . . ; and thanks to a great general's triumph [like Alexander's], Rome was no longer at war" (Pollitt 1978, 168).

It is unclear from Pliny's account how the substitution of Augustus's head for Alexander's would have been received by the general Roman populace. In one sense, however, Claudius's action simply made explicit the implicit analogy between Alexander the Great and Augustus. Perhaps the transformation of Apelles' panels might even be considered only the final act in what had been an ongoing performance of memory, since the paintings had first been collected and displayed. Once Augustus's head replaced Alexander's, however, the panels' meanings were drastically altered: Augustus replaced Alexander both as the companion of Castor, Pollux, and Victory, and also as the triumphant general who has bound War.

Reinscribing the Stele of Naram-Sin

The preceding Roman example is a visual transformation, and thus easily recognizable as such. Reinscription, however, is an equally powerful method of transforming the meaning of an object. Modern society has generally seen a division between texts and images. Verbal and visual language, while parallel forms of communication, tend to be analyzed using different sets of tools: iconography versus hagiography, formal analysis versus literary criticism. In the ancient Near East, however, the relationship between image and text was much closer, and Bahrani suggests that the Assyrians and Babylonians considered the distinction between these forms of communication, verbal and visual, as fluid and unstable (Bahrani 2003, 99, 119).

When examining Near Eastern objects, where representation and inscription often exist side by side, it is possible to see the two elements as part of a larger whole. We might even think about royal inscriptions in the same way that we think about royal images: that these stand in for the presence of ruler himself. In the case of a secondary inscription, one that becomes part of the object well after its creation, this correlation between word and image allows us to speak in terms of biographical transformations.

Bearing this in mind, let us return to Susa, where much of the booty was reinscribed; on those objects without secondary inscriptions (such as the Code of Hammurabi) often a space had been cleared away for an inscription that was never executed (Harper 1992, 159). The Stele of Naram-Sin actually bore two inscriptions: one in Akkadian, which was largely effaced. Today, only just enough of the original text remains to verify the fact that it was, in fact, a victory monument. The secondary inscription, which is well preserved, was carved at the time of abduction of the stele to Susa, and reads as follows.

> I am Shutruk-Nahhunte, the son of Halludush-Inshushinak, king of Anshan and Susa, the enlarger of my realm, the caretaker of Elam, sovereign of Elam. As Inshushinak, my god, bade me, I have destroyed Sippar and taken the Stele of Naram-Sin in hand. I have taken it away and brought it to Elam. I have placed it before Inshushinak, my god, for dedication. (My translation from König 1965, 76)

This seems to be the standard formula for these inscriptions: Shutruk-Nahhunte identifies himself first, followed by a reference to Inshushinak, at whose behest he undertook a specific action (for example, "I destroyed Sippar"). Finally, he identifies what it was he seized as booty, and, in this case, dedicates the statue to Inshushinak.

In many ways this could almost seem a primary inscription, like a votive dedication; but the wording makes very clear the fact that this is a second stage in the object's life history, and that this is an important point to be made. This type of inscription links the king to the object's past; he appropriates it and associates himself with it. Thus, Naram-Sin and Shutruk-Nahhunte appear together on the same stele.

Thinking in terms of the relationship between the word and the image, the placement of this Elamite inscription on the stele is also quite telling. Instead of being in some inconspicuous part of the image, Shutruk-Nahhunte's inscription is placed prominently in the middle of the stele, on the depiction of the tall mountain before which Naram-Sin stands. The Elamite king transforms this object for all who see it; he makes Naram-Sin's victory his own simply by inserting his words, and thus himself, into the victory narrative.

Reinscriptions and recarvings such as these are memory performances of the highest degree, related, but not identical, to those examined before. The structure and wording of the Elamite reinscription and the repainting of Apelles' panels show the marked subjugation of the past (as was the case with the defaced and mutilated objects), but there is in both examples also a marked admiration for that past. Alexander the Great and Naram-Sin both were imagined as figures with compelling narratives worthy of emulation. Effectively, the Elamite king's performance of memory has deftly inserted him into a quasi-divine Akkadian narrative, along with all of the trappings that this narrative involves. The emperor Claudius achieved the same effect, albeit on behalf of someone else, by inserting Augustus's own face into a narrative that had contained Alexander the Great. These "memory insertions" provide a new avenue for thinking about the relationships among objects, memories, and acts of legitimization.

Conclusions

Although there are probably as many ways to perform memory as there are people and objects to perform them, I have argued that it is possible to pinpoint specific moments in time and place where a memory performance has altered the life history of some object or monument. More important, however, a pattern emerges from this study that shows that people are well aware of the power of images and are adept at manipulating and using this power to situate themselves in relation to their pasts.

At times this power to manipulate both object and memory asserts itself as a claim of ownership, either on behalf of oneself or the gods. The destruction of objects, however, exerts a different type of power—the power to overcome, to vanquish, and to neutralize. One of the more interesting aspects of this study has been the evidence that the immediacy of such iconoclastic acts rests in the power of altering memory rather than destroying it entirely. Finally, there were also acts that inserted the actor himself both onto the object and into the previous narrative of that object, associating himself with a variety of meanings.

These visible memory performances tend to be crystallized into the object's life history at times of cultural and social stress, a pattern also present in Susan Alcock's survey of memory in the Greek landscape

(Alcock 2002). The majority of the junctures of memory and object that I have presented are found in times of war, political strife, and disruption. It may well be that the best evidence for memory in the ancient world derives from these stress fractures of history. Perhaps memory is a common thread that people are able to hold in the midst of turmoil. It may also be that these moments in history mark precisely the times when a ruler has greatest need to consolidate his claims to power. In these examples, the ruling elite effectively employ the power inherent in human relationships with objects to mark their ascendancy over the past in the minds of those around them.

If nothing else, this study has illustrated that the material world is not a passive slate to be acted upon, but that this world also shapes and reshapes our own experiences and memories. The life history of the Stele of Naram-Sin did not end when the sculptor stepped back from his creation and decided that it was good, nor should we think of it merely in terms of its value in learning about the Akkadians. At the same time, it is also more than Elamite booty or an artifact in the Louvre.

Bibliography

Alcock, Susan E. 2002. *Archaeologies of the Greek Past: Landscape, Monuments, and Memories.* Cambridge: Cambridge University Press.

Appadurai, Arjun. 1986. Introduction: Commodities and the Politics of Value. In *The Social Life of Things: Commodities in Cultural Perspective,* ed. Arjun Appadurai, 3–63. Cambridge and New York: Cambridge University Press.

Assmann, Jan. 2001. *The Search for God in Ancient Egypt.* Trans. David Lorton. Ithaca, N.Y. and London: Cornell University Press.

Bahrani, Zainab. 2003. *The Graven Image: Representation in Babylonia and Assyria.* Philadelphia: University of Pennsylvania Press.

Bartman, Elizabeth. 1991. Sculptural Collecting and Display in the Private Realm. In *Roman Art in the Private Sphere,* ed. Elaine Gazda, 71–95. Ann Arbor: University of Michigan Press.

Bergmann, Bettina. 1995. Greek Masterpieces and Roman Recreative Fiction. In *Greece in Rome: Influence, Integration, Resistance.* Harvard Studies in Classical Philology. Vol. 97:79–120.

Bieber, Margarete. 1977. *Ancient Copies: Contributions to the History of Greek and Roman Art.* New York: New York University Press.

Black, J. A., and W. J. Tait. 1995. Archives and Libraries in the Ancient Near East. In *Civilizations of the Ancient Near East IV,* ed. Jack Sasson, 2197–2209. New York: Scribner.

Bol, Peter C. 1972. *Die Skulpturen des Schiffundes von Antikythera*. Mitteilungen des Deutschen Archäologischen Instituts, Athänische Abteilung, 2. Beiheft. Berlin: Gebr. Mann Verlag.

Budde, Ludwig. 1951. *Jugendbildnisse des Caracalla und Geta*. Orbis Antiquus, Heft 5. Münster: Aschendorffsche Verlagsbuchhandlung.

Burke, Peter. 1989. History as Social Memory. In *Memory: History, Culture and the Mind*, ed. Thomas Butler, 97–113. Oxford and New York: Blackwell.

Cassius Dio. 1914. *Dio's Roman History*. Trans. Earnest Cary. Loeb Classical Library Series. London: W. Heinemann. (Orig. ca. AD200–222.)

Cauville, Sylvie. 1990. *Le Temple de Dendera: Guide Archéologique*. Le Caire: Institut français le archéologie orientale.

—— 1999. Dendera. In *Encyclopedia of the Archaeology of Ancient Egypt*, ed. Katherine Bard, 252–54. London and New York: Routledge.

Csikszentmihalyi, Mihaly. 1993. Why We Need Things. In *History from Things: Essays on Material Culture*, eds. Steven Lubar and W. David Kingery, 20–29. Washington: Smithsonian Institution Press.

Flower, Harriet. 2000. Damnatio Memoriae and Epigraphy. In *From Caligula to Constantine: Tyranny and Transformation in Roman Portraiture*, ed. Eric C. Varner, 9–26. Atlanta: William C. Carlos Museum.

Frankfurter, David. 1998. *Religion in Roman Egypt: Assimilation and Resistance*. Princeton: Princeton University Press.

—— 2004. The Vitality of Egyptian Images in Late Antiquity: Christian Memory and Response. Paper given at *The Sculptural Environment of the Roman Near East: Reflections on Culture, Ideology and Power*. International conference, November 7–10, 2004, Ann Arbor, Mich.

Freedberg, David. 1989. *The Power of Images: Studies in the History and Theory of Response*. Chicago: University of Chicago Press.

Gazda, Elaine. 2002. Beyond Copying: Artistic Originality and Tradition. In *The Art of Emulation: Studies in Artistic Originality and Tradition from the Present to Classical Antiquity*, ed. Elaine Gazda, 1–25. Ann Arbor: University of Michigan Press.

Grayson, Albert K. 1991. Assyrian Civilization. In *The Cambridge Ancient History*, 2nd ed., Vol. 3, pt. 2, *The Assyrian and Babylonian Empires and Other States of the Near East from the Eighth to the Sixth Centuries*, eds. John Boardman et al., 104–228. Cambridge: Cambridge University Press.

Grossman, Peter. 1991. Dandarah. In *The Coptic Encyclopedia*, vol. 3, ed. Aziz S. Atiya, 690–91. New York: Macmillan.

Harper, Prudence. 1992. Mesopotamian Monuments Found at Susa. In *The Royal City of Susa: Ancient Near Eastern Treasures in the Louvre*, eds. Prudence Harper, Joan Aruz, and Françoise Tallon, 159–82. New York: Metropolitan Museum of Art.

Joyce, Rosemary. 2003. Concrete Memory: Fragments of the Past in the Classic Maya Present (500–1000 A.D.). In *Archaeologies of Memory*, eds. Ruth M. Van Dyke and Susan E. Alcock, 104–27. Malden, Mass.: Blackwell.

König, Friedrich-Wilhelm. 1965. *Die Elamischen Königinschriften*. Graz: Archiv für Orientforschung Beiheft 16.

Koortbojian, Michael. 2002. Forms of Attention. Four Notes on Replication and Variation. In *The Art of Emulation: Studies in Artistic Originality and Tradition from the Present to Classical Antiquity*, ed. Elaine Gazda, 173–204. Ann Arbor: University of Michigan Press.

Kopytoff, Igor. 1986. The Cultural Biographies of Things: Commoditization as a Process. In *The Social Life of Things: Commodities in Cultural Perspective*, ed. Arjun Appadurai, 64–90. Cambridge and New York: Cambridge University Press.

Langdon, Susan. 2001. Beyond the Grave: Biographies from Early Greece. *American Journal of Archaeology* 105:579–606.

Mattusch, Carol C., with Henry Lie. 2004. *The Villa dei Papiri at Herculaneum: Life and Afterlife of a Sculpture Collection*. Los Angeles: J. Paul Getty Museum.

Meskell, Lynn. 2004. *Object Worlds in Ancient Egypt: Material Biographies Past and Present*. London: Berg.

Neudecker, Richard. 1998. The Roman Villa as the Locus of Art Collections. In *The Roman Villa: Villa Urbana*, ed. Alfred Frazer, 77–91. Philadelphia: University of Pennsylvania Press.

Nylander, Carl. 1980. Earless in Nineveh: Who Mutilated Sargon's Head? *American Journal of Archaeology* 84 (3): 329–33.

Pape, Magrit. 1975. Griechische Kunstwerke aus Kriegsbeute und ihre öffentliche Aufstellung in Rom: von der Eroberung von Syrakus bis in augusteische Zeit. Ph.D. diss., University of Hamburg.

Parpola, Simo. 1983. Assyrian Library Records. *Journal of Near Eastern Studies* 42 (1): 1–29.

Pearce, Susan. 1994. The Urge to Collect. In *Interpreting Objects and Collections*, ed. Susan Pearce, 157–59. New York and London: Routledge.

——— 1995. *On Collecting: An Investigation into Collecting in the European Tradition*. New York and London: Routledge.

Perry, Ellen. 2005. *The Aesthetics of Emulation in the Visual Arts of Ancient Rome*. Cambridge and New York: Cambridge University Press.

Pliny. 1938. *Natural History*. Trans. Harris Rackham. Loeb Classical Library Series. Cambridge, Mass.: Harvard University Press. (Orig. ca. AD 77.)

Pollitt, Jerome J. 1978. The Impact of Greek Art on Rome. *Transactions of the American Philological Association* 108:155–74.

——— 1986. *Art in the Hellenistic Age*. Cambridge: Cambridge University Press.

Potts, Daniel T. 1999. *The Archaeology of Elam: Formation and Transformation of an Ancient Iranian State*. Cambridge and New York: Cambridge University Press.

Root, Margaret C. 1979. *The King and Kingship in Achaemenid Art: Essays on the Creation of an Iconography of Empire*. Leiden, Belgium: Brill.

Rowlands, Michael. 1993. The Role of Memory in the Transmission of Culture. *World Archaeology* 25:141–51.

Saggs, Henry W. F. 1984. *The Might That Was Assyria*. London: Sidgwick and Jackson.
Strabo. 1917. *Geography*. Trans. Henry L. Jones. Loeb Classical Library Series. Cambridge, Mass.: Harvard University Press. (Orig. ca. early 1st century AD.)
Strong, Donald E. 1994. *Roman Museums: Selected Papers on Roman Art and Architecture*. London: Pindar Press.
Suetonius. 1914. *Divius Augustus*. In *The Lives of the Caesars*. Trans. John C. Rolfe. Loeb Classical Library Series. Cambridge, Mass.: Harvard University Press. (Orig. ca. AD 121.)
Van Dyke, Ruth M., and Susan E. Alcock, eds. 2003. *Archaeologies of Memory*. Malden, Mass.: Blackwell.
Varner, Eric R. 2000. Tyranny and the Transformation of the Roman Visual Landscape. In *From Caligula to Constantine: Tyranny and Transformation in Roman Portraiture*, ed. Eric C. Varner, 9–26. Atlanta: William C. Carlos Museum.
Warden, Gregory P., and David G. Romano. 1994. The Course of Glory: Greek Art in a Roman Context at the Villa of the Papyri at Herculaneum. *Art History* 17 (2): 228–54.
Wojcik, Maria Rita. 1986. *La Villa dei Papiri ad Ercolano: contributo alla ricostruzione dell'ideologia della nobilitas tardorepubblicana*. Rome: L'Erma di Bretschneider.
Zanker, Paul. 1988. *The Power of Images in the Age of Augustus*. Trans. Alan Shapiro. Ann Arbor: University of Michigan Press.

3 Unforgettable Landscapes
ATTACHMENTS TO THE PAST IN HELLENISTIC ARMENIA

Lori Khatchadourian

Historical cartographers are quintessential memory specialists. Given the task of determining the relative importance of one hamlet, village, town, or city from another, those who map the past exercise the right to erase the memory of a place itself, along with the memories of the peoples, histories, and monuments through which that place was constituted. As reviewers of the *Barrington Atlas of the Greek and Roman World* recently wrote, "All maps—in one way or another, aggressively or unconsciously—'lie' to us" (Alcock, Dey and Parker 2001, 458). This discriminating duty of the cartographer, when paired with the narrow approach of traditional classical scholarship on southwest Asia during the Hellenistic era[1] (ca. 323–31 BC), has resulted in rather peculiar maps of the period: undiscovered places that are mentioned in Greek and Roman sources are marked, while archaeological sites whose names do not appear in this particular body of literature are not. The dominant narrative concerning Hellenistic southwest Asia has privileged cities thought to have been centers of Hellenism, due to the celebrated works of Greek art their inhabitants produced. For the student of classical archaeology, the likely impression of this region in the enigmatic period between the collapse of the Persian Empire and the rise of the Roman Empire is like that of a photograph with well-focused, foregrounded, Hellenized hubs—such as Pergamon, Antioch, Ephasos—set against a soft-focused, hazy background of places that were perhaps touched by the ripple effects of Hellenism, or stagnantly persisted as vestigially Persian.

But studies of Hellenistic southwest Asia are changing, and the welcome transformations that are underway make this epoch more difficult to define than ever before. Nearly every component of traditional scholarship, which characterized the Hellenistic world along clear temporal, cultural, and geographic parameters, has come under scrutiny. While early conventions date the start of the era by the death of Alexander the

Great, recent studies stress continuities from the Achaemenid or Pharaonic periods and call into doubt such an absolute temporal rupture (Sherwin-White and Kuhrt 1993; Briant 1982). Culturally, the traditional notion that the Hellenistic period was one of Hellenization through an exclusionary Greco-Macedonian elite is being supplanted by the recognition that more complex social processes were at work, which included varying degrees of assimilation and the persistence of local, non-Greek traditions. Geographic conceptions are similarly becoming more nuanced. Whereas the Hellenistic world was once thought to encompass the vast swath of territory conquered by Alexander, it is increasingly recognized that this notion of a monolithic Greek sphere is not sustainable. In this changing scholarly atmosphere, the soft-focus background can begin to come to the fore, and forgotten places can reemerge in the cartographies of southwest Asia in the final centuries BC.

Hellenistic Armenia

With the death of Alexander the Great in 323 BC, southwest Asia became an arena of dynastic politics dominated by Macedonian monarchs. Prominent families such as the Ptolemies and the Seleucids were surrounded by smaller dynastic polities—such as those of the Armenian plateau—whose authorities either answered to these monarchs or vied with them for autonomy.[2] Alexander did not pass through the upland plains and daunting mountains of the South Caucasus (Hammond 1996), yet his conquests brought Armenia into contact with the eastern reaches of Hellenism, heralded by the Seleucid successors of Alexander who held sway over much of southwest Asia in the third and second centuries BC. However, for the communities living on the Armenian highland, as palpable as the present benefits and challenges of contact and exchange may have been, so too were the opportunities and pressures of the past. These communities inhabited a landscape replete with monuments that spoke to the triumphs and failures of past regimes.

On hills and outcrops of the fertile Ararat plain stood the fortresses that once constituted the northern province of the kingdom of Urartu. This power is thought to have emerged in eastern Anatolia from a conglomeration of smaller polities during the late second and early first millennia BC. Between the mid-ninth and late eighth centuries BC, Urartu expanded to encompass the South Caucasus and northern Iran (Smith 2003).

Occupation in Armenia spanned from the second decade of the eighth century until Urartu's decline some time in the late seventh or early sixth centuries BC (Smith 2003). Some of Urartu's citadels were reduced to ruins at this time; others continued for centuries to boast formidable defensive structures and sturdy constructions.

Soon after Urartu's decline Armenia was incorporated into the expansive Achaemenid Persian Empire. Textual sources suggest that a local power, named the Yervandid dynasty after a series of eponymous kings, emerged as vassals to the Persian court. Relatively little is known about the archaeology of Armenia during the reign of this Yervandid dynasty from the fifth through fourth centuries BC. Although Alexander's eastern campaign in the fourth century precipitated the collapse of the Persian Empire, the Yervandid dynasty seems to have survived the political upheavals that ensued after Alexander's death in 323 BC and appears to have continued to rule into the Hellenistic period for more than a century, albeit under close Seleucid surveillance. This period of semi-autonomous Yervandid rule will be referred to here as the late Yervandid period (323–212 BC). The geographer Strabo would have us believe that toward the end of the third century, the late Yervandid dynasty was succeeded by a new dynastic family, the Artaxiads, after the Seleucid king Antiochus III conquered the last Yervandid king and placed Artaxias I on the throne (Str. 11.14.11).

Whether the subjects and authorities of Hellenistic Armenia (that is, Late Yervandid and Artaxiad) would have recognized Urartian- and Achaemenid-period remains as the work of two distinct predecessors depends in part upon the life span of social memories. Richard Bradley, in his elegant studies on social memory, has emphasized that memories become unstable within spans of time far briefer than most archaeological research can detect (Bradley 2003, 2002). Memories are constantly shifting, and the very act of their construction is by necessity selective. Although the process of social forgetting can be stalled through various strategies—whether writing texts, inscribing artifacts, or constructing monuments—nevertheless, these memories will be unstable and subject to ever-changing meanings.

Writing is clearly not the only way to codify memories, yet archaeological studies of social memory have quite reasonably tended to draw a distinction between the way commemorative acts operated in historic and prehistoric contexts, and indeed, the way today's observer can interpret commemorative acts on either side of the narrative turn (Van Dyke and Alcock 2003). Oral traditions can be mimetic in rendering the meaning of the past; however, in the absence of written narrative to codify these meanings the content of the past is no longer likely to be recalled. In archaeological studies of social memory that deal with prehistory, "the past" that is being remembered becomes a timeless abstraction whose remembrance cannot easily be moored to specific motivations even if it can be clearly identified, whereas historic studies tend to specify what part of the past is being remembered or forgotten and can better probe to what end.[3]

A study of social memory in Hellenistic Armenia does not fit comfortably on either side of the historic versus prehistoric divide. There are no known contemporary narrative texts from Armenia that could elucidate what parts of the past were being remembered, how intentionally, and for what purposes (although there is an important set of inscriptions that will be discussed later). At the same time, in the late first millennium BC there is sufficient historical information available from Greek, Roman, and Persian sources to bracket the past into discrete heuristic temporal eras, in this case the Urartian and Achaemenid periods. Whether this same division would have been meaningful to communities living in Armenia in the last three centuries BC is as yet unknowable. In this setting, where memories were transmitted orally, we could suggest that remembering the content of the Urartian past in an unmythologized form would be exceedingly unlikely, whereas recollections of the Achaemenid past would still be in transmission. This distinction between actual and mythologized memories has its limitations, however. It glosses over the notion that memories are constantly mutating, not only over centuries or between generations, but within life spans and between individuals.

From our perspective, the archaeological and epigraphic records suggest that in the Hellenistic period the political calculations and social relationships of elites and non-elites alike hinged, at least in part, upon a commemoration of both the Achaemenid and Urartian past, just as they did upon an accommodation of the ideological and social demands of the present. Indeed, expressing commitment to the past may have been instrumental to meeting the challenges of the present. On the level of the elite, the late Yervandid and Artaxiad kings of Hellenistic Armenia made materially visible choices through which they interacted with the built spaces and perceived associations of the past. These authorities constructed a new elite identity precisely by picking and choosing from the smorgasbord of old and new places, languages, iconographies, and, indeed, pedigrees that lay before them. Although situated at the edges of the imposing Seleucid and then Roman realm, and incorporating some elements of the regal vocabulary of Macedonian kings, Hellenistic-era elites in Armenia practiced politics and projected authority within landscapes that incorporated the enduring remains of the Urartian and Achaemenid eras. Embedded within the physical vestiges of the Urartian and Achaemenid polities were the grounds on which later elites staked a claim to legitimacy and briefly realized the promise of empire.

Archaeological research in Armenia has tended to focus on monumental fortresses of the Ararat plain and their palatial or administrative centers, making the commemorative choices of elites particularly open to investigation. Elite arenas are indeed privileged sites of social production to which others respond. At the same time, social forms are substantially determined by subject behavior. Little is known about the social organization of the communities discussed in this chapter. Nevertheless, there is sufficient (though fragmentary) evidence for non-elite practices during the Hellenistic period—gleaned from the tantalizing digressions of top-down archaeological efforts—to suggest that past landscapes offered an important sense of place across the social spectrum. Though perhaps differently motivated, elite and non-elite commemorative acts in Hellenistic Armenia display similar trajectories in their memorialization of the past, reflecting the recursive relationships that shape decision making among elite and subject groups.

The social memories discussed here were constructed through text, place, and ritual behavior (Van Dyke and Alcock 2003, 4). The texts, which will be the focus of part one of this study, are a series of stelae dating to the reign of Artaxias I (189–160 BC), the eponymous first king of the Artaxiad dynasty. These stelae, which illustrate that pedigree and name are fertile terrain for memory and identity manipulation, offer direct evidence of Artaxias I's awareness of, and reliance upon, the Urartian and Yervandid Achaemenid past. The second part of this study looks at settlements of the last three centuries BC, and in particular the different ways in which two new political centers, Armavir and Artashat, interacted with preexisting Urartian fortresses in the kingdom's heartland on the Ararat plain. Certain Urartian citadels were reused with different degrees of modification, while others remained vacant. Even these neglected Urartian fortresses, however, became sites of activity. This phenomenon is examined in the third part of this study, which turns to funerary practices to suggest that the subjects of Hellenistic Armenia, just as their rulers, engaged in a deliberate discourse with the lived spaces of the Urartian past.

Royal Recollections: The Stelae of Artaxias I
(189–160 BC)

It is by now commonly held in scholarship on identity politics that little of our social matrix is to be understood as fixed and immutable. Class, ethnicity, religion, status, and even gender are subject to change and choice. The manipulation of these vectors of identity resides ultimately in the hands of individuals, whose choices may or may not represent wider group identities. Elite individuals figure prominently in classical and Near Eastern discourses. Colorful personalities are often well known, thanks in part to their own loquacity. In the stelae of Artaxias I we see such a loquacious ruler whose proclamations reveal a number of identity choices, including ones that extended to his very lineage. The stelae to be discussed tell the story of an individual king who used the seemingly lasting medium of carved stone in an attempt to safeguard the memory of his declared identity. These stelae are the only substantial corpus of written artifacts from Hellenistic Armenia. They are pragmatic monuments that exhibit a concerted effort on the part of a single individual to make an overt claim to territory and the right to demarcate it. The texts inscribed on them conveyed a message deemed important enough to be copied more than ten times and spread across a wide territory, in some cases providing the only material evidence for the presence of Artaxiad rule in regions as yet unexplored archaeologically.

The stelae have been found sporadically in Armenia since 1906, dispersed throughout the country, with the northernmost stele found at Spitak, the southernmost at Zangezur, and a cluster around Lake Sevan (fig. 3.1). Although their sizes vary, all of the stelae are roughly similar in shape—a rectangular stone, sometimes having a lug for a base, that widens toward the top and is crowned with three blunt crenellations (fig. 3.2), recalling a dentate crown-type form, which Root regards as an "incontrovertible hallmark of Achaemenid Persian iconography and formal resolution" (Root 1999, 164). The stelae are inscribed in Aramaic, the language of the Achaemenid Persian court, and the letter forms

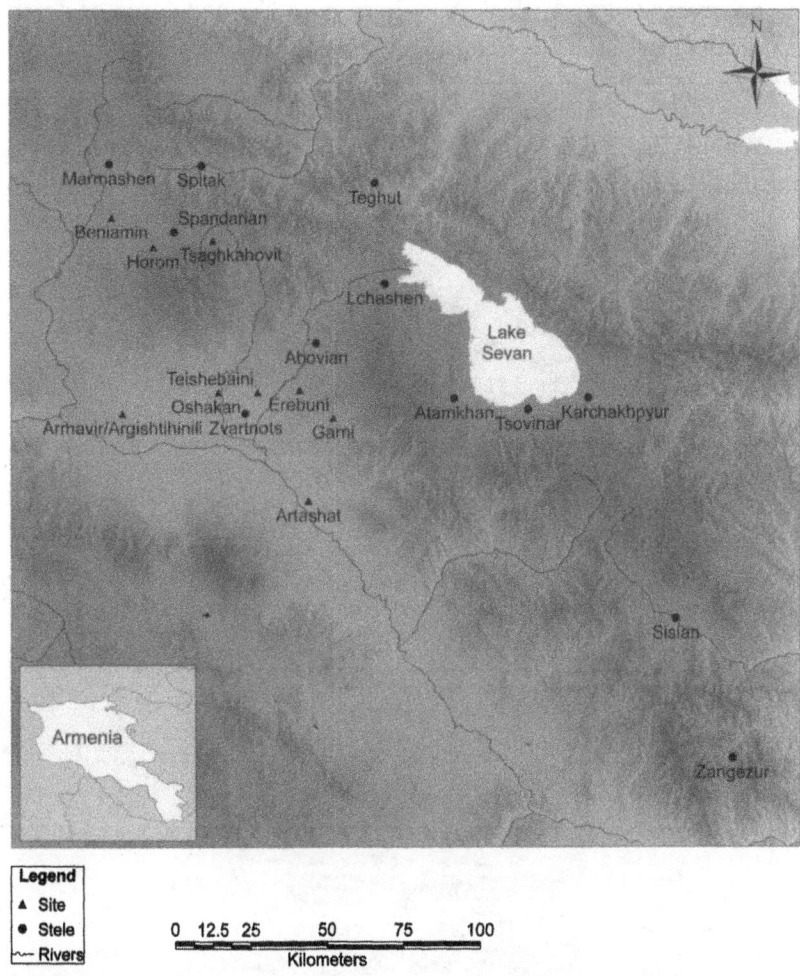

FIGURE 3.1 Map of Armenia

follow the tradition of the Achaemenid imperial office, although they point to a roughly second-century BC date, consistent with Artaxias I's regnal years, 189–160 BC (Tiratsyan 1977, 255). The inscriptions on these stelae are nearly identical in content. Each contains two elements: the title of the king and a practical statement addressing the occasion of the inscriptions. For example, the inscription from Teghut reads:

> In year ten of Artaxerxes, king, Yervandid, son of Zareh the Majestic, bearer of the crown, ally of Xšaθra [power?], Vanquisher of all who

encourage/engender Evil, Artaxerxes, king, Yervandid, son of Zareh, divided the land between the villages. (Perikhanian 1971, 170 [my translation from Perikhanian's French translation])

Within this formulaic arrangement are notable nuances, particularly in the rendering of the king's name. In the Sevan and Zangezur inscriptions

FIGURE 3.2 Artaxiad stele from Spitak (Tiratsyan 1977, 255)

his name occurs as "Artaxšasi," which is the Persian word for the Greek Artaxerxes (Tiratsyan 1977, 256). On the Teghut stele the scribe has used the Greek version, "Artaxerxes," but still rendered with Aramaic characters. In the Spitak inscriptions, the scribe employed the Persian name, but with no final suffix—"Artaxšas." This is the version that would come to be closest to the Armenian, Artashes (Tiratsyan 1977, 256). Thus, in several contemporary inscriptions the identity of the king himself—insofar as nomenclature is a marker of identity—is given different emphasis. Whether or not these stelae are the work of a single scribe, they are clearly the commission of a single individual. The otherwise strict conformity among the various stelae brings the variations in the rendering of the king's name into even greater relief.

There are two possible interpretations of this variation, both equally significant in their implications for Artaxiad elite identity. The use of Greek and Persian names for the same king may have been a deliberate gesture on the part of Artaxias I to draw upon the multiple languages of the region. In this instance we can understand Artaxiad identity construction not as a consistent, elite-dictated mandate for Hellenization or Persianization, but an undertaking marked by a degree of flexibility that might have been essential for anyone hoping to derive legitimacy in the heterogeneous cultural landscape of Hellenistic southwest Asia. If this interpretation pushes the evidence of a single name too far, an alternative analysis could read the use of Greek and Persian versions of the king's name as nothing more than scribal error or the work of multiple scribes whose competencies in one or another language varied. In this case, we might suggest that "ethnic" identity, at least as far as language is concerned, was inconsequential. To Artaxias I, who presumably commissioned the stelae, whether his name was rendered in Greek or Persian was not as important as might be expected among observers today, who are accustomed to polarizing Greek versus Persian identity as absolute and mutually exclusive qualities. The second interpretation appears somewhat more likely, but in either case the ultimate message is very much the same: even when set in stone, the identity of the king was not fixed.

Against this picture of deliberate mutability or linguistic indifference are a number of other factors that reveal the significance of these stelae not only as administrative texts but as commemorative artifacts. The use of the Aramaic alphabet reflects, for example, a choice on the part of the king and not the inevitable continuity of Achaemenid administrative practices. By the second century BC, Greek would have been another option for official correspondence. A set of roughly contemporary Greek rock-cut inscriptions from the site of Armavir demonstrates that this language was already introduced into this region (Robert and Robert 1952, 184–85). Among these Greek inscriptions is a list of the months of the year, whose order corresponds to that of the official Seleucid calendar (Sherwin-White and Kuhrt 1993, 195). This and other references in Greek sources make it clear that the authorities of Hellenistic Armenia were in diplomatic contact with the Macedonian powers to the west. In light of this, the choice to use Aramaic in the stelae constitutes an overt alignment with the Achaemenid past.

The feature of the stelae that best illuminates Artaxias I's use of the past to project his own identity is the king's title. There are numerous, if disparate, indications, in addition to the testimony of Strabo mentioned earlier, that Artaxias I ushered in a change in Armenian dynastic politics of the second century BC and was not a part of the preceding Yervandid dynastic line.[4] In the preceding Teghut inscription, however, Artaxias I declares himself a Yervandid. This claim to Yervandid descent appears on every one of the Artaxiad stelae, including the many abbreviated inscriptions in which certain elements of Artaxias I's titulature, such as "vanquisher of those who engender evil," are eliminated. The indispensable assertion, "Artaxšasi, king, son of Zareh, Yervandid" (Perikhanian 1971, 172), is always retained.

Artaxias I, in marshaling the memory of the Yervandid dynasty, exemplifies the ways in which previous political constellations can offer a repertoire of associations—in this case replete both with notions of empire and sovereignty—that are suitable to the task of choreographing identity. In 1959, G. A. Tiratsyan interpreted Artaxias I's deliberate affiliation with the Yervandid dynasts as an act of legitimation by association with Achaemenid grandeur. "To be a relative of the Yervandids," he wrote, "therefore meant to be a relative of the Achaemenids" (Tiratsyan 1959, 90 [my translation]). Artaxias I's declaration of putative Yervandid descent is an indication that the past was harnessed for the political capital it offered to the present.

Such declarations, however, only become capital when there is an audience to be persuaded. It is improbable that Aramaic could be read by the greater part of the viewers who looked upon Artaxias I's stelae, although nothing for certain is known about the audience of these monuments. The benefit to be gained by parading the apparently uncommon skill of writing across the Armenian plateau may have exceeded that obtained by adherence to the content of the inscriptions themselves. Nevertheless, given the pragmatic content of the stelae, primarily focused on some form of land parceling, we can at least assume a cohort of Artaxiad-period elites for whom these inscriptions, with their references to the Yervandid Achaemenid past, were comprehensible and meaningful acts of commemoration.

Artaxias I was not the first to inscribe his identity across the Armenian plateau in this way, although his inspiration does not seem to have been the Yervandids, whose administrative language and political legacy he otherwise celebrated in these inscriptions. Archaeological research in Armenia has not revealed any stelae dating to the Achaemenid period, suggesting that while the *content* of the texts calls upon the Yervandid past, the *form* of the stelae does not.[5] The concept of inscribing royal declarations on stone was first employed in the Armenian highland by the Urartians, and nearly fifty stone inscriptions written in Urartian cuneiform have been found in modern Armenia (only a small fraction of the hundreds of Urartian inscriptions found in Turkey and northwestern Iran [Harutunyan 2001]). Many of these inscriptions are found on building stones associated with fortresses; a prominent collection of such blocks was found at Armavir and would have been plainly visible to the Hellenistic inhabitants of the site. Numerous other inscriptions, however, were also scattered across the landscape on cliffs across Armenia, at such sites as Abovian, Marmashen, Lchashen, Atamkhan, and Tsovinar (Harutunyan 2001). These inscriptions would have been noticeable to later generations of antiquity just as they are today. More analogous still to the Artaxiad stelae is a set of Urartian stone stelae with cuneiform inscriptions. Most of these have been found in Turkey, although two examples from Armenia—one discovered on the Ararat plain at Zvartnots and the other in the south, near Sisian—offer convincing parallels to the Artaxiad examples. All of the Urartian stelae have worked, rounded crowns and

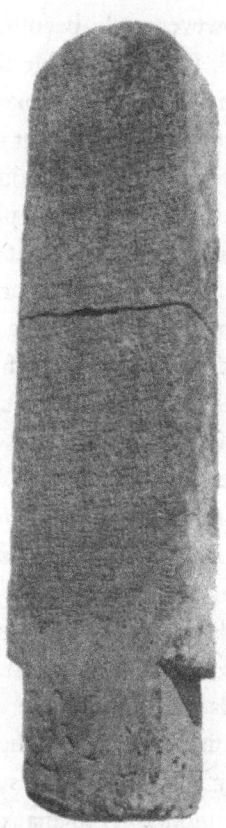

FIGURE 3.3 Urartian stele from Zangezur (Harutunyan 2001, plate CXLIX)

some, like the Artaxiad versions, have lugs at their base (fig. 3.3). Artaxias I's decision to deploy rock-cut Aramaic inscriptions on stelae across Armenia was, I suggest, modeled on the cuneiform rock-cut inscriptions that were found similarly dispersed across the Armenian landscape.

In content and in form, therefore, Artaxias I drew from both the Urartian and Yervandid past, materializing the resonances offered by these polities in the durable medium of stone. Neither he nor his commemorative act, however, was immune to later gestures of social forgetting. Another stele was recently found near the southern shore of Lake Sevan, tucked behind a wax-covered votive stand in an active shrine associated with a small cemetery. The artifact is unmistakably an Artaxiad stele, with its hallmark crenellated top and lugged base. The Aramaic inscription, however, has been effaced, and in its place a cross has been carved in high relief, effectively converting the Artaxiad monument into an irregularly shaped Armenian *khatchkar*, or Christian cross stone. Artaxias I's stele, which sought to memorialize both his own identity and the Yervandid past, was turned into the most common sacred symbol of modern Armenia, in effect subverting or annexing the memory of Armenia's pre-Christian past. This stele is an instructive reminder of the relentless and shifting nature of the work of social memory.

On the Summits of Urartu: Capital Cities in Hellenistic Armenia

With the exception of the Artaxiad stelae, the durable imprint of Hellenistic Armenia's discourse with the past is visible in physical space rather than in text. Authorities of this period built their political centers on a landscape dotted with monumental architecture dating from as early as the Late Bronze Age. The placement of political centers such as Armavir and Artashat in the last three centuries BC suggests that it was the built landscape of Urartu that preoccupied the commemorative energies of the political elites who governed the Armenian highland in the last three centuries BC. Yet the silence of the historical record on the matter of Urartu would have us believe that this polity was all but forgotten after its collapse, at the end of the seventh century. The Achaemenid Persians had some recollection of a place named Urartu in the region of Armenia, judging by the Bisitun inscription.[6] This text, however, is the last historical reference to Urartu, and after the Urartian collapse most of the Urartian lands are bound to the Achaemenid Persian Empire, though how closely is not clear.

The built remains of Urartu, however, remained as potent reminders to subsequent authorities that they were not the first to rise, nor would they be the last to fall. On the Ararat plain, Urartian citadels stood visible and in different conditions: one, a dilapidated heap of melted mud brick with stone foundation courses (for example, Teishebaini); others, palatial complexes with still-formidable defensive capabilities (for example, Argishtihinili, Artashat, Erebuni, Oshakan) (fig. 3.1). Of these, at least two were reoccupied in the Achaemenid period (Erebuni, Oshakan). Urartu may have been forgotten by Armenia's neighbors, whose scribes and authors are our only written sources on Armenia in the late first millennium BC.

But for those living among the ruins of Urartu's fortresses, it would be difficult not to acknowledge the legacy of a once-cohesive and formidable power.

To be sure, there are several factors that can explain the reuse of Urartian fortresses in the Hellenistic period, including economic, strategic, and environmental considerations. The reoccupation of an Urartian fortress does not necessarily signal a deliberate policy to memorialize or co-opt an earlier political tradition. Nor are the various factors that help explain settlement patterning mutually exclusive. It is nevertheless notable that no single major Hellenistic site on the Ararat plain is located apart from a preexisting Urartian fortress. The challenge for future research will be to identify independent lines of evidence that can further support the notion explored here, of a purposeful reoccupation of certain Urartian landscapes.

There is a striking and ironic distinction between Urartian and Hellenistic regard for the built past. The Urartians obliterated the memory of their forerunners by literally scraping and razing all preceding occupation levels at a given site before building directly on bedrock—"a technology of political memory and forgetting" (Smith 2003, 168). In contrast, authorities of the late first millennium interacted with Urartian spaces through a combination of non-destructive abandonment and varying degrees of reuse. The configuration of Hellenistic capitals suggests an effort on the part of late Yervandid and then Artaxiad elites to establish themselves as independent political entities, while at the same time drawing upon the symbolic resources of Urartu. Such calculations played themselves out most obviously on the Ararat plain, which appears to have been a central focus of settlement activity throughout the first millennium BC.

Significant challenges beset the study of post-Urartian settlements in Armenia. Archaeological research has focused largely on the Ararat plain. Even there, despite considerable research at Argishtihinili, Armavir, Erebuni, Oshakan, and Teishebaini, some sites are as yet uninvestigated or unpublished.[7] The recent excavations at Horom (Badaljan et al. 1995) and Beniamin (Khachatryan 1991, 1998), and the recent survey and excavations on the Tsaghkahovit plain (Smith et al. 2004) are beginning to fill the gap in knowledge of the north, as are recent survey projects in the south.⁸ This study focuses on the Ararat plain, both because it has benefited from decades of study and because it was (and still is) a political heartland. Enough data are available on the Ararat plain to suggest that Hellenistic-period authorities organized their polities through a communication with the past and a regard for the political necessities of the present.

Erebuni

Among these political necessities may have been the establishment of a new capital, a practice hardly uncommon among successive powers in southwest Asia, but apparently new to the Armenian highland. Erebuni had effectively been a capital for over five hundred years, first as an Urartian political center beginning in the eighth century BC and then possibly as a satrapal outpost within the Achaemenid Empire. The site underwent significant changes in the Achaemenid period, with the expansion of columned halls that resemble, on a smaller scale, the monumental structures at Persepolis (Tiratsyan 1960; Ter-Martirosov 2001). By the Hellenistic period, Erebuni's identity as an Urartian fortress was substantially transformed and perhaps forgotten given the more recent associations with Achaemenid hegemony that had defined the site for over two centuries.

Erebuni was abandoned at some point after the collapse of the Achaemenid Empire. There is scarcely any evidence for occupation in the Hellenistic period. For reasons that are not yet clear, both the late Yervandid and the Artaxiad authorities dissociated from a settlement that had served as a capital for over half a millennium. It is tempting to suppose that the intermediate Achaemenid-era use of the site was somehow a factor in Erebuni's abandonment, and it is noteworthy that other Urartian fortresses that were substantially reoccupied in the Achaemenid period, namely the sites of Oshakan and Altıntepe (Summers 1993), were also neglected as centers of authority in the Hellenistic period. However, all instances of abandonment cannot uncritically be explained as a deliberate rejection of a part of the past. As I hope to make clear in this section, we can go no further than to speak from the positive evidence, which demonstrates that Hellenistic authorities restricted their capitals to landscapes first built in the Urartian period.

From Argishtihinili to Armavir

The new capital at Argishtihinili would have projected the resonance of former supremacy. Argishtihinili was founded in 776 BC by the Urartian king Argishti I. Situated in the western Ararat plain, five kilometers north of the modern course of the Araxes River, the settlement's location catered to Argishti's apparent ambition to situate his fortresses at all four corners of the plain. Argishtihinili became one of the largest Urartian complexes on the Armenian plateau. The settlement's life as an Urartian fortress came to an end in the late seventh or early sixth century.

The site is made up of two complexes that consist of an extended ridge to the west and an adjacent basalt outcrop to the east. Both complexes have undergone thorough investigation (Martirosyan 1974; Tiratsyan 1988). On the eastern complex, referred to as Armavir, a Hellenistic settlement dating from the third through first centuries BC was identified amidst the Urartian constructions (Tiratsyan 1988, 11). This corresponds with the account of the controversial early Armenian historian Moses Khorenatsi, who reports that Armavir became a capital of Armenia after the Achaemenid collapse. The veracity of his description is questionable given that almost a millennium separates Khorenatsi from his subject.[9] Nevertheless, it is archaeologically demonstrated that Armavir was a prominent Hellenistic center, with a probable elite residence at the summit of the hill and a lower settlement to the west of the fortress (Tiratsyan 1979, 163). Given its appearance in Ptolemy's *Geographia* (Ptol., *Geog.* V.12), Armavir must have been a reasonably sizeable and important settlement in the late first millennium BC.

The Urartian structures of the Armavir citadel, including those that archaeologists identified as dwelling quarters, palatial structures, and temple buildings, were reused with little or no modification in the late first millennium (Tiratsyan 1988, 82) (fig. 3.4). The Urartian fortifications were also adopted, with only minor restoration to the mud-brick superstructures that rested above the semi-ashlar stone foundations and the addition of a tower that restricted access to the entrance (Tiratsyan 1979, 164). The masonry technique observable in the construction of this tower and in some other modified walls, namely the use of swallowtail clamps, is found elsewhere in Hellenistic Armenia and the wider Hellenistic and Achaemenid realms, helping to date these restorations to the post-Urartu era.

The precise relationship between Hellenistic and Urartian constructions varies across the fortress, with the most substantial modifications in the western area (Tiratsyan 1988; Kanetsyan 1998); however, the architectural plans detailing the configuration of the Hellenistic levels in this area are complicated by the poor state of preservation.

What is important for our purposes is the nearly wholesale adoption of the Urartian buildings and fortifications that effectively organized spatial relationships at this site in the Hellenistic period and that served as constant reminders of Armavir's connection with the distant past. The choice to reconstruct walls and build towers in a technique that differed from Urartian methods and instead drew on new masonry styles with Mediterranean associations, while operating in a largely undisturbed Urartian settlement, reveals the mix of past and present associations that shaped Hellenistic Armavir. The late Yervandid kings of the fourth century abandoned Erebuni, perhaps to distance themselves from the satrapal connotations of that place. They reached further back into the past to capitalize on the unprecedented potency of a clearly old and dominant presence, just as they asserted their new identity as rulers of an independent polity.

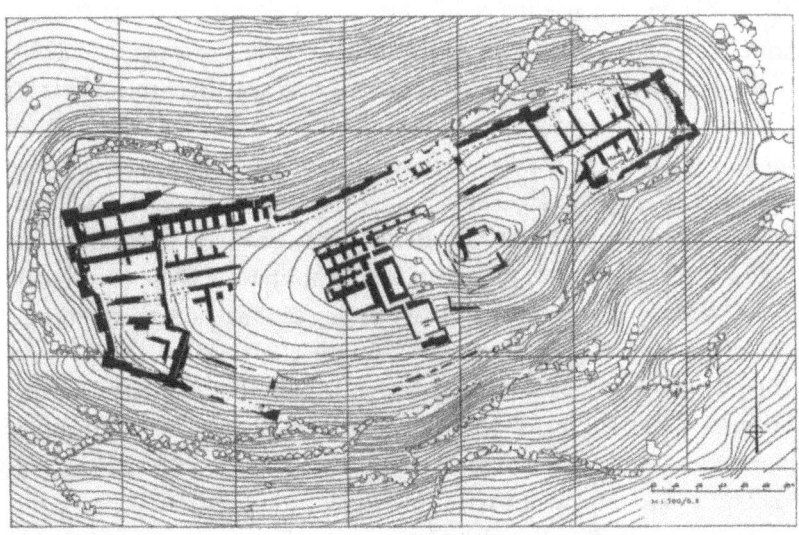

FIGURE 3.4 Plan of Armavir (Kanetsyan 1998, 14)

Artashat (Greek Artaxata)

> Hannibal the Carthaginian, after Antiochus had been conquered by the Romans, left him and went to Artaxas the Armenian.... Observing that a section of the country which had the greatest natural advantages and attractions was lying idle and neglected, he drew up a plan for a city there ... whereupon a very great and beautiful city arose there, which was named after the king, and proclaimed the capital of Armenia. (Plut. *Luc.*, 31)

The natural advantages to which Plutarch refers are those discussed several decades earlier by his probable source, Strabo—namely the Araxes River and the broad, fertile Ararat plain that stretches out in all directions from the site of Artashat.[10] While his description of the place as "idle" and "neglected" recalls the sort of hyperbole that precedes many Urartian declarations of fortress building in Armenia (see Smith 2003, 163–65), it is in fact archaeologically demonstrable that Artashat had been idle for some time, not having been occupied in the Achaemenid period. In their descriptions, however, both Plutarch and Strabo omit an important, additional advantage of this place. On the highest of the twelve hills that make up the site was an Urartian fortress with the distinctive buttressed walls that are the hallmark of Urartian fortifications (fig. 3.5). Like Armavir before it, this second capital city of Hellenistic Armenia, founded at the time of the installation of a new dynastic family in the early second century BC, was grafted atop the Urartian citadel that had been abandoned for over four hundred years. It should be pointed out that Artashat would have offered an attractive settlement location regardless of its past associations, with its conglomeration of adjacent twelve hills rising from the flat fertile plain, and well watered by the Araxes River. Nevertheless, Hellenistic authorities, in their movements and settlement choices, were also responding to the tenor of resilient and enduring authority that Urartian spaces project.

However, in contrast to Armavir and, indeed, to all the Urartian fortresses that came before, the Hellenistic settlement at Artashat was unprecedented in form and scale. With the exception of a brief capital-building project at Tigranokerta (in modern southeastern Turkey) during the reign of Tigranes the Great in the first century BC, Artashat remained the capital until the fourth century AD. The city was large and

Attachments to the Past in Hellenistic Armenia 61

FIGURE 3.5 Plan of Artashat (Tonikian 1992, 170)

imposing, and though the hill that supports the Urartian fortress is the largest of the twelve, it is consumed by the broader design of the site, which is demarcated by an embracing fortification wall. The entire site has been elaborately mapped, and two of the twelve hills have been excavated completely: hill one, which seems to have been a military barrack and outpost; and hill eight, which consists of domestic quarters. Four hills were destroyed by intensive blasting for marble quarrying in the Soviet period, and the remaining hills have been investigated only partially or not at all. Unfortunately, the second hill (where the Urartian citadel stood) has received limited attention to date, which prohibits a close comparison of Urartian and later constructions. It appears that some parts of the Urartian fortress were repaired or modified, particularly its defensive walls, "according to old Urartian methods of fortification, which by that time were obsolete" (Tonikian 1992, 173). These walls were incorporated into the general defensive system of the Hellenistic settlement.

In many respects, Artashat appears to represent a departure from the Urartian past. Some have compared the city of Artashat with Hellenistic cities of Asia Minor such as Pergamon and Priene in terms of how the city plan accommodates the natural setting with manmade spaces—a common feature of Hellenistic urban planning. This sense of departure from the Urartian past is also shaped by the personality of Tigranes II (95–56 BC), the great-grandson of Artaxias I, who was renowned in ancient literary sources for his philhellenism, and during whose reign Armenia would be brought into close contact with Rome. Under Tigranes II and his successors, Artashat would be a place where coins were minted for the first time, relations with Rome were managed, and plays of Euripides allegedly performed.[11] Nevertheless, the physical and metaphorical constructions of Urartu provided a springboard for the Hellenistic capital, and Urartian traditions can be traced in the layout of the forts of the citadel that persisted for as long as the city was in use (Tiratsyan 1979, 174). The spatial and architectural relationships that may one day be discovered on hill two will further clarify our understanding of the correlation between the Urartian occupation and the Hellenistic city.

Houses of the Dead: Remembering Urartu through Funerary Practice

Mortuary landscapes are fertile ground for the glorification of the past, as numerous studies that have probed the ritual veneration of ancestors have shown (Jonker 1995; Kuijt 1996; Barrett 1988; Morris 1988; Bradley 2002). For the communities living on the Ararat plain in the final three centuries BC, funerary landscapes were indeed primary venues for the veneration of the past. The foci of commemoration, intriguingly, were not the deceased ancestors themselves but, it appears, the living spaces they once inhabited. At different points on the Ararat plain, burials dating from the third through first centuries BC have been found embedded within the ruins of Urartian settlements. In each case, the primary complexes of the Urartian fortresses were left vacant. These monumental constructions served as commanding backdrops as attention instead turned to the living quarters associated with those citadels, which (with one exception) had not been inhabited since the Urartian collapse in the late seventh century BC. In two of these cases (Teishebaini and Oshakan), the settlements associated with the Hellenistic burials have not yet been located, but it is clear that the Urartian spaces where the burials were placed were not themselves occupied in the Hellenistic period and instead were utilized solely as settings for funerary ritual.

Across the Ararat plain, Hellenistic-era mortuary rituals were played out in the living spaces of the Urartian past, in some cases, as at Teishebaini, with such careful attention to the original configuration of these spaces that individual rooms each accommodated only one burial. Once-lived landscapes were converted into cemeteries through a process that preserved the integrity of the past and injected its quotidian landscapes with the connotations of mortuary space. The Urartian settlements became liminal zones, where the transformation from life to death was exercised in funerary ritual just as it was represented in physical space.

Argishtihinili

As discussed above, the Hill of Armavir was reinhabited in the late fourth century BC and became an important political center until the founding of a new capital at Artashat in the early second century BC. Excavations at Argishtihinili proper, however, where the main complex of the Urartian fortress stood, did not reveal reoccupation levels dating to the late first millennium BC. Nevertheless, Hellenistic interactions with Urartian Argishtihinili did extend to the western boundaries of the site.

In the residential blocks and detached houses of the Urartian fortress, A. Martirosyan uncovered a series of burials contemporary with the post-Urartian occupation at Armavir (Martirosyan 1974, 55–58). The forms of the burials correspond to those found at other Hellenistic cemeteries in Armenia. In room number four of the residential complex called House number two, for example, a jar burial and a stone-lined burial—both similar in form and arrangement to securely dated Hellenistic burials at Teishebaini—were nestled within the Urartian stratum. Two more burials were found in room number two of House number three, belonging to the same residential complex. One was another stone-lined grave located in the same stratigraphic level as that in House number two, this one containing a few items of bronze jewelry. The other was a pit burial with ceramics. Six or seven more stone-lined burials were identified within Urartian levels in the central residential quarter at Argishtihinili. Some of these were covered with hardened clay formed from the destroyed mud-brick walls of the Urartian buildings.

The total number of identified burials at this site is limited (around ten, although the site report is unclear on precise numbers). It bears mentioning that not all of the domestic spaces at Argishtihinili have been fully excavated. The burials are modest, with few grave goods. For the non-elite families who buried their deceased within this abandoned Urartian town, the domestic spaces of Argishti's fortress provided an appropriate setting despite several centuries of dereliction, suggesting that the vacant fortress was imbued with particular associations in the late first millennium. Whether or not those associations related to its Urartian identity, they were sufficiently commanding to attract not only the late Yervandid elite, who saw in Armavir a new political center, but also families who regarded Argishtihinili's residential surroundings—evocative as they must have been of the living past—a fitting place in which to commemorate their dead.

Oshakan

An identical phenomenon can be observed at the Urartian site of Oshakan, located in the northwest corner of the Ararat plain. The site is made up of an imposing hill on which the main fortress is situated, and a smaller hill to the northeast, on whose north slope archaeologists S. A. Esayan and A. A. Kalantaryan excavated a Hellenistic cemetery with over forty burials (Esayan and Kalantaryan 1988, 32). The burials were located amidst the ruins of a large, agglutinative living complex built in the eighth century BC and destroyed at the same time as Argishtihinili and Teishebaini, in the late seventh century BC. However, as at

Erebuni, some form of activity continued at the site until the end of the fifth century BC.

Of the excavated burials, some were located outside the complex area. Over thirty burials, however, were spread across fifteen rooms of the thirty-nine-room complex, with most rooms containing more than one burial, and a concentration of burials in room XII (fig. 3.6). Most of the burials were of the stone-box type covered with stone slabs, in which the body was lying on its left side—a burial form also seen at Argishtihinili and Teishebaini. In many of the stone boxes there were traces of burning attesting to graveside ceremonies. Some of the burials discovered within the Urartian rooms were cromlechs—a burial form consisting of one or more stone circles, often with central capstones.[12] Several jug burials were also found within the rooms. In one such burial (number thirty-eight) the jug was placed inside a stone box, which was itself covered with a cromlech; such combinations of burial forms are not uncommon at Oshakan.

The ceramics from the inventory of the burials include several forms that are highly distinctive of post-Urartian pottery, in particular a set of painted flasks that can be securely dated to the third through first centuries BC (Esayan and Kalantaryan 1976, 31). Some of the burials had been robbed, while about half of the unrobbed tombs had no inventory whatsoever. The remaining contained an evenly distributed collection

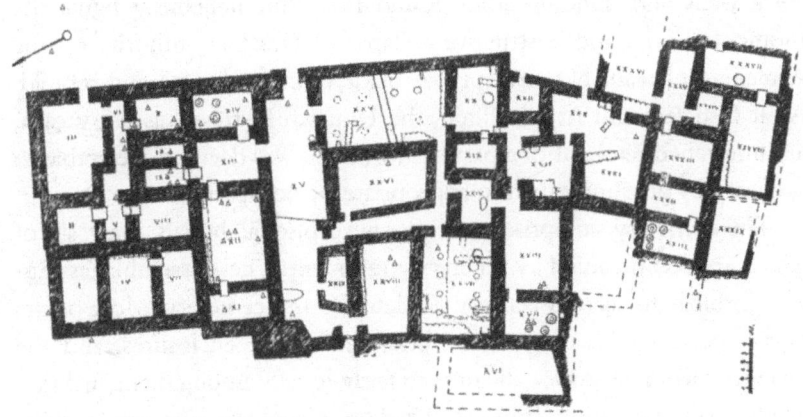

FIGURE 3.6 Plan of Oshakan settlement with approximate locations of burials (marked by triangles)(Esayan and Kalantaryan 1988, plate XI)

of bronze, iron, and gold jewelry or paste beads, with the exception of a few burials (for example, number eleven and number thirty-six), which were disproportionately rich in jewelry. The design and method of manufacture of two bracelets from this corpus, when considered along with a blown-glass flask, suggest that the cemetery was in use until the third century AD. (Esayan and Kalantaryan 1976, 39).

For several hundred years, therefore, beginning in the Hellenistic period, the rooms of this complex, which once served as the residence of an Urartian elite, became modest and fragmented contexts for mortuary activity—constricted and divided by the spatial organization of the Urartian constructions. Commemorating the dead at Oshakan, as at Argishtihinili, became linked with the acknowledgement of the lived spaces of the past.

Teishebaini

Situated in the northeastern part of the Ararat plain, Teishebaini was a large fortified complex built by the Urartians in the early seventh century BC and destroyed at the end of that same century. The ruins of Teishebaini are still visible today, as they would have been in the third century BC, when a community established a cemetery inside the abandoned Urartian settlement (fig. 3.7) (Tiratsyan and Vayman 1974). The settlement is located at the foothills of the citadel, whose ruined mudbrick walls and standing stone foundations simultaneously signal the momentous rise and destructive collapse of Urartian authority on the Armenian plateau. No attempt was made to clear the site and rebuild. As at Oshakan and Argishtihinili, the Urartian fortress was left vacant, an untouched remnant of a past with which it was deemed preferable to associate by proximity than to appropriate by occupation.

The cemetery comprises several unexceptional burials, only six of which are accompanied by funerary equipment. These assemblages suggest a third- to second-century BC date for the cemetery. Most of the burials consist of pentagonal or hexagonal stone enclosures, and the inventory from the graves, distributed fairly equally among them, includes beads, a silver seal-ring, iron spearheads, and some bronze jewelry similar to that found in the Oshakan cemetery. Unlike Oshakan, no two burials were placed in the same room; however, as at Oshakan, funerary

FIGURE 3.7 View of Teishebaini fortress from lower settlement (photo: L. Khatchadourian)

rituals are choreographed according to the spatial configuration of the Urartian town (fig. 3.8).

On the whole the Teishebaini cemetery signifies a local commitment to a place and its past. Yet though some characterizations of the Hellenistic world have gone rather far in portraying this period as one of unprecedented globalization in the wake of Alexander, the final three centuries BC do appear to have ushered in new opportunities for travel and contact between and within the eastern and western Mediterranean (Walbank 1992). One of the Teishebaini burials speaks to this new atmosphere and offers an important reminder that the past is not all that mattered to the Hellenistic-era communities of the Ararat plain. Along with two bronze bracelets, in this burial a silver drachma of Alexander the Great, bearing on the obverse the distinctive bust of Heracles adorned in his lion skin and on the reverse an enthroned Zeus with scepter and eagle, was placed in the mouth of a deceased child as "Charon's Fee" (fig. 3.9). This Greek burial practice of offering payment to the ferryman Charon for leading the soul of the deceased over the river Styx is men-

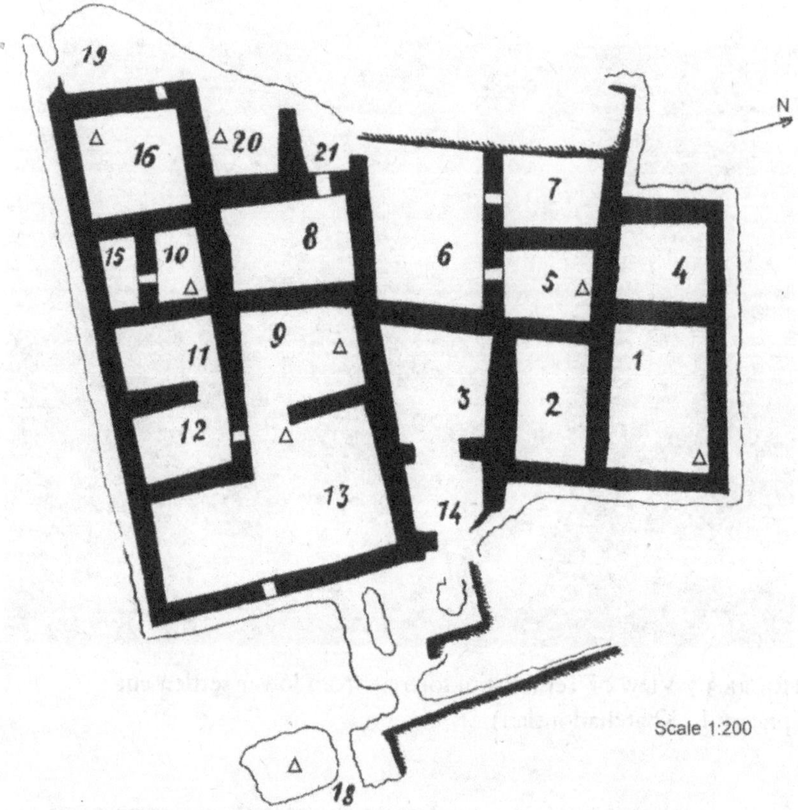

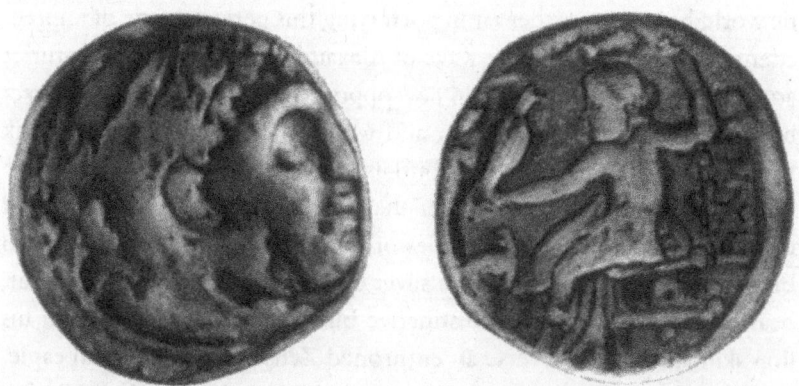

FIGURE 3.8 Plan of Teishebaini settlement with approximate locations of burials (marked by triangles)(Tiratsyan and Vayman 1974, 68)

FIGURE 3.9 Alexander the Great coin from child's burial at Teishebaini (Tiratsyan and Vayman 1974, 63)

tioned by a number of Greek sources including Aristophanes, Strabo, and Lucian, and is first noted archaeologically in Athenian graves of the Hellenistic period. Contemporary with the Teishebaini burial is a fourth-century burial at Olynthos, where the deceased—here too a child—was found with a bronze coin in its mouth (Kurtz and Boardman 1971). The Teishebaini burial is not the only instance of this practice on the Armenian plateau; other such burials have been found in eastern Turkey and at the Armenian site of Garni, where yet another coin of Alexander the Great was buried with the deceased (Tiratsyan 1976).

For the family of this child at Teishebaini, the symbols of the Macedonian conqueror and the social changes introduced by his campaign across the east influenced funerary ritual behavior just as did the commanding Urartian fortress at whose foot the child was buried. Allegiances to past and present, and commitments to local and global senses of belonging, converge in this one burial and evoke the competing pressures and associations that continuously shape social memory in the past.

Conclusion

Adam Smith recently wrote that "military defeat in the late seventh century B.C. led to a political collapse so complete that even the memory of the Urartian empire virtually disappeared" (Smith 2003, 254). This study, which has tried to demonstrate the materially visible and multifaceted reuse of Urartian landscapes in Hellenistic Armenia, would seem at first glance to challenge Smith's claim of wholesale forgetting.

What is at issue, however, in this seeming incongruity between the remembering and forgetting of Urartu is the distinction between form and content in the production of social memories. This contrast was explicitly presented in the discussion on the Artaxiad stelae, where the content of the inscriptions unambiguously pointed to an attachment to the Yervandid past, while the form of the stelae most probably was derived from the numerous (though presumably incomprehensible) cuneiform Urartian stelae and stone inscriptions dispersed throughout Armenia. Similarly, the repeated occurrence of Urartian fortresses and settlements across the Ararat plain, distinctive and evocative both in their physical setting and technological achievement, unmistakably captured the attention of elites and non-elites in the Hellenistic period. It is the *form* of these reused and modified landscapes—the relationship between old and new constructions, settlement plans, and functional uses of space—that open them to interpretation as venues for the commemoration of the past. It is doubtful, however, that the *content* or meaning of these spaces as specifically Urartian was retained among the communities who interacted within them in the last three centuries of the first millennium BC. In the commemoration of monuments, "there is a certain tension between the enduring character of these buildings" Bradley notes, "and the changing ways in which they were actually used" (Bradley 2003, 223). The meanings of places change over time, even if their forms remain the same. It is in this light that Smith's proposition cannot be contested.

Social memories, however, are always selective, in response to the specific needs of the present, and transformative in the way they shape the meaning of the past, even in the most literate of communities and across the shortest of time spans. The meanings of Urartu's landscapes in the Hellenistic period of course differed substantially from what they may have been several centuries before. Whether such spaces were generative of mythologies, they were clearly nodal points for collective activities among different social groups across the Ararat plain in this later period.

For the elite groups who established the capital cities of Armavir and Artashat amidst Urartian ruins, these ruins were meaningful in ways we can only conjecture, perhaps as sites of a stable and long-term authority with the demonstrable ability to harness considerable human resources. There would have been good reason to project an image of stability and authority in the final three centuries BC. In this period, Armenia came into contact and conflict with formidable militaristic powers such as the Seleucids, the Romans, and the Parthians. These powers interfered regularly in Armenian affairs. According to Strabo, Artaxias I was given the throne by the Seleucid king Antiochus III after the latter had defeated the last Yervandid king and brought Armenia under direct satrapal control in 212 BC. (Strabo 11.14.11). Antiochus III was defeated by Rome in 190 BC at the Battle of Magnesia, and it is at this time, Strabo tells us, that Artaxias I declared himself an independent king and established the new capital at Artashat. After the campaigns of Pompey, Armenia became a Roman protectorate, and the country was often in the middle of Rome's constant struggles with the Parthians. In the fragile political period immediately after Achaemenid collapse, and the aggressive milieu that was fostered by Roman interventions in the east, we can surmise the ideological capital that was gained, at home and abroad, from affiliating with the legacy of such an authority as Urartu.

The stelae of Artaxias I suggest that this king drew upon the legacy of the recent Yervandid dynasty in establishing his legitimacy; yet in reoccupying Urartian fortress sites, Hellenistic authorities also reached further back, memorializing the physical forms of an earlier polity. With the content of Urartian political traditions now forgotten, elites could appropriate these landscapes and inscribe them with new meanings. The forms and contents of the Urartian and Yervandid pasts could be merged to produce a new political identity that drew differently from both antecedents.

This elite proclivity toward Urartian fortress sites took place in dialogue with subject responses toward the Urartian past. The demands and motivations behind the establishment of cemeteries in the once-lived Urartian spaces of Argishtihinili, Oshakan, and Teishebaini are less easily inferred. Many of the burials, especially at Oshakan, were composed from the worked stones of the Urartian rooms, suggesting a functional explanation for this practice; however, this was not always the case. When we consider the numerous jar burials and the graves whose stone slabs were not taken from the Urartian constructions, an alternative explanation based on a collective attachment to the past becomes more compelling.

Ruth Van Dyke and Susan Alcock have pointed out that while "in archaeological contexts it is easiest to see the top-down machinations of elite groups using memory to [create and support a sense of individual and communal identity], memory is also employed in the service of resistance" (Van Dyke and Alcock 2003, 3). The notion of legitimacy inherently assumes an audience before whom a case must be made, which means alternative constructions can never be too far off. It is notable that all of the Hellenistic cemeteries are located near fortresses that were not reinhabited as Hellenistic power centers. Through these cemeteries subject communities appropriated *their own* Urartian landscapes, whose commanding citadels were otherwise neglected. Although not necessarily a statement of resistance in any formal sense, the Urartian towns used as Hellenistic cemeteries do mark distinct loci for commemoration, existing apart from the instruments of the polity.

Across the Ararat plain, and across social boundaries, at least two different conversations with the past operated simultaneously, although in different ways and in separate spaces. As elites and non-elites interacted with different parts of the built past, their commemorative acts converged around a common attachment to the unforgettable landscapes of Urartu.

Acknowledgments

Various units of the University of Michigan, including the Center for Russian and East European Studies, the Armenian Studies Program, the International Institute, and the Interdepartmental Program in Classical Art and Archaeology, have provided support for my research in Armenia. I would also like to thank Mkrditch Zardaryan and Ruben Badalyan for their continuing guidance. I greatly appreciate the comments offered on earlier drafts of this chapter by Susan Alcock, John Cherry, Adam T. Smith, and Norman Yoffee.

Notes

1. The term *Hellenistic* is used here as a shorthand to denote the final three centuries of the first millennium BC. The cultural associations triggered by the word *Hellenization* are not implied by my use of the term *Hellenistic*, intended here as a chronological designator.

2. The "Armenian plateau" refers to the uplands of modern eastern Turkey and the Republic of Armenia. This study focuses on the eastern parts of the plateau, in modern-day Armenia, particularly on the Ararat plain, which is only one part of the larger Armenian highlands.

3. To illustrate this point, contrast case studies in Bradley 2002 with those in Alcock 2002.

4. Another indication that Artaxias I marks a new dynastic line is that, prior to him, every reference to the Yervandid kings of Armenia—whether in Greek or Aramaic sources—identifies them by the name (or title) Orontes/Yervand. This makes Artaxias's name a point of departure. Also, the account of the early Armenian historian Moses Khorenatsi, though deeply controversial and problematic in many regards, records animosity between Artaxias and the last Yervandid king. Whether Khorenatsi is accurate or not, his testimony indicates that in the fifth century AD, the memory of this earlier period is one of discord, not continuity, between the Yervandids and Artaxias (Thomson 1978).

5. The practice of writing appears to have disappeared from the Armenian highland in the Achaemenid period. Two Elamite tablets that address the Gilgamesh legend were found at the site of Armavir and stand as possible exceptions to this claim. Although the dating of the tablets is disputed between an eighth- and a sixth-century BC date, even the latter estimated date is close to 550 BC, before the consolidation of the Achaemenid Empire (Diakonoff and Jankowska 1990; Vallat 1997).

6. The Babylonian version of the Bisitun inscriptions mentions a place called Urartu, corresponding with Armenia in the Old Persian and Elamite versions of the same inscription (LeCoq 1997).

7. Metzamor and Voskevaz are unpublished. Dovri and Artashat are largely uninvestigated. Aramus is currently undergoing excavation.

8. Recent research in southern Armenia has been carried out by Western archaeologists in collaboration with Armenian scholars. One project is headed by Dr. Stephan Kroll and Dr. Pavel Avetisyan. For more information see http://www.vaa.fak12.uni-muenchen.de/Armenia/Armenia.html. The other project, called the Vorotan Project, is directed by Dr. Susan Alcock, Dr. John Cherry, Dr. Mkrditch Zardaryan, and Dr. Armen Tonikian (Alcock and Cherry 2005).

9. There is much controversy concerning the date of Moses Khorenatsi's *History of the Armenians*. See Thomson 1978.

10. Strabo says of Artashat: "The cities of Armenia are Artaxata, also called Artaxiasata, which was founded by Hannibal for Artaxias the king, and Arxata, both of the Araxes River. . . . Artaxata is near the Araxene plain, being a beautiful settlement and the royal residence of the country. It is situated on a peninsula-like elbow of land and its walls have the river as protection all round them, except at the isthmus, which is enclosed by a trench and a palisade." (Str. 11.14.6)

11. See Plutarch's *Life of Crassus*, 33. Crassus's head is delivered to the Armenian and Parthian kings while they are viewing a production of the *Bacchai*.

12. This burial type is common in the Late Bronze and Early Iron ages but unusual for the Hellenistic period.

Bibliography

Alcock, Susan E. 2002. *Archaeologies of the Greek Past: Landscape, Monuments, and Memories*. Cambridge: Cambridge University Press.

Alcock, Susan E., and John Cherry. 2005. New Fieldwork in Armenia: The Vorotan Project, 2005. *Kelsey Newsletter* (Fall 2005): 6–7.

Alcock, Susan E., Hendrik D. Dey, and Grant Parker. 2001. Sitting Down with the Barrington Atlas. *Journal of Roman Archaeology* 14:454–61.

Badaljan, Ruben S., Phil L. Kohl, and Stephan E. Kroll. 1997. Horom 1995: Bericht über die amerikanisch-armenisch-deutsche archäologische Expedition in Armenien. *Archäologische Mitteilungen aus Iran und Turan*. 29:191–228.

Barrett, John C. 1988. The Living, the Dead, and the Ancestors: Neolithic and Early Bronze Age Mortuary Practices. In *The Archaeology of Context in the Neolithic and Early Bronze Age: Recent Trends*, ed. John C. Barrett and Ian A. Kinnes, 30–41. Sheffield: Sheffield Department of Archaeology and Prehistory.

Bradley, Richard. 2002. *The Past in Prehistoric Societies*. London and New York: Routledge.

——— 2003. The Translation of Time. In *Archaeologies of Memory*, eds. Ruth M. Van Dyke and Susan E. Alcock, 221–27. Malden, Mass.: Blackwell.

Briant, Pierre. 1982. *Rois, tributs et paysans: études sur les formations tributaires du Moyen-Orient ancient.* Paris: Les Belles Letters.

Diakonoff, I. M., and N. B. Jankowska. 1990. An Elamite Gilgameš Text from Argištihenele, Urartu (Armavir-blur, 8th century BC). *Zeitschrift für Assyriologie und Vorderasiatische Archäologie* 80:102–23.

Esayan, Stepan, and Aram Kalantaryan. 1976. Antichnyi nekropol' oshakana. *Vestnik obshchestvennykh nauk* 12:27–40.

——— 1988. *Oshakan.* Yerevan: Izdatel'stvo Armianskoi SSR.

Hammond, Nicholas G. 1996. Alexander and Armenia. *Phoenix* 50 (2): 130–37.

Harutunyan, Nikolai V. 2001. *Korpus Urartskikh klinoobraznykh nadpicei.* Izdatel'sztvo "gitutiun" NAN RA.

Jonker, Gerdien. 1995. *The Topography of Remembrance: The Dead, Tradition and Collective Memory in Mesopotamia.* New York: E. J. Brill.

Kanetsyan, Amina. 1998. Città e insediamenti nell'Armenia di età classica. In *Ai piedi dell'Ararat: Artaxata e l'Armenia ellenistic-romana,* ed. Antonio Invernizzi, 3–94. Firenze: Le lettere.

Khachatryan, Hamazasp. 1991. Hellinisticheskoe poselenie Beniamina. *Tezisy dokladov. Nauchnaia sessia, posviaschennaia itogam polebykh arkheologicheskikh issledovanii v RA. Izd. AN RA.* Erevan 1989–1990: 90–92.[In Armenian]

——— 1998. Beniaminskaia keramika ellinisticheskogo vremeni. *Tezisy dokladov. Respublikanskaia nauchnaia sessia, posviaschennaia pamiati prof. Kafdariana 'Kul'tura drevnei Armenii' Izd. RA NAN.* Erevan 11:31–32. [In Armenian]

Khachatryan, Zhores. 1998. Artaxata: Capitale Dell'Armenia Antica (II sec. A.C.-IV D.C.) In *Ai piedi dell'Ararat: Artaxata e l'Armenia ellenistic-romana,* ed. Antonio Invernizzi, 95–151. Firenze: Le lettere.

Kuijt, Ian. 1996. Negotiating Equality through Ritual: A Consideration of Late Natufian and Pre-Pottery Neolithic A Period Mortuary Practices. *Journal of Anthropological Archaeology* 15:313–36.

Kurtz, Donna C., and John Boardman. 1971 *Greek Burial Customs.* Ithica, N.Y.: Cornell University Press.

LeCoq, Pierre. 1997. *Les Inscriptions de la Perse achéménide.* Paris: Gallimard.

Martirosyan, Harutyun A. 1974. *Argishtihinili.* Yerevan: Izdatel'stvo Armianskoi SSR.

Morris, Ian. 1988. Tomb Cult and the "Greek Renaissance": The Past in the Present in the 8th Century B.C. *Antiquity* 63:750–61.

Perikhanian, Anahit. 1971. Les inscriptions Araméennes du roi Artachès. *Revue des études Arméniennes* 8:169–74.

Robert, Jeanne, and Louis Robert. 1952. Bulletin Epigraphique. *Revue des études grecques* 65:124–202.

Root, Margaret C. 1999. The Cylinder Seal from Pasargadae: Of Wings and Heels, Date and Fate. In *Neo-Assyrian, Median, Achaemenian and Other Studies in Honor of David Stronach,* ed. Rémy Boucharlat, John E. Curtis, and Ernie Haerinck. *Acta Iranica* 34:157–90.

Sherwin-White, Susan, and Amélie Kuhrt. 1993. *From Samarkhand to Sardis: A New Approach to the Seleucid Empire*. Berkeley: University of California Press.

Smith, Adam T. 2003. *The Political Landscape: Constellations of Authority in Early Complex Polities*. Berkeley: University of California Press.

Smith, Adam T., Ruben Badalian, Pavel Avetisyan, Mkridtch Zardaryan, et al. 2004. Preliminary Report on the 2002 Archaeological Investigations of Project ArAGATS in the Tsakahovit Plain, Armenia. *American Journal of Archaeology* 108:1–41.

Summers, David. 1993. Archaeological Evidence for the Achaemenid Period in Eastern Turkey. *Anatolian Studies* 43:85–105.

Ter-Martirosov, F. 2001. The Typology of Columnar Structures of Armenia in the Achaemenid Period. In *The Royal Palace Institution in the First Millennium B.C.: Regional Development and Cultural Interchange between East and West*, ed. Inge Nielsen, 155–63. Aarhus, Denmark: Aarhus University Press.

Thomson, Robert W. 1978. *Moses Khorenats'i: History of the Armenians*. Cambridge, Mass.: Harvard University Press.

Tiratsyan, Gevork A. 1959. Novonaidennaia nadpis' Artashesa 1-go, tsaria Armenii. *Vestnik drevnei istorii* 1:88–90.

―――. 1960. Arin-berdi syunazard dahlije ev satrapakan kentronneri hartse haikakan lernashkharhum. *Teghekagir Hasarakakan Kitutyunneri* 7–8:99–114.

―――. 1976. Novye arkheologicheskie materialy posleurartskogo vremeni na territorii Zapadnoi Armenii (Turtsiia) i ikh mesto v istorii drevnearmianskoi kultury. *Drevnii vostok* 2:134–57.

―――. 1977. Artashes I-ini evs mek noragyut arameakan ardzagrutyun. *Patma-banasirakan handes* 4:254–59.

―――. 1979. Goroda Armenii ellinisticheskogo vremeni v tsvete arkheologicheskikh issledovanii. *Vestnik drenvei istorii* 2:160–75.

―――. 1988. *Kul'tura drevnei Armenii: VI v. do n.e.-III v. n.e.: po arkheologicheskim dannym*. Erevan: Izd-vo AN Armianskoi SSR.

Tiratsyan, Gevork A., and A. A. Vayman. 1974. Karmir-blurskii nekropol' ellinisticheskogo vremeni. *Lraber Hasarakakan Gitutyunneri* 8:60–70.

Tonikian, Armen V. 1992. The Layout of Artashat and Its Historical Development. *Mesopotamia* 27:161–87.

Vallat, F. 1997. La lettre élamite d'Arménie. *Zeitschrift für Assyriologie und Vorderasiatsche Archäologie*. 87:258–70.

Van Dyke, Ruth M., and Susan E. Alcock, eds. 2003. Archaeologies of Memory: An Introduction. In *Archaeologies of Memory*, 1–13. Malden, Mass.: Blackwell.

Walbank, Frank W. 1992. *The Hellenistic World*. Cambridge, Mass.: Harvard University Press.

4 Mortuary Studies, Memory, and the Mycenaean Polity

Seth Button

In excavating human remains and the contexts in which they were deposited, archaeologists sometimes encounter artifacts, architecture, and features that past people seem likely to have connected with still earlier people and events. Often, our confidence in our ability to make specific statements about who remembered what in connection with particular places, features, artifacts, and sets of human remains, and to evaluate the validity of these conjectures, is low. However, variability in mortuary arrangements and in later activities at grave sites is sometimes patterned in a way that suggests architecture or material culture physically associated with specific dead individuals or groups was treated in identifiably different ways than architecture, features, and material culture associated with other dead people and groups of dead people belonging to the same society. In certain cases there appear to have been changes over time in the treatment of such architecture, features, and material culture.

It is a central tenet of mortuary analysis that the treatment and manner of disposal of a dead person often reflects something about that person, who he or she was, and what he or she did in life (Brown 1979; Saxe 1971; Binford 1972; Peebles and Kus 1977; O'Shea 1984, 1996). This tenet is entirely compatible with the idea, frequently asserted in recent literature, that the treatment of the dead reflects decisions and choices made by the living, which may also take into account such factors as their own ambitions, emotional states, or the circumstances under which people died (Hodder 1982; Meskell 1999; Parker Pearson 2000; Brown 2006). Likewise, we have recognized for a long time that archaeologists' interpretations of the mortuary record are complicated not only by natural site formation processes, but also by past cultural activity. In addition to the looting or destruction of earlier burials, the ethnographic and archaeological records are full of cases where the bodies of the dead are not immediately deposited in an archaeological context, or are eventually or periodically removed from such a context. In discussing cultural changes to mortuary contexts, John O'Shea (1984, 25–26) mentions the eviction of old burials from medieval English cemeteries to make room for the more recent dead, the repeated use of chamber tombs in European and Mediterranean prehistory (Keswani 2004) and Hopewell charnel houses (Brown 1979). One might also point to the periodic rewrapping and reinterment of the dead in communal tombs in Madagascar (Bloch 1971; Feeley-Harnik 1984) and mummies paraded through the streets in the Andes (Cobo 1990).

Treatments of the dead and associated architecture or objects that amount to deliberate changes to the original arrangement for disposal create interpretive difficulties, but they are potentially informative about the societies, groups, and individuals who made the changes, especially if such changes result in observable patterns in the archaeological record. In the following pages I argue that we can identify evidence for activities at the time of burial and evidence for subsequent deliberate modifications to mortuary landscapes, both of which have to do with memory, and that the presence of such evidence in some graves, grave groups, or cemeteries and its absence in others relates to specific differences in how, for how long, and with what modifications information about individuals or groups was remembered.

In terms of the Greek Bronze Age (see table 4.1), I am tempted to agree with those (for example, Wright 1987; Voutsaki 1995, 1999) who have suggested that the manipulation of memory attached to the mortuary landscape is probably concomitant with the growth and increasing centralization of the Mycenaean polity from the early second millennium to the thirteenth century BC. Furthermore, it seems plausible that when centralized polities again began to emerge several centuries after the destruction of Mycenae in the twelfth century BC, new elites used mythical genealogies and the impressive physical traces of Bronze Age tombs and other architecture as sources of legitimacy and power (Morris 1988; Antonaccio 1996; Boardman 2002; Prent 2003). However, we must be careful in inferring causality. Just as not every trace of activity at a previously inhabited site represents an intentional and meaning-laden memory act (Blake 2003), not all social continuity or change can be attributed to memory or forgetting. I have tried to avoid making claims that are irrefutable either because they are so general or so vague as to be almost certainly true (for example, people had memories), or because no

TABLE 4.1 Chronological Table for Mainland Greece

	Period	approximate dates in calendar years BC	
		High	Low
Middle Bronze Age	Middle Helladic (MH I, II, and III)	2050/2000–1680	2000–1600
Late Bronze Age	Late Helladic I (LH IA and B)	1680–1600/1580	1600–1510/1500
	Late Helladic II (LH IIA and B)	1600/1580–1425/1390	1510/1500–1390
	Late Helladic III A (LH IIIA)	1425/1390–1340/1330	1390–1340/1330
	Late Helladic III B (LH IIIB)	1340/1330–1190/1180	1340/1330–1185/1180
	Late Helladic III C (LH IIIC)	1190/1180–1065/1060	1185/1180–1065
	Submycenaean	1125–1050 (in Attica; dates vary by region)	
Early Iron Age	Protogeometric	1050–900 (in Argolid; dates vary by region)	
	Early Geometric	900–825 (in Argolid; dates vary by region)	
	Middle Geometric	825–750 (in Attica; dates vary by region)	
	Late Geometric	750–700 (in Attica; dates vary by region)	

Source: Manning 1999, 2001; Warren and Hankey 1989

evidence can be brought to bear (some people might have remembered thing X in way Y, but perhaps not). I have also attempted to make clear where I discuss ideas about memory whose validity I cannot determine how to evaluate against the available archaeological evidence.

This discussion is framed largely in terms of the manipulation of the physical remains of the past by different groups of elites, not because their use of the past is more important or more widespread than non-elites' (Richards 2000; Van Dyke and Alcock 2003), but because elites were in a better position to "inscribe" their versions of the past in enduring ways susceptible to recovery by archaeologists (Khatchadourian, this vol.; for the "inscription" of memory, see Van Dyke and Alcock 2003).

This chapter has six parts. The first is this introduction. In the second, I provide a brief description of the site of Mycenae (figs. 4.1 and 4.2) and its importance in the archaeology of the Greek Bronze Age. In the third and fourth sections I briefly review the evidence for the prehistoric cemetery and the two grave circles at Mycenae, including both the original use of the graves and subsequent modifications to these mortuary precincts. The fifth section is a discussion of the use and post-depositional histories of the shaft graves at Mycenae as evidence for "memory activities." The sixth part discusses the treatment of Mycenaean material culture by later, Iron Age Greeks, and the last is my conclusion.

Mycenae

The site of Mycenae is situated on a low hill in the northern Argive plain (Argolid), in the eastern Peloponnesus, the near-island that constitutes the southern part of the Greek mainland (fig. 4.1). The site is considered one of the most important in Greek prehistory. The best-preserved period at the site is the Late Bronze Age (table 4.1), and the societies of the Late Bronze Age on the mainland of Greece are generally referred to as Mycenaean, though they were not entirely homogeneous. I have thought it prudent to restrict my discussion to Mycenae and its immediate neighborhood and not attempt to generalize about the rest of the Greek mainland.

By the third phase of the Late Bronze Age (LH III—see table 4.1), Mycenae and other major sites in southern and central Greece conventionally referred to as palaces were highly complex polities, as attested by the settlement patterns in their respective regions, and by administrative

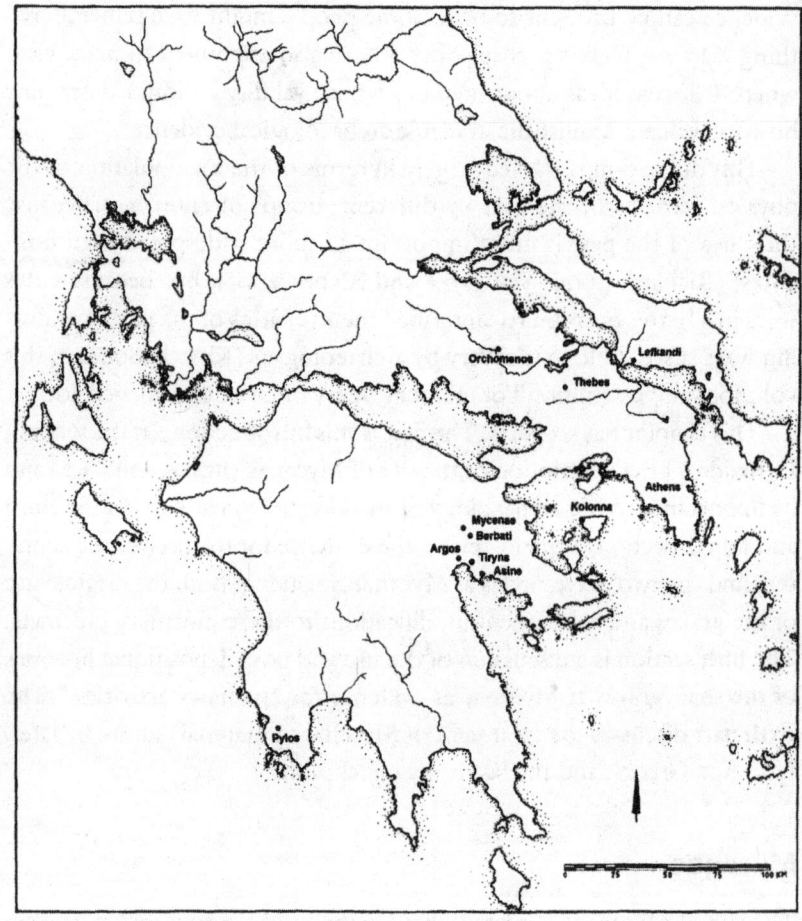

FIGURE 4.1 Map of Greece showing sites mentioned in the text (Rutter 2001a, 127, fig. 12)

records of the mobilization and redistribution of resources, which were written in the Linear B script and archived in the palaces. The palaces seem all to have been destroyed at about the same time, at the end of LH IIIB, probably very early in the twelfth century BC. The cause of this destruction is unknown. Although Athens and Thebes, both sites of Mycenaean palaces, later became politically important centers in the mid-first millennium BC, Mycenae never again controlled the amount of territory it had in the Late Bronze Age.

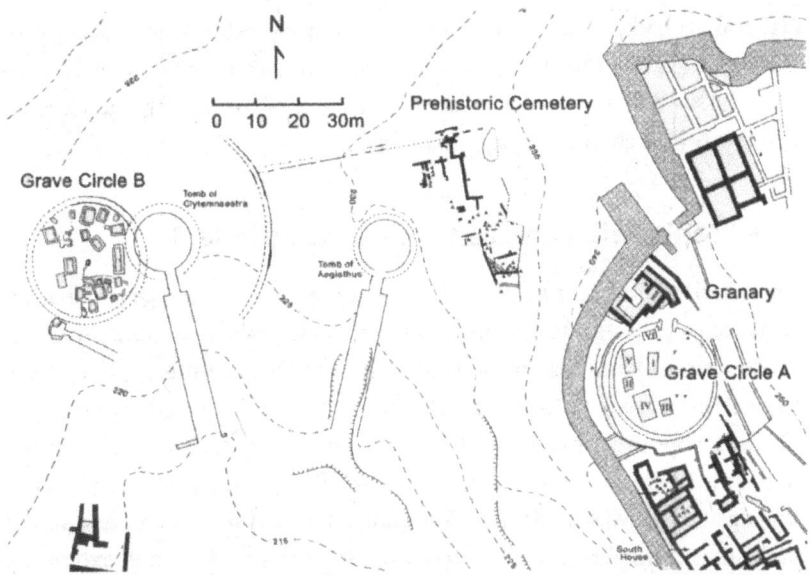

FIGURE 4.2 Partial site plan of Mycenae, showing the locations of the prehistoric cemetery, Grave Circles A and B, and two tholos tombs (sheet map by M. Pringle in Alden 2000)

The first archaeological work at Mycenae was undertaken in the 1870s by Heinrich Schliemann, who also excavated at Tiryns in the Argolid and Troy (Hissarlik) in western Asia Minor. Schliemann maintained a steady faith in the accuracy of stories about the Bronze Age as preserved in Early Iron Age epic poetry (especially the *Iliad* and *Odyssey*) and in the later Greek writers Thucydides, Euripides, and Pausanias (Schliemann 1877, 344–49). It has been suggested that both his archaeological ethics and his field methods were questionable even by the permissive standards of his day (Calder and Traill 1986; Traill 1993; but see Dickinson 2005), and students of Mycenaean archaeology understand his excavations less well than they would like. Sophie Schliemann, Heinrich's wife, is said to have directed specific projects, such as the clearing of the Tomb of Clytemnestra (fig. 4.2), though the truth of these claims is debated (Traill 1993, 238–41). Panagiotis Stamatakis, a representative of the Greek Archaeological Service, was charged with supervising Schliemann's excavations: he attempted to impose some order on them and to encourage better recording. Later excavators include some of the most prominent classical archaeologists of the twentieth century: Alan Wace, director of the British School in Athens; Carl Blegen, of the University of Cincinnati; Lord William Taylor; George Mylonas; Ioannis Papademetriou; Elizabeth French; and Spyros Iakovidis.

The Prehistoric Cemetery and Grave Circle B

There is little evidence for the nature of the Early Bronze Age occupation at Mycenae, though it is attested by scattered finds of ceramic material. Protonariou-Deilaki has argued (1990; contra Dickinson 1977) that in the Early Bronze Age (ca. 3100–2200 BCE) three tumuli covered the area west of the acropolis of Mycenae (fig. 4.2). Few if any traces of these putative tumuli remain. The earliest secure mortuary evidence from Mycenae belongs to the Middle Bronze Age (table 4.1) and is concentrated in the prehistoric cemetery, which covered the west slope of the hill, extending at least as far south as the location of the much later Citadel House and perhaps as far west as Grave Circle B (fig. 4.2). The prehistoric cemetery is less likely to have represented a single cemetery as such, and more likely a loosely defined area for the disposal of the dead, some of whom were buried within the walls of structures and others without (Alden 2000, 18–19), as at other Middle Bronze Age sites. Eventually, smaller plots of the prehistoric cemetery—for example, the area of Grave Circle B—were apparently partitioned off for the use of specific groups.

Chronological control over these early Middle Bronze Age graves is relatively poor since (1) many of them were apparently destroyed in prehistory, (2) until recently, ceramic sequences for the Middle Bronze Age were poorly understood, and (3) of the intact graves, many contained little or no datable pottery or other artifactual material. Many of the graves are cists, relatively shallow cuttings in the earth and bedrock typically lined with slabs of limestone, though cists with walls of dry stone or brick, or partially of brick, are also known to exist (Alden 2000, 20). People were also buried in simple pits and ceramic jars, or *pithoi*; the latter were most often used for children's burials (Alden 2000, 21).

Some graves seem to have been deliberately reopened and reused, whereas others were disturbed by later cists that cut into them (Alden 2000, 17, 25). The positions of at least some of these graves would have been evident years or decades after the first interment in them, as in the case of one marked by three orthostates above the level of the fill (Alden 2000, 25). It would be valuable to know whether those graves obviously marked were more frequently reused for burial, but we should hesitate to identify any graves as unmarked, since they might have been marked in ways no longer evident, such as with pots, a practice known from later Greek cemeteries; with organic materials such as wood; or with stones that the excavators did not recognize as markers. Some deposits of bones not found in situ seem to have been removed from their original graves, either as a result of intentional destruction or deliberate reuse (Cavanagh and Mee 1998; Alden 2000, 21).

In the early Middle Bronze Age graves at Mycenae, as at Asine (Nordquist 1990, 36), the effort apparently expended on the construction of a given grave does not correlate with the grave goods, whether in their number or "value." Artifacts associated with graves often include ceramic cups and other vessels appropriate to eating and drinking, and some graves include animal bones apparently deposited at the time of burial (Alden 2000, 29). Taken together, these suggest feasting in a funerary context (Hamilakis 1998, 116–22; on feasting in the Late Bronze Age, see Wright 2004b). A funerary feast is likely to have something to do with memory; it is possible that further systematic study of the remains of feasting in mortuary contexts would yield interesting results.

Although the "poverty" of MH graves relative to those of the Late Bronze Age seems to indicate that societies in mainland Greece were small in scale and relatively egalitarian in the Middle Bronze Age, there is good reason to suspect increasing status differentiation in the latter part of this period (especially the third phase of the Middle Bronze Age, MH III). Evidence for differential site sizes may reflect a settlement hierarchy of at least three tiers—though the survey evidence from the hinterland of Mycenae is not as detailed as for other centers such as Pylos in Messenia (Wright 2004a; Rutter 2001a; Cherry and Davis 2001). At the site of Asine, about twenty-four kilometers southeast of Mycenae on the coast, several large Middle Bronze Age houses seem to be contemporary with more modest homes (Nordquist 1990, 38). The most dramatic evidence, however, comes from the shaft graves of Grave Circles A and B, which taken together cover a period from the later Middle Bronze Age to the second phase of the Late Bronze Age (MH III–LH II: see Dickinson 1977; Dietz 1991; Graziadio 1988), and which present a striking picture of increasing wealth and social complexity. It is important to reiterate, however, that the mortuary record is not the only evidence for the emergence of strong social ranking at this time.

The shaft graves of Grave Circle A were excavated by the Schliemanns and Stamatakis, those of Grave Circle B by George Mylonas, Ioannis Papademetriou, Antonios Keramopoullos, and Spyridon Marinatos. Shaft graves are deep pits in the bedrock, originally roofed, which allowed for successive inhumations in the same chamber. Taken together, the grave circles span the Middle to Late Bronze Age transition. The artifacts deposited in them included decorated weapons, tools, articles of personal adornment, gold funerary masks, and equipment for feasting, including gold and silver vessels, some of which might have been made specifically for a mortuary context, to judge from their thinness. Unfortunately, because of the methods of excavation, and because the shaft graves contain multiple burials, it is often impossible to associate particular objects with specific people. The graves and associated finds have been described and analyzed in great detail (Schliemann 1877; Evans 1929; Karo 1915, 1930–33; Wace 1949, 59–63; Hammond 1967; Mylonas 1972–73; Dickinson 1972; Muhly 1973; Angel 1973; Gates 1985 with bibliography; Laffineur 1989, 1990, 1995; Graziadio 1988, 1991; Dietz 1991). My purpose here is not to deal with the chronological sequence of the shaft graves or to use them as evidence for increasing social complexity in the Argolid, but to discuss the ways their builders and users dealt with the physical traces of the past, and how later people dealt with the shaft graves.

Grave Circle B is located to the west of the prehistoric cemetery (fig. 4.2). There seem to have been Middle Bronze Age structures in the area (Alden 2000, 16; Mylonas 1972–73, 8–18), but burial in and among the houses of a settlement was not itself unusual in the Middle Bronze Age (Cavanagh and Mee 1998). The shaft graves belonging to the grave circle represent perhaps three generations (Graziadio 1988, 372). There are many more male than female burials, though some of the female burials were accompanied by outstanding quantities of grave goods (Graziadio 1991, 430). The adult individuals were big and healthy, if not significantly longer-lived than everyone else; in some cases their skeletal remains exhibit evidence of violent trauma (Angel 1973, 379–97).

The differential treatment accorded some individuals is obvious: while many people were buried with pots, others were interred with weapons, gold and silver jewelry and vessels, and other artifacts plausibly interpreted as valuable. These "expensive" goods are mostly found together and appear only rarely in otherwise "poor" burials (Graziadio 1991, 430). Age does not apparently correlate with the amount of wealth deposited: the young girl in Grave Xi, for example, was covered with jewelry. Giampaulo Graziadio infers (1991, 430) that status was ascribed. This inference seems plausible, but the kinds of calculations that are standard in mortuary analysis are complicated here by the practice of multiple burial and our uncertainty about whether artifacts (or indeed, entire sets of human remains) were removed from graves in the course of later burials (see Keswani 2004, who dealt with a similar situation in Bronze Age tombs on Cyprus). Mylonas thought that pots were taken out to make room for new corpses, based on the sherds he found in the fill (1957, 134–5); many "valuable" artifacts were pushed to one side but left in the grave. Graves characterized by multiple burials appear to be "richer" than single inhumations, though the frequency of reuse of graves drops off in LH I (Graziadio 1988, 372). Grave Beta, for example, was relatively "poor," and was never reopened, while Grave Gamma received four inhumations and impressive quantities of grave goods.

Stone stelae were erected in the grave circle, though not over every grave. Grave Iota, for example, had no stele, but was marked with an outline of stones, and by a small deposit of animal bones and seashells that might be evidence for a funerary meal (Mylonas 1957, 151). Some stelae were sculpted, others were not (for a fuller discussion of these stelae, see Younger 1997). Shaft graves were prone to caving in, at which point a stele erected over the grave might fall down. It might be set back up when the hole was filled in, as in the case of Grave Gamma (Mylonas 1957, 135).

At some point during its use, Grave Circle B was surrounded with a wall of big, rough cobbles (see Mylonas 1957, 131). This wall was later destroyed in several places: on the eastern side in LH III when the Tomb of Clytemnestra was built, and in the southwest when a round structure dating to the Early Iron Age (Geometric period) was built (Mylonas 1957, 130). The spatially bounded nature of Grave Circle B, in contrast to other Middle Bronze Age graves at Mycenae, is likely to be highly significant. Lynne Goldstein's reformulation (1976, 61) of the Saxe-Binford hypothesis number eight is as follows: "If a permanent, specialized, bounded disposal area for the exclusive disposal of a group's dead exists, then it is likely that this represents a corporate group who has rights over the use and control of critical but restricted resources." Unlike Saxe's original statement, Goldstein's formulation does not demand that control of resources be so marked, but simply admits this possibility. The precincts of Grave Circles A and B certainly seem to separate their occupants from the rest of the dead; the exact nature of the social groups represented remains an open question.

Graziadio has argued that in the first phase of the Late Bronze Age (LH I) Circle B was "a secondary burial area, mainly reserved for middle- if not low-ranking men and for some women of relatively high rank who could not be buried in Circle A" (1991, 440). However, even if the grave circles were in use for only 100 years, as Oliver Dickinson (1977) argues, then the dead population of twenty-seven individuals suggests four to five adults interred in each generation (perhaps twenty years). This in turn implies that the two circles could conceivably represent one large extended family or perhaps two branches of the same family.

Grave Circle A and Later Activity

The most common interpretation of Grave Circle A is that the individuals buried there in LH I were from the ruling family or families of Mycenae, and of higher status than those buried in grave Circle B at the same time (Graziadio 1991). This is based partly on the proximity of Grave Circle A to the citadel, partly on the spectacular quantities of gold and other grave goods recovered from these shaft graves by Schliemann (who, however, thought that they represented reinterments of people originally buried in the *tholos* tombs such as the so-called Treasury of Atreus and Tomb of Clytemnestra). Like Grave Circle B, Grave Circle A was modified after the last of the shaft-grave burials, but unfortunately the stratigraphy that corresponds to the time between the first shaft-grave burials in late MH/LH I and the last period of the Mycenaean palaces in LH IIIB (table 4.1) is ambiguous, and the records of the original excavation are unhelpful. What is clear, however, is that some time in LH IIIB an extension to the western fortification wall, along with several structures interpreted as houses, were built over graves on the western part of the hill on which Mycenae is situated; around the same time, Grave Circle A was surrounded with a double ring of monumental slabs, or orthostates (figs. 4.3 and 4.4). Unless one imagines non-elites rebuilding the wall of the citadel on their own initiative—interfering with elite graves in the process—this project must have been authorized and directed by elite Mycenaeans. Although we have some information about Mycenaean palatial administration from the Linear B tablets, it is not known who at Mycenae was directly responsible for supervising construction projects of this nature.

The floor level of Grave Circle A immediately after this construction project is uncertain: was it at or near the base of the slabs, or did it reach their tops? This is an important question, for if the level of fill reached the tops of the orthostates, then the stelae found by Schliemann could have been buried and invisible in LH IIIB (though Charles Gates argues

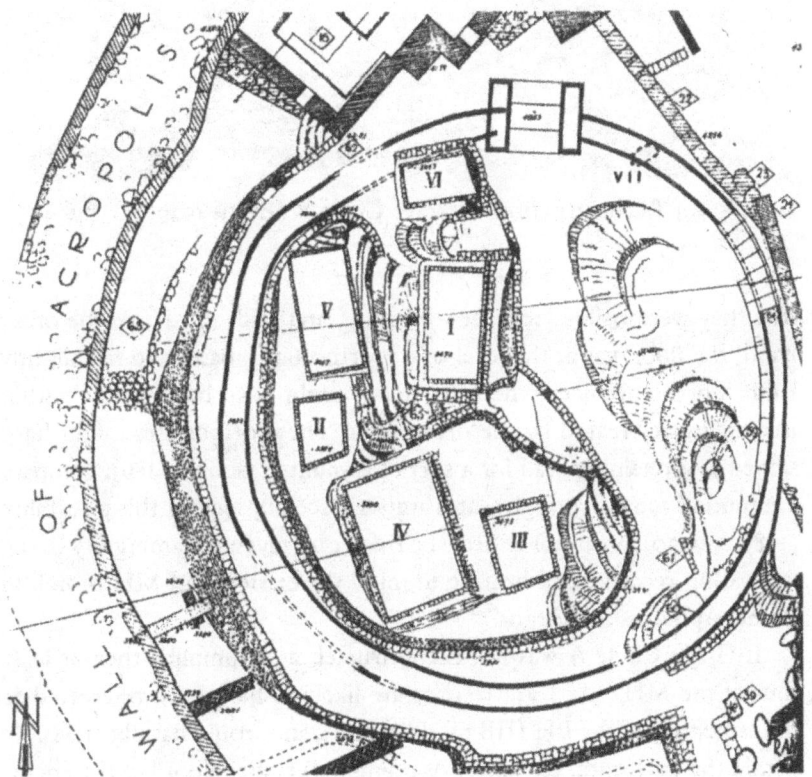

FIGURE 4.3 Plan of Grave Circle A after final phase of LH IIIB modifications (Gates 1985, 266, ill. 1)

FIGURE 4.4 Reconstruction of Grave Circle A (Evans 1929, 60, fig. 44)

that they were visible [1985, 268–74 and Gates's Ill. 2]). If, on the other hand, the floor was at the level of the orthostates' bases and the slightly later "north entrance," then the stelae might have been visible within the enclosure created by the orthostates. These orthostates might have served as a retaining wall for a sort of tumulus (Tsountas 1895; compare Hammond 1967). Though Gates argues forcefully against this possibility (1985, 269–70), it cannot entirely be ruled out, given the ambiguity of the excavation records, and bearing in mind the existence of MH tumuli at Vrana, Aphidna, and Argos.

If Grave Circle A was not reconstructed as a tumulus, then at least four of the MH/LH I grave stelae are likely to have been re-erected at the same time as the LH IIIB modifications, and would have been visible within the enclosure. As Gates has pointed out, the "floor" of the enclosure would have sloped more than a meter from east to west and about a meter from north to south, meaning that the stelae would have been buried at different depths. When the entrance was added to Grave Circle A, a modification that apparently postdates the erection of the orthostates, the whole enclosed area, about thirty meters in diameter, would have been able to be entered (Belger 1893). Though it was not reused as a burial ground, it has been suggested that it served at this time as a venue for assemblies (Gates 1985, 271–72) or ritual behavior connected with the remembered dead.

In the fill in which he found the stelae, Schliemann also discovered a circular stone construction about a meter high, like a wellhead, which he decided was an "altar" at which people buried in the shaft graves were worshipped by later Mycenaeans, an interpretation followed by at least some later excavators (Wace 1949). It is possible that it served to mark the location of Shaft Grave IV, but as Mylonas (1957, 112) showed, the altar is likely to have been below the surface at the time of the later construction projects. Mylonas hoped to find an "altar" in Grave Circle B, but he did not (1957, 153).

There were apparently no new burials in Grave Circles A or B after LH II (the second phase of the Late Bronze Age, see table 4.1). It was after this date that some Mycenaeans began to be buried in monumental, vaulted *tholos* tombs built of blocks of cut stone. William Cavanagh and Christopher Mee suggest that these *tholoi* developed from piled earth tumuli, of which many examples elsewhere in southern Greece date to the Middle Bronze Age (1998, 45). The tholos tombs represented a significant investment of labor: ten men working for 240 days could have cleared the ground for the Tomb of Aegisthus, but it might have taken as long, or longer, for the tomb itself to be built (Wright 1987, 173–74). The tombs were used for multiple interments, usually deposited in simple cists. Tholoi were built over some areas of the old prehistoric cemetery, almost certainly destroying old graves in the process. We have already seen how the Tomb of Clytemnestra encroached on Grave Circle B (fig. 4.2).

The natural inclination of Schliemann, Evans, and other early scholars was to believe that these tholoi were "royal" tombs. Cavanagh and Mee, however, have argued that tholoi were not exclusive to the rulers of Mycenae, since multiple tholoi were in use at one time, both at Mycenae and elsewhere in the Mycenaean world, at Kakovatos, Pylos, Koukounara, and Peristeria (1998, 56). In any event, most Mycenaeans, even among the elite, were not buried in tholos tombs: a more common arrangement was the chamber tomb, a subterranean room with a narrow passage, or *dromos*. Like the shaft graves and the tholoi, these were reused.

Memory and the Mortuary Landscape at Mycenae

Clearly, both the destruction and the reuse of old graves were common practices in the Middle Bronze Age. Destruction may have been accidental, expedient, or both; reuse may have been expedient or opportunistic, but cannot have been wholly accidental. The locations of some graves were marked, which would have permitted reuse, but not all were reused. Starting with the null hypothesis that there is no meaningful correlation between artifacts recovered from graves, their size, or the amount of labor apparently invested, versus subsequent reuse, one might be able to test whether graves that were bigger, "richer" in terms of artifacts per individual, or more elaborate in their construction were reused more frequently than would be expected. At first glance this test seems to support the null hypothesis, but the result is problematic because we really do not know how long most of the reused graves were in use, how many burials they had held at the time of the last interment, or what artifacts were removed from them in prehistory.

In any case, it is possible to infer that in the Middle Bronze Age a significant part of the population did not choose to mark graves in a way that was intended to be permanent, and therefore they expected the locations of the graves eventually to be forgotten, in contrast to tumuli elsewhere in Greece that the builders must have known would persist for a very long time. This inference could be called into question by archaeologically, ethnographically, or historically attested cases where "permanent" marking was understood to persist after the deterioration of a physically perishable marker.

Alden writes, "Dismantling graves in a ceremony amounting to a second funeral may be part of the process of constructing memory and forgetting the individual" (2000, 25, citing Cavanagh 1978 and Cavanagh and Mee 1998). This is compatible with Brown's understanding: "Where interment of the dead has been created from secondary burials, social identities are no longer carried with them out of necessity" (2006, 208).

Secondary burial in the Greek Bronze Age may also reflect both practical concerns and beliefs about the supernatural: where the decomposing bodies of the dead might have presented a threat to the community in terms of public health as well as ritual pollution, their clean bones could be handled with relative impunity (Cavanagh 1978; Cavanagh and Mee 1998). The suggestion is interesting, though it is difficult to see how it could be subjected to critical evaluation, given the state of the evidence. I cannot find any archaeologically recoverable feature of secondary burial practice in Greek or other societies that either infallibly indicates the presence of cultural ideas about ritual pollution attached to the dead, or is present in the archaeological record at Mycenae. We are also left with a large number of sets of human remains that evidently did *not* receive this secondary burial treatment. This variability is most likely significant: it might reflect differences among the dead, differences among groups of survivors, or both.

Nordquist argues that in the Middle Bronze Age at Asine, it was "possible to very closely define each person's individual place within the society," a feature Nordquist claims is typical of small-scale societies; larger-scale societies, on the other hand, signal group membership (1990, 38). Questions of individuality and group membership are relevant in the context of memory. Although it may be possible under ideal circumstances to separate those aspects of funerary equipment and ritual that mark an individual as a member of a group from those that are idiosyncratic gestures made by the community in reference to a dead individual's life, I do not see specific evidence at Mycenae that the graves of the early Middle Bronze Age express "individuality" rather than group membership at all, to judge from the artifacts in them. As compared with later periods, the grave goods deposited in the first part of the Middle Bronze Age (MH I–II) are relatively homogeneous, and few if any obviously reflect the roles or social personae of the deceased. Of course, cloth and other organic artifacts that might have been informative have typically deteriorated. Greek archaeologists suspect that burial shrouds were important in later Greek practice (in the *Odyssey*, Penelope famously weaves and unravels an elaborate burial shroud for Odysseus's father; for more on later Greek funerary textiles see Barber 1991). Textiles might also have played a role in a hypothetical reburial ceremony, as in the case of the *famidahana* in Madagascar, in which old bones are removed from a tomb and rewrapped (Bloch 1971; Kottak 1980; Feeley-Harnik 1984).

Partly because we cannot know what is missing, it is impossible to rule out the possibility that memory was strongly marked in the material record in the early Middle Bronze Age at Mycenae. It is fair to say that even in the case of multiple inhumation, which I have argued relates directly to memory, there is considerable variation that does not at first glance seem to correlate with any other observable variation, such as grave size, degree of elaboration, number of artifacts deposited, or distance from the citadel. This is not, however, the case for the shaft graves.

Graziadio has argued that the strong spatial association among individuals deposited in the same grave indicates that descent was becoming more important in structuring social relations at the end of the Middle Bronze Age (1991, 405). The preceding evidence reviewed suggests that funerals were occasions during which not only the recently dead, but his or her ancestors, might be remembered (Hamilakis 1998). Since shaft graves seem to have been designed to be reused multiple times (or at least were apparently reused with greater frequency than cist graves), their locations had to be remembered. As we have seen, this could be achieved with rocks or perishable markers, but also with limestone stelae. The sculpted stelae set up in Grave Circles A and B depict people with weapons, some in chariots, and apparent fighting among people and between people and wild animals (Younger 1997). It seems likely that the images on the stelae refer to the social personae of at least some of the people buried in the shaft graves, since some of the dead were interred with quantities of weapons: the stelae therefore might communicate some memory of the dead (whether individually or collectively) to viewers.

As noted, the faunal evidence and broken pottery in the fill of cist and shaft graves are sometimes interpreted as evidence for a funerary meal, or for later meals commemorating the dead. In Bronze Age Greece, the funeral of an important person, or subsequent commemorative events, might have been occasions for a particularly big or well-attended feast. For this reason it would be interesting to investigate whether graves that reflect apparently greater investment of labor, larger numbers of "valuable" goods, or which are otherwise outstanding, are more frequently associated with physical evidence reasonably attributable to feasting, or greater quantities of such remains (for example, more cups, the bones of more or larger animals). If so, one might entertain the hypothesis that family—or faction—members were using the funerary feast to display or reinforce patronage relationships vis-à-vis humbler members of the community or to mobilize labor for the construction of elaborate tombs.

However, James Brown has recently cautioned against simply assuming that large construction projects are indicative of coercion rather than collaboration at Cahokia (2006), and the same caveat applies equally well in Greek prehistory. It is also important to note that funerary ritual involving consumption can have the effect of redistributing wealth from the rich to the poor, or serve as a "leveling mechanism" by consuming most or all of the dead person's accumulated wealth: compare the different economic results of funerals in Madagascar (Kottak 1980).

The preceding section has dealt with evidence (and the lack of evidence) for "memory activities" at the time of burial or shortly thereafter; in the following paragraphs I will turn to the later modification of extant mortuary contexts, which I believe are potentially informative. In the thirteenth century BC, people at Mycenae, or at least the elites in charge, apparently took a selective interest in the physical vestiges of the past. Grave Circle B was infringed upon by the construction of the Tomb of Clytemnestra, but Grave Circle A was refurbished at the same time the new fortification wall was built, and surrounded with the unusual wall of orthostates. The changes in the appearance of Grave Circle A over a period of 500 years or so, from the time of the shaft graves down to shortly before the destruction of the citadel (ca. 1680 to 1200 BC) are clearly exceptional. If subsequent physical treatment of graves is a kind of remembering, then the people buried there were remembered in a different way from other members of Mycenaean society. To Wace, the significance of the modifications was clear:

> The Grave Circle [A] . . . became a temenos (sacred precinct) where the due rites could be paid to the deceased kings at the rock altar in the center so that their spirits could still watch over the fortress they had ruled in life. The cult of the dead seems to have persisted, for no later buildings were ever built over the graves and the tradition recorded by Pausanias and interpreted by Schliemann regarded this area as the place where Agamemnon, Cassandra, and their murdered comrades

were buried. Once the royal graves were so hallowed and protected, the rest of the cemetery was built over. (1949, 63)

Wace's interpretation is, of course, highly speculative, especially regarding the rock "altar." But some evidence suggests that the putative association of present power with the remembered dead in LH III was not exclusive to Mycenae: the association of the gateway and tholos tomb at Pylos might reflect a similar situation there (Wright 1984, 1987). This does not, of course, imply detailed and accurate knowledge of the past on the part of thirteenth-century Mycenaeans. From his review of the evidence, Gates suggests that at this time "knowledge of the Shaft Graves and Mycenaean civilization was considerably diluted, already dissolving into legend" (1985, 272).

Here I will move into the Early Iron Age (table 4.1), leaving Mycenae, but drawing on examples from its geographical neighborhood, the Argive plain. Activity at Bronze Age graves by Early Iron Age people, particularly apparent ritual activity (Morris 1988; Antonaccio 1996; Prent 2003), is potentially significant in terms of memory. In the Early Iron Age, emergent elites in Greece attempted to use the past as a source of legitimacy—as is clear from the mythical genealogies and claims of autochthony preserved in textual sources. But interest in the past was apparently not restricted to elites, to judge from the Iron Age offerings, which include modest pottery and clay figurines. Ian Morris has argued (1988) that Mycenaean tombs were potentially sources of social tension because they could provide a common ancestor for members of the emergent polis, or "city-state," just as easily as a heroic pedigree for aristocrats; that these two groups were often at odds is inferred from historical sources. This apparent tension has led Morris to argue that "we must look more closely at the plurality of readings of the rituals available to competing groups" (1988, 758).

Carla Antonaccio has tried to disentangle the evidence for contended readings of the past in Early Iron Age Greece. "Rather than a single, unified concept," she argues, "ancestral and hero cult articulated different versions of the past" (Antonaccio 1996, 389). Antonaccio's model gives us two categories of people: those articulating kinship-based identities by venerating ancestors at an old Mycenaean tomb, and those seeking to create regional identities by encouraging the worship of a local hero. We should further suspect the existence of people who did both these things at different times, but how to recover the motivation behind individual offerings is unclear (unless they carry lengthy dedicatory inscriptions or implicitly refer to the dedicator's motives—as when clay models of body parts were dedicated at later Greek sanctuaries by people seeking relief from specific ailments).

If Morris and Antonaccio are correct, then the physical remains of the past and the questions of which remains were worth reusing, who could use them, and for what ends, had real importance in Early Iron Age Greece, just as they apparently had in LH IIIB Mycenae. The existence of a deceased ancestor, even a purely conjectural or anonymous one (compare Boardman 2002, 60) buried on a particular plot of land, might have been used to legitimize one's claim to that land or to a heroic pedigree. Where no Bronze Age tomb or other architecture existed, it might be faked: at the Argive Heraion a "mock-Mycenaean platform" seems to have been built in the eighth century using traditional Bronze Age construction techniques (Morgan and Whitelaw 1991, 84; contra Boardman 2002, 45). This sort of investment suggests the physical remains of the past had some currency.

As has been noted, the range of variability in how people remember and use the past is enormous: directly contradictory interpretations and conflicting uses of the past probably existed more often than not. Where we are able to identify these, they may be of some interest. As Lynn Meskell has argued, "Disjuncture need not be negative or contradictory, and variability need not be smoothed over for the sake of a mistaken unity that may lend spurious weight to a convincing argument" (1999, 222). A useful next step in recovering the "plurality of readings" available to Late Geometric Greeks might be a detailed analysis of the kinds of dedications that appear at the sites listed by Morris. Unfortunately, however, it is often impossible to separate competing groups at these sites by the kinds of material culture they deposited. Many of the actual artifacts, rather than belonging to people from one of Antonaccio's two groups, could equally well be interpreted as the results of general piety on the part of anonymous farmers, some of whom may not even have had in mind a specific name for the hero whose tomb they venerated, let alone a desire to incorporate him into their family tree (Boardman 2002; 52, 60). It is worth drawing attention to a fifth-century BC potsherd that found its way into Grave Circle A: the sherd was inscribed, "I belong to the hero" (Schliemann 1877; Jeffery 1961; 174, no. 6). Did the dedicator have in mind the mythical King Agamemnon remembered in the fifth century in oral epic, visual art, and tragedies? If so, he or she did not specify.

A final problem in evaluating the significance of Iron Age dedications at Bronze Age tombs is even later cultural interference with the Iron Age material. Members of some groups may have taken deliberate steps to homogenize the versions of the past available at tombs and sanctuaries by altering the artifactual record in ways difficult to detect. Adam Smith (2003, 167) has identified attempts on the part of Urartian elites to eliminate a "rival sense of place" by actively destroying inconvenient traces of the past. Editing of information about the past was probably done verbally and textually as well as physically (Lyon Crawford, this vol.).

Conclusion

We may wonder to what degree archaeologists project their own obsession with the past onto the people they study. But the practice of multiple burial, the state-sponsored modifications to Grave Circle A in the Late Bronze Age, and Iron Age dedications at Bronze Age sites are phenomena not easy to explain unless people were thinking in some way about the past. Some problems of equifinality exist: we might recognize that people could remember something in way X as opposed to way Y, but would the two ways leave identifiable and different traces in the material record? Unlike ritual, which is by definition structured and therefore has some tendency to produce patterning in the material record (Marcus, forthcoming), activities related to memory may be more idiosyncratic, and often tend not to produce intelligible patterning.

I have suggested that a study of memory-related behavior might usefully be based on evidence of variation in graves and in later modifications to graves. At the site of Mycenae, Middle Bronze Age graves were marked in a variety of ways or not at all, some were used for multiple burials while others were not, and reuse does not seem to correlate with other observed aspects of variation, such as the number of artifacts or the size of the grave.

With the Middle to Late Bronze Age shaft graves, however, there is a significantly higher incidence of multiple burial, in spatially bounded areas, correlating with overall "wealth"—in other words, we are able to perceive patterned variation. It is my contention that this reflects a kind of memory practice, and a consensus about such practice, that is markedly different from the preceding period. Memory practice in a mortuary sphere is likely to have been susceptible to influence from other spheres of social life (Howey and O'Shea 2006)—such as the evident material inequality that the shaft graves probably reflect.

The different fates of the two grave circles, one partly destroyed and built over, the other surrounded by a new wall, probably indicate that Late Bronze Age elites in the thirteenth century BC—those who were in a position to authorize the construction of the Tomb of Clytemnestra or the wall of orthostates around Grave Circle A—remembered the groups that the shaft graves represented in different ways. Those buried in Grave Circle A might have been venerated, whereas those in Grave Circle B may have been almost entirely forgotten. Finally, Iron Age activity at Bronze Age graves in the form of added dedications—although difficult to parse in terms of the people involved and their motives—also represents evidence for memory activity. The lack of strong patterning suggests a variety of personal and idiosyncratic practice on the part of Early Iron Age Greeks, related to memories attached to Late Bronze Age tombs.

Acknowledgments

I wish to thank Norman Yoffee, Jack Davis, Emily Holt, Henry Wright, the other contributors, and the anonymous reviewers for helpful comments. Errors and problems in this chapter are entirely my fault.

Bibliography

Alcock, Susan E., and John Cherry. 2006. No Greater Marvel: A Bronze Age Classic at Orchomenos. In *Classical Pasts: The Classical Traditions of Greco-Roman Antiquity*, ed. Jay Porter, 69–86. Princeton, N.J.: Princeton University Press.

Alden, Maureen. 2000. *The Prehistoric Cemetery: Pre-Mycenaean and Early Mycenaean Graves* [*Well-built Mycenae* fasicule 7]. Oxford: Oxbow Books.

Angel, J. L. 1973. Human Skeletons from Grave Circles at Mycenae. In *Ho Taphikos Kyklos ton Mykenon*, G. E. Mylonas, 379–97. Athens: He En Athēnais Archaiologikēs Hetaireias.

Antonaccio, Carla. 1995. *An Archaeology of Ancestors*. Lanham, Md.: Rowham and Littlefield.

——— 1996. Contesting the Past: Hero Cult, Tomb Cult, and Greek Epic in Early Greece. *AJA* 98:389–410.

Barber, Elizabeth J. W. 1991. *Prehistoric Textiles: The Development of Cloth in the Neolithic and Bronze Ages with Special Reference to the Aegean.* Princeton, N.J.: Princeton University Press.

Belger, Christian. 1893. *Mykenische Lokalsage von den Gröben Agamemnons und der Seinen in Zusammenhange der griecheschen Sagenentwicklung.* Berlin: R. Gaertners Verlagsbuchhandlung.

——— 1895. Mykenische Studien. I. Erbauung und Zerstörung des mykenischen Plattenringes. *JdI* 10:114–27.

Binford, Lewis, ed. 1972. Mortuary Practices: Their Study and Their Potential. In *An Archaeological Perspective.* New York: Seminar Press.

Blake, Emma. 2003. Byzantine Era Reuse of Sicily's Prehistoric Rock-Cut Tombs. In *Archaeologies of Memory*, eds. Ruth M. Van Dyke and Susan E. Alcock, 203–20. Malden, Mass.: Blackwell.

Bloch, Maurice. 1971. *Placing the Dead.* London and New York: Seminar Press.

——— 1977. The Past and the Present in the Present. *Man* 12:278–92.

Boardman, John. 2002. *The Archaeology of Nostalgia: How the Greeks Re-Created Their Mythical Past.* London: Thames and Hudson.

Bradley, Richard. 2002. *The Past in Prehistoric Societies.* London and New York: Routledge.

Brown, James. 1979. Charnel Houses and Mortuary Crypts: Disposal of the Dead in the Middle Woodland. In *Hopewell Archaeology*, eds. D. S. Brose and N. Greber, 211–19. MCJA Special Paper no. 3. Kent, Ohio: Kent State University Press.

——— 2006. Where's the Power in Mound Building? An Eastern Woodlands Perspective. In *Leadership and Polity in Mississippian Society*, eds. B. Butler and P. Welch, 197–213. Occasional paper 33. Carbondale: Center for Archaeological Investigations, Southern Illinois University, Carbondale.

Button, S. 2005. Review of *The Mycenaean Feast*, ed. J. Wright, in *Bryn Mawr Classical Review* 2005.04.49.

Calder, William, III, and David Traill. 1986. *Myth, Scandal, and History: The Heinrich Schliemann Controversy and a First Edition of the Mycenaean Diary.* Detroit: Wayne State University Press.

Cavanagh, William. 1978. A Mycenaean Second Burial Custom? *BICS* 25:1–72.

Cavanagh, William, and Christopher Mee. 1998. *A Private Place: Death in Prehistoric Greece.* SIMA 125. Jonsered, Sweden: Paul Astroms Forlag.

Cherry, John, and Jack Davis. 2001. Under the Sceptre of Agamemnon: The View from the Hinterlands of Mycenae. In *Urbanism in the Aegean Bronze Age*, ed. K. Branigan, 141–53. Sheffield Studies in Aegean Archaeology 4. London: Sheffield Academic Press.

Cobo, Bernabé. [1653]1990. *Inca Religion and Customs.* Trans. R. Hamilton. Austin: University of Texas Press.

Dabney, Mary, and James Wright. 1990. Mortuary Customs, Palatial Society and State Formation in the Aegean Area: A Comparative Study. In *Celebrations of Death and Divinity in the Bronze Age Argolid*, eds. R. Hagg and G. C. Nordquist, 45–53. Stockholm: Paul Astroms Forlag.

Deshayes, Jean. 1966. *Argos: les Fouilles de la Deiras. Études Péloponnésiennes* IV. Paris: J. Vrin.

Dickinson, Oliver. 1972. The Shaft Graves and Mycenaean Origins. *BICS* 19:146–47.

——— 1977. *The Origins of Mycenaean Civilisation*. SIMA 49. Göteborg, Sweden: Paul Astroms Forlag.

——— 1999. Invasion, Migration and the Shaft Graves. *BICS* 43:97–107.

——— 2005. The "Face of Agamemnon." *Hesperia* 74 (3): 299–308.

Dietz, Søren. 1980. Asine II. Results of the Excavations East of the Acropolis, 1970–1974. SkrAth 24:2. Stockholm: Paul Astroms Forlag.

——— 1991. *The Argolid at the Transition to the Mycenaean Age: Studies in the Chronology and Cultural Development of the Shaft Grave Period*. Copenhagen: Aarhus University Press.

Dietz, Søren, and Nicoletta Divari-Valakou. 1990. A Middle Helladic III/Late Helladic I Grave Group from Myloi in the Argolid (Oikopedon Manti). *OpAth* 18:45–62.

Evans, Arthur. 1929. *The Shaft Graves and Bee-hive Tombs of Mycenae*. London: MacMillan and Company.

Feeley-Harnik, Gillian. 1984. The Political Economy of Death. *American Ethnologist* 11 (1): 1–2.

Flannery, Kent V. 1973. Archaeology with a Capital S. In *Research and Theory in Current Archaeology*, ed. C. L. Redman, 47–53. New York: Wiley.

Gates, Charles. 1985. Rethinking the Building History of Grave Circle A at Mycenae. *AJA* 89:263–74.

Goldstein, Lynne. 1976. Spatial Structure and Social Organization: Regional Manifestations of Mississippian Society. Ph.D. diss., Northwestern University.

Graziadio, Giampaulo. 1988. The Chronology of the Shaft Graves of Circle B at Mycenae: A New Hypothesis. *AJA* 92:343–72.

——— 1991. The Process of Social Stratification at Mycenae in the Shaft Grave Period: A Comparative Examination of the Evidence. *AJA* 95:403–40.

Hamilakis, Yannis. 1998. Eating the Dead: Mortuary Feasting and the Politics of Memory in the Aegean Bronze Age Societies. In *Cemetery and Society in the Aegean Bronze Age*, ed. Keith Branigan, 115–32. Sheffield Studies in Aegean Archaeology 1. Sheffield, U.K.: Sheffield University Press.

Hammond, N. G. L. 1967. Tumulus Burial in Albania, the Grave Circles of Mycenae, and the Indo-Europeans. *BSA* 62:77–105.

Hiller, Stephan. 1989. On the Origins of the Shaft Graves. In *Transition: Le monde égéen du Bronze moyen au Bronze récent*, ed. R. Laffineur, 137–44. Aegaeum 3. Liège, France: Université de Liège.

Hodder, Ian. 1982. *Symbols in Action: Ethnoarchaeological Studies of Material Culture*. Cambridge: Cambridge University Press.

Howey, Meghan C. L., and John M. O'Shea. 2006. Bear's Journey and the Study of Ritual in Archaeology. *American Antiquity* 71 (2): 261–82.

Iakovidis, Spyros. 1981. Royal Shaft Graves outside Mycenae. *TUAS* 6:17–28.

Jeffery, Lillian H. 1961. *Local Scripts of Archaic Greece.* Oxford: Clarendon Press.

Karo, Georg. 1915. Die Schachtgräber von Mykenai. *Ath. Mitt.* 40:113–230.

—— 1930–33. *Die Schachtgräber von Mykenai,* 1 and 2. Munich: F. Bruckmann.

Keswani, Priscilla. 2004. *Mortuary Ritual and Society in Bronze Age Cyprus.* Monographs in Mediterranean Archaeology. London and Oakville, Conn.: Equinox.

Kottak, Conrad. 1980. *The Past in the Present: History, Ecology, and Cultural Variation in Highland Madagascar.* Ann Arbor: University of Michigan Press.

Laffineur, Robert, ed. 1989. Mobilier Funéraire et Hiérarchie Sociale aux Cercles des Tombes de Mycènes. In *Transition.* Aegaeum 3. Liège, France: Université de Liège.

—— 1990. Grave Circle A at Mycenae: Further Reflections on Its History. In *Celebrations of Death and Divinity in the Bronze Age Argolid,* eds. R. Hägg and G. C. Nordquist, 201–6. Stockholm: Paul Astroms Forlag.

—— 1993. Material and Craftmanship in the Mycenaean Shaft Graves: Imports vs Local Productions. *Minos* 25–26:245–95.

—— 1995. Aspects of Rulership at Mycenae in the Shaft Grave Period. In *The Role of the Ruler in the Prehistoric Aegean,* ed. P. Rehak, 81–94. Aegaeum 11. Liège, France: Université de Liège.

Lolos, Yannis. 1989. The Tholos Tomb at Koryphasion: Evidence for the Transition from Middle to Late Helladic in Messenia. In *Transition: Le monde égéen du Bronze moyen au Bronze récent,* ed. R. Laffineur, 171–75. Aegaeum 3. Liège, France: Université de Liège.

Lowenthal, David. 1985. *The Past Is a Foreign Country.* Cambridge: Cambridge University Press.

Manning, S. W. 1999. *A Test of Time: The Volcano of Thera and the Chronology and History of the Aegean and East Mediterranean in the Mid-Second Millennium BC.* Oxford: Oxbow Books.

—— 2001. The Absolute Chronology of the Aegean Early Bronze Age: Archaeology, History and Radiocarbon. *Monographs in Mediterranean Archaeology* 1. Sheffield, U.K.: Sheffield Academic Press.

Marcus, Joyce. Forthcoming. Rethinking Ritual. In *The Archaeology of Ritual,* ed. E. Kyriakidis. Los Angeles: Cotsen Institute of Archaeology, UCLA.

Marinatos, Spiridon. 1953. Peri tous neous Basilikous taphous ton Mukênôn. In *Geras Antôniou Keramopoullou,* ed. Antonios Keramopoullou, 54–88. Hetaireia Makedônikôn Spoudôn 9. Athens: Typographeion Myrtide.

Mee, Christopher. 1998. Gender Bias in Mycenaean Mortuary Practices. In *Cemetery and Society in the Aegean Bronze Age,* ed. K. Branigan, 165–70. Sheffield, U.K.: Sheffield University Press.

Meskell, Lynn. 1999. *Archaeologies of Social Life: Age, Sex, Class et cetera in Ancient Egypt.* Oxford: Blackwell.

Morgan, Catherine, and Todd Whitelaw. 1991. Pots and Politics: Ceramic Evidence for the Rise of the Argive State. *AJA* 95:79–108.

Morris, Ian. 1986. The Use and Abuse of Homer. *Classical Antiquity* 4:81–138.

——— 1988. Tomb Cult and the "Greek Renaissance": The Past in the Present in the 8th Century B.C. *Antiquity* 62:750–61.

Muhly, James. 1973. On the Shaft Graves at Mycenae. In *Studies in Honor of Tom B. Jones*, eds. M. A. Powell Jr. and R. H. Sack, 311–23. Neukirchen-Vluyn, Germany: Neukirchener Verlag.

Mylonas, Giorgios E. 1957. *Ancient Mycenae: The Capital City of Agamemnon*. Princeton, N.J.: Princeton University Press.

——— 1972–73. *O Taphikos kuklos B tōn Mykenōn*. Athens: He En Athēnais Archaio logikēs Hetaireias.

Nordquist, Gullög. 1990. Middle Helladic Burial Rites: Some Speculations. In *Celebrations of Death and Divinity in the Bronze Age Argolid*, eds. R. Hägg and G. C. Nordquist, 35–41. Stockholm: Paul Astroms Forlag.

——— 1991. New Middle Helladic Finds from Asine. *Hydra* 8:31–34.

O'Shea, John. 1984. *Mortuary Variability: An Archaeological Investigation*. Orlando, Fla.: Academic Press.

——— 1996. *Villagers of the Maros: A Portrait of an Early Bronze Age Society*. New York and London. Plenum Publishing.

Parker Pearson, Michael. 2000. *The Archaeology of Death and Burial*. College Station, Tex.: Texas A&M University Press.

Peebles, Chris, and Susan Kus. 1977. Some Archaeological Correlates of Ranked Societies. *American Antiquity* 42:421–48.

Prag, A. J. N. W., et al. 1995. Seven Faces from Grave Circle B at Mycenae. *BSA* 90:107–36 and plates 14–18.

Prent, Mieke. 2003. Glories of the Past in the Past: Ritual Activities at Palatial Ruins in Early Iron Age Crete. In *Archaeologies of Memory*, eds. Ruth M. Van Dyke and Susan E. Alcock, 81–103. Malden, Mass.: Blackwell.

Protonariou-Deilaki, Evangelia. 1990. Burial Customs and Funerary Rites in the Prehistoric Argolid. In *Celebrations of Death and Divinity in the Bronze Age Argolid*, eds. R. Hägg and G. C. Nordquist, 69–83. Stockholm: Paul Astroms Forlag.

Richards, Janet. 1999. Conceptual Landscapes in the Egyptian Nile Valley. In *Archaeologies of Landscape: Contemporary Perspectives*, eds. Wendy Ashmore and A. Bernard Knapp, 83–100. Malden, Mass.: Blackwell.

——— 2000. Modified Order, Responsive Legitimacy, Redistributed Wealth: Egypt, 2260–1650 B.C. In *Order, Legitimacy and Wealth in Ancient States*. New Directions in Archaeology. Eds. J. Richards and M. van Buren, 36–45. Cambridge: Cambridge University Press.

Rutter, Jeremy. 1992. Cultural Novelties in the Post-Palatial Aegean: Indices of Vitality or Decline? In *Crisis Years: The 12th Century B.C. from beyond the Danube to the Tigris*, eds. W. A. Ward and M. Joukowski, 61–78. Dubuque, Iowa: Kendall/Hunt.

—— 2001a. The Prepalatial Bronze Age of the Southern and Central Greek Mainland. *Aegean Prehistory: A Review. AJA* supplement 1. Ed. T. Cullen, 95–147.

—— 2001b. The Prepalatial Bronze Age of the Southern and Central Greek Mainland. Addendum: 1993–1999. *Aegean Prehistory: A Review. AJA* supplement 1. Ed. T. Cullen, 148–55.

Sahlins, Marshall. 1972. *Stone Age Economics*. Chicago: Aldine-Atherton.

Saxe, Arthur. 1971. Social Dimensions of Mortuary Practices in Mesolithic Populations from Wade Halfa, Sudan. In *Approaches to the Social Dimensions of Mortuary Practices*, ed. J. A. Brown. *Memoirs of the Society for American Archaeology* 25:39–56.

Schliemann, Heinrich. 1877. *Mycenae: A Narrative of Researches and Discoveries at Mycenae and Tiryns*. New York: B. Blom.

Shelmerdine, Cynthia. 2001a. Review of Aegean Prehistory VI: The Palatial Bronze Age of the Southern and Central Greek Mainland. *Aegean Prehistory: A Review. AJA* supplement 1. Ed. T. Cullen, 329–78.

—— 2001b. Addendum: 1997–1999. *Aegean Prehistory: A Review. AJA* supplement 1. Ed. T. Cullen, 378–81.

Smith, Adam. 2003. *The Political Landscape: Constellations of Authority in Early Complex Polities*. Berkeley: University of California Press.

Traill, David, ed. 1993. Chapter 17. *Excavating Schliemann: Collected Papers on Schliemann*. Atlanta: Scholars Press.

Tsountas, Christos. 1893. *Mukênai kai Mukênaios Politismòs*. Athens: Bibliopoleio tes Hestias.

—— 1895. Zu einegen mykenischen Streitfragen. *JdI* 10:143–51.

Van Dyke, Ruth M., and Susan E. Alcock, eds. 2003. Archaeologies of Memory: An Introduction. In *Archaeologies of Memory*. Malden, Mass.: Blackwell.

Voutsaki, Sophia. 1995. Social and Political Processes in the Mycenaean Argolid: The Evidence from Mortuary Practices. In *Politeia: Society and State in the Aegean Bronze Age*, eds. R. Laffineur and W. D. Niemeier. Aegaeum 12. Liège, France: Université de Liège.

—— 1999. Mortuary Display, Prestige and Identity in the Shaft Grave Era. In *Eliten in der Bronzezeit: Ergebnisse zweier Kolloquien in Mainz und Athen*. Römisch-Germanisches Zentralmuseum Forschungsinstitut für Vor- und Frühgeschichte, Monographien 43 (1): 103–18.

Wace, Alan. 1921–23. Excavations at Mycenae VII: The Lion Gate and Grave Circle Area. *BSA* 25:103–26.

—— 1949. *Mycenae: An Archaeological History and Guide*. Princeton, N.J.: Princeton University Press.

—— 1950. Excavations at Mycenae, 1939. *BSA* 45:203–28.

Warren, P., and V. Hankey. 1989. *Aegean Bronze Age Chronology*. Bristol, U.K.: Bristol Classical Press.

Wright, James. 1984. Changes in Form and Function of the Palace at Pylos. In *Pylos Comes Alive: Industry and Administration in a Mycenaean Palace*, eds. C. W. Shelmerdine and T. G. Palaima, 19–29. New York: Fordham University Press.

——— 1987. Death and Power at Mycenae. In *Thanatos,* ed. R. Laffineur, 171–84. Aegaeum 1. Liège, France: Université de Liège.

——— 1995. Empty Cups and Empty Jugs: The Social Role of Wine in Minoan and Mycenaean Societies. In *The Origins and Ancient History of Wine*. Food and Nutrition in History and Anthropology. Eds. P. E. McGovern, S. J. Fleming, and S. H. Katz, 287–309. Philadelphia: Gordon and Breach.

——— 2004a. Comparative Settlement Patterns During the Bronze Age in the Peloponnesos. In *Side-by-Side Survey: Comparative Regional Studies in the Mediterranean,* eds. J. Cherry and S. Alcock, 114–31. Oxford: Oxbow.

———, ed. 2004b. *The Mycenaean Feast. Hesperia* ex. pub. 73.2.

Younger, John. 1997. The Stelai of Mycenae Grave Circles A and B. In *TEXNH,* eds. Robert Laffineur and Paul Betancourt, 229–41. Aegaeum 16. Liège, France: Université de Liège.

5 Identity under Construction in Roman Athens

Sanjaya Thakur

Although Roman Greece, and specifically Athens during the reign of the Roman emperor Augustus (31 BC–AD 14), has traditionally received little attention from scholars,[1] Augustan Athens provides an exemplary period in which to study the relationship between social identity and monumental building. This chapter focuses on a single monument, the Temple of Roma and Augustus, and the effects its construction had on the landscape of Athens and the acropolis, and upon those individuals who came in contact with it.

The reign of Augustus, Rome's first emperor, was typified by building projects that dramatically restructured civic and public space. The Temple of Roma and Augustus is no exception. The goddess Roma, a personification of the city, had been worshipped in Athens for two hundred years, but her association with the ruler and her worship on the acropolis was an Augustan innovation (on Roma, see Mellor 1975, 1981). A monumental construction, for the first time, housed worship of a living person on the acropolis (fig. 5.1).

I demonstrate how much planning went into the design of the temple and discuss the complexity of its effects on landscape, identity, and memory (past, present, and future). A brief historical background of Athens in the Augustan period contextualizes the political and social conditions under which the monument was built, investigating factors contributing to the temple's construction and identifying groups in the city who interacted with the monument and were motivated to support its construction. In the following sections I look closely at the choice of location of the monument, its physical features, some of the emotions it inspired, and memories it drew upon and subsequently altered. My aim is to understand the relationships among the monument, the greater landscape of the acropolis, and those we may call the audience for the Augustan material transformations.

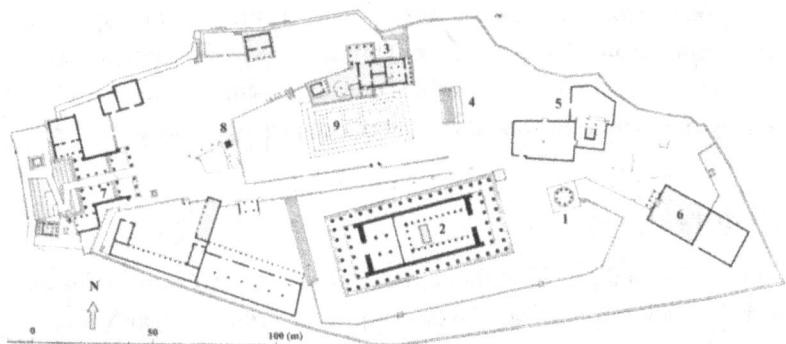

FIGURE 5.1 Restored overhead plan of the acropolis (adapted from G. P. Stevens 1958). (1) Temple of Roma and Augustus, (2) Parthenon, (3) Erechtheion, (4) great altar, (5) temple and sanctuary of Zeus Poleius, (6) sanctuary of Pandion, (7) Propylaia, (8) statue of Athena Promachos, (9) old temple of Athena.

Using ancient Greece as a case study, Susan Alcock has recently studied "how people made use of their past" and shown that "what people remember of the past fashions their sense of community and determines their allies, enemies and actions" (Alcock 2002, 1). I expand these concerns in this chapter by considering the reception of a monument, that is, how people's decisions about the past affected their rituals, civic behavior, and social identity.

Alcock (2002, 1) has also delineated the connection between identity and memory: "people derive identity from shared remembrance—social memory—which in turn provides them with an image of their past and a design for their future." These issues can be pursued in Augustan Athens, where local social changes were occurring in an empire that was experiencing dramatic change. The Temple of Roma and Augustus illustrates how alterations in identity occur through the transformation of landscape and appropriation of memory. The temple provides a case study to determine whether shared remembrance can be created, and how a foreign power is able to share in the memories of its conquered people (Schama 1995; Sinopoli 2003). Previous scholarship has studied historical information on individuals in Augustan Athens (Graindor 1923; Geagan 1979b, 1992, 1997; Schmalz 1994; Follet 2002). I discuss shared memories of groups (termed "memory communities" by Alcock 2002, 65–75) and detail what specific memories the monument draws upon, alters, and provokes. I also consider how the monument, and modifications in landscape, affect group identity and the experience of other monuments in a sacred space. The temple provides a physical example of elites using monumental construction to present identity and ideology among themselves, the populace, and the empire as a whole.

History

Athens was a unique city in the Roman world, not only because of its special history, but also for its critical relationship with Rome.[2] Athens's rich political and philosophical history formed important models for Romans, especially in the late Republic and early Empire. The city of Athens, although located within the new Roman province of Achaia, was granted free status, meaning it was not subject to direct imperial control. Despite this special free status, relations between elites of Athens and Rome were important.

By the end of the Republic the city's military prowess had long since dissipated, and Athens had basically become a college town. Athens was "a city where sophists and philosophers had replaced generals and orators as the most notable citizens [and] the sons of many a Roman senator and numerous eminent men of letters came" (Shear 1981; 357, 361; Cicero *de Or.* III.43; also see Schmalz 1994, 87; Alcock 1993, 196–97). Athens had become a fashionable spot for the philosophical and oratorical training of noble Roman youth. These schools had become the major industry in the city and brought a large population of young Romans from elite families to the city. This created an opportunity for Athenians to develop connections to future Roman nobles, which was a motivating factor in courting Roman favor. Similarly, by demonstrating a receptive attitude to Rome's leaders, Athenians hoped for Roman support.

In the previous century Athens had had a turbulent relationship with the political powers in Rome, allying itself to losing sides in four consecutive wars—having joined the causes of Mithridates, Pompey, Brutus and Cassius, and Antony. In 88 BC Rome was involved in a war with Mithridates VI, King of Pontus; since Athens sided with Mithridates, in 86 BC, it incurred punishment from the Roman general Sulla. Despite the importance of its previous history, Athens felt Rome's wrath. Sulla sacked the city, significantly damaging parts of it, notably the agora and acropolis (Shear 1981, 370; Lawrence 1996, 123; Hoff 1997; contra Hurwit 1999, 266). Even by Augustus's reign many areas of the city damaged by

Sulla had not been repaired (Thompson 1987, 4; Schmalz 1994, 7; Camp 1986, 106, 181; Hoff 1997; Shear 1997, 508).

Athens received little attention until 63 BC, when the Roman general Pompey donated fifty talents to help restore the city (Plutarch *Pompey* 42.6). As the rivalry for political supremacy grew between Julius Caesar and Pompey, Caesar initiated funding for a new Roman agora in 51 BC (Cicero *Att.* VI.I.25) because the classical agora had been damaged in Sulla's sack, but it was also a way to gain support through personal patronage. Caesar was attempting to generate sympathy and support, since Pompey controlled the eastern half of the Republic. This attempt to curry favor was apparently unsuccessful, as Athens allied with Pompey during the Roman civil war. Not surprisingly, Caesar ceased funding the project. After defeating Pompey at Pharsalos in 48 BC, Caesar did not sack Athens, as Sulla had done nearly forty years before. Instead he demanded reparations (*restitutio*) from all the eastern cites (Cassius Dio XLII.49.1–4). Caesar did this, not because he wished to spare Athens in particular, but because virtually every city in the East was allied with Pompey. Thus the Athenians did not have sufficient funds to continue the massive project (or start others) after paying Caesar for their indiscretion, and he had no desire to help them. Although Athens subsequently erected statues in Caesar's honor (Hoff 1989, 272), and despite the fact that Caesar sponsored many building projects throughout the empire in his short reign (48–44 BC), there is no evidence that he paid Athens any particular attention. Athenian attempts at reconciliation were too late to redeem its previous opposition to Caesar.

After Caesar's assassination (44 BC), war broke out again, between Brutus and Cassius, the conspiracy leaders, and Mark Antony (Caesar's former right-hand man) and Octavian, his adopted son (later given the title Augustus).[3] As cities in the East were former allies of Caesar's rival Pompey, they were quick to laud the conspirators and ally themselves with them. Athens was no exception.[4] When Octavian and Mark Antony were victorious at the battle of Philippi in 42 BC, Athens was again on the losing side. As time passed Mark Antony and Octavian became rival and fought a war in which propaganda played a large role, highlighted by Octavian's identification as *divi filius,* or son of a god. On this basis Augustus could claim divine heritage and worship. In 31 BC events between Mark Antony and Octavian culminated at Actium, where

Octavian defeated his rival. As in the preceding war, Octavian had strong support in the West, and the East continued to support the losing side. Antony, having allied himself with the forces of Cleopatra and the East, had alienated Rome and the western provinces, and he paid the price. For the fourth time Athens chose the wrong side.

Ancient sources place strong emphasis on Antony's presence in Athens, where he was headquartered for a time. He is described as an Easterner, who became an Athenian citizen, and even symbolically married Athena.[5] Even though, throughout the late Republic, the leaders of Athens tried to associate the city with powerful military figures, no sacred spaces were dramatically altered, nor were any monumental buildings erected in the city or on the acropolis.

After decades of war, Augustus's victory brought a prolonged peace. In Greece, which had been the scene of much of the fighting, there was now the opportunity to rebuild. Initially Athens did not receive special attention from Augustus, and he did not turn his attention to the East until about ten years after Actium (Schmalz 1996, 384). We do not see any activity in Athens, or the East, until about 22 or 21 BC, when Augustus visited Athens. It is possible that during this visit the Temple of Roma and Augustus was dedicated, but if so, we do not know who was responsible for the construction of the temple. Although Alcock (2002, 66) states, "to establish who built, or who financed, a particular monument is only to begin the discussion of its commemorative significance," the act of construction does provide a starting point for discussion of a monument's impact and reception. It is generally thought, due to the poor state of the city's finances, that local Athenian elite benefactors (*euergetai*) sponsored the project (Day 1942, 126–27; Schmalz 1994, 16). The dedicatory inscription on the monument (IG II² 3173, figs. 5.2 and 5.3) states that it was given by the Athenian people, signifying public approval of the project. However, it is generally agreed that high-level civic magistrates, such as the hoplite general Pammenes mentioned in the inscription, would provide financial support, an obligation of their position and indication of elite status (Graindor 1927, 157; Geagan 1967, 18–31 and 1997, 21–24; Schmalz 1994, 20). The monument can be seen as a logical attempt by the elite, new and/or old, to appease the emperor (especially while he was in the East). Athenian elites were presumably influenced by projects in Rome and in other imperial cities; recently scholars have argued that

FIGURE 5.2 Remains of the Temple of Roma and Augustus with the east façade of the Parthenon in the background (photo: S. Thakur)

the temple was modeled after a similar temple seen in Roman coinage (Schmalz 1994; Baldassarri 1998; Rose 2005).

Despite these arguments, it is likely some degree of imperial involvement existed in the temple's construction. Athens was in need of repair, and only through imperial support could large-scale projects be undertaken, as we see in the reconstruction of the Erechtheion on the acropolis (fig. 5.1; Burden 1999, 31–75). Caryatids, modeled after those in the south porch of the Erechtheion, were incorporated into Marcus Agrippa's (Augustus's second in command) Pantheon in Rome, and the presence of a dedicatory equestrian statue to him at the entrance of the Propylaia may indicate that he was the benefactor of the Erechtheion refurbishment. If this were the case, a certain degree of imperial influence can be envisioned in the Temple of Roma and Augustus's design. Its message and images were consistent with those the Roman government imparted in provincial cities. Further support can be seen in the axial alignment of the temple (see "Relationship to Other Monuments" section that follows), for "the principles of axial design (were) most favored by Roman architects" (Shear 1981, 362). It was

FIGURE 5.3 A reconstruction of the Temple of Roma and Augustus (adapted from Kawerau 1888). The dedicatory inscription (IG II² 3173), as translated by the author, reads "The people [of Athens dedicate this monument] to the goddess Roma and Augustus Caesar; when the hoplite general was Pammenes, son of Zenon, from Marathon, priest of Roma and Augustus the savior on the acropolis; when Megiste, daughter of Asklepedes, from Halai was priestess of Athena Polias; when Areius, son of Dorion, from Paiania was archon."

also characteristic for Augustan projects to dramatically reapportion open sacred spaces (Walker 1997; Alcock 2002, 51). This is the case in the construction of the Temple of Roma and Augustus on the Athenian acropolis.

The Physical Characteristics of the Temple of Roma and Augustus

Very little remains of the Temple of Roma and Augustus (fig. 5.2). Pausanias (a travel writer of the second century AD) does not mention the temple, and it does not appear in literature. A few fragments of the temple do remain, allowing assessments of its size and appearance (fig. 5.3). Archaeological work on the site started with Georg Kawerau (1888) and has most recently been continued by Wolfgang Binder (1969). Kawerau found that many of the elements of the temple had been reused as spolia and been distributed throughout the acropolis site, making the task of collection and reconstruction extremely difficult. All that remained at the site of the temple was the square foundation, which measures about twelve meters per side. The temple was monopteral, had nine Ionic columns, a "steeply sloping conical roof" (Travlos 1971, 494), and a dedication to Augustus (IG II^2 3173) on its architrave (fig. 5.2). The height of the temple's columns (7.4 meters) was nearly the exact dimension of its interior diameter, providing a symmetrical appearance to the structure.

Although most Roman temples of this period used Corinthian capitals, the temple has Ionic columns. This was presumably influenced by the nearby Erechtheion, whose north porch had a similar column type (Travlos 1971, 494; Schmalz 1994, 15; Shear 1997, 508; Burden 1999, 65). The association goes beyond similarity, as the dimensions of the column capitals are virtually identical. This indicates a conscious decision and intention by the designers. As Shear (1997, 507) states, "indeed one gets the impression that the builders of the acropolis monopteros actually measured their dimensions from the columns of the east porch of the Erechtheion."

The columns of the temple were not engaged, so that the interior contents of the temple were visible from all angles of approach. This "open" nature of the temple distinguishes it from the other temples on the acropolis and, indeed, most ancient temples and monuments, where interior elements are presented to the audience in a controlled and regulated fashion. It is most likely that the statues within the temple were intended to be seen by all passersby. Although we know little about the precise contents of the temple, we can make some informed guesses based on comparable cult shrines in other cities.[6] The temple must have contained cult images, presumably bronze statues of Augustus and the goddess Roma.

Relationship to Other Monuments

The position of the Temple of Roma and Augustus on the acropolis is itself significant (fig. 5.1).[7] The temple was located in the center of the open eastern plateau, directly in front of the east (main) entrance to the Parthenon (fig. 5.2). The temple and cult statues housed within were in direct alignment with the Parthenon. If an observer stood west of the Temple of Roma and Augustus, he stood between symbols of Athenian and Roman identity. To an observer east of the temple, his view of the Parthenon would have been obstructed. Furthermore, to enter the Parthenon, visitors had to encounter the Temple of Roma and Augustus, because the temple filled the previously open space in front of the Parthenon. Figure 5.4 demonstrates the axial alignment of the Roma and Augustus temple to the Parthenon. In addition, the figure illustrates the distances between the steps of the Parthenon to the inner and outer tangents of the Temple of Roma and Augustus. Schmalz (1994, 14) argues that the shorter distance is that of the width of the inner cella of the Parthenon, while the longer distance corresponds to the full Parthenon's width. The construction of an elaborate foundation for the temple demonstrates the designers' interest in creating specific spatial relationships. Rather than choosing a naturally flat spot on the plateau, the foundation is built on a sloped area; the importance of the site is dictated by its relationship to the Parthenon.[8] This precise alignment demonstrates the designers' goal of creating spatial relationships with the most important monument on the acropolis.

The siting of the temple was significant in another respect. Both the Parthenon and the Erechtheion are strongly associated with the origins of Athens. The Parthenon was, as it is now, the symbol of Athens. The west pediment of the Parthenon depicted Athena's defeat of Poseidon to become Athens's main civic deity, and the east pediment depicted the birth of Athena. The goddess was centrally depicted alongside Zeus, emphasizing the strong association between the two and hence between Athens and the divine world. By placing the Roma and Augustus

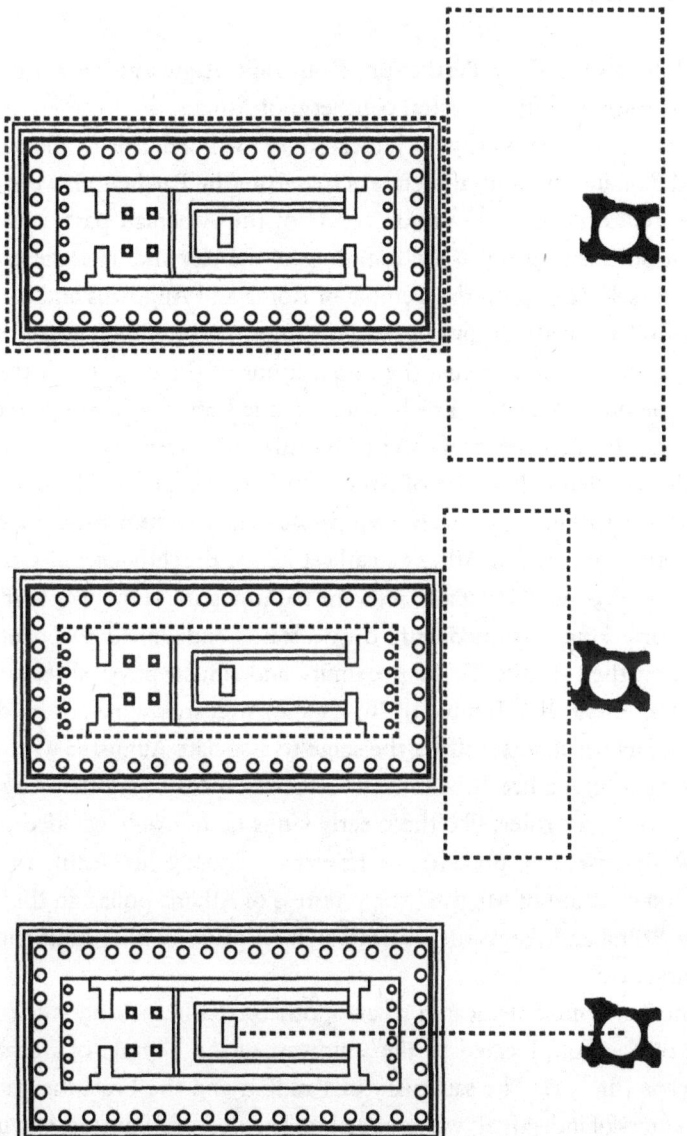

FIGURE 5.4 Spatial relationships between the Parthenon and the Temple of Roma and Augustus. (*Top*) The distance from the Parthenon east facade to the eastern edge of the Roma and Augustus foundations equals the width of the Parthenon's foundations. (*Middle*) The distance from the Parthenon facade to the western edge of the Roma and Augustus foundations equals the width of the Parthenon cella. (*Bottom*) The center of the temple of Roma and Augustus is in axial alignment to the center of the Parthenon cult image (adapted from Schmalz 1994).

temple in front of the Parthenon, Roma and Augustus were, in effect, also inserted into the ancestral pantheon of Athens.

In the Erechtheion (fig. 5.1), located on the north side of the acropolis and flanking the central avenue across from the Parthenon, were many of the relics relating to famous events of the Athenian past, as well as certain objects relating to the founding of the city and its earliest kings. Previous scholarship on the Temple of Roma and Augustus and the Erechtheion has failed to move beyond the importance of their shared architectural features and discuss the implications of the contents within the Erechtheion. Inside the Erechtheion (named after Athens's legendary first king, Erechtheus) were the primordial olive tree given by Athena, the old wooden cult statue of Athena in her civic persona (*polias*), and tombs of early kings. As one of its purposes, the Erechtheion was a site of the worship for two of Athens's earliest kings, Erechtheus and Cecrops. Interestingly, and particularly relevant to Augustus, is the fact that both these early kings assumed semi-divine status and joined the pantheon following their deaths. By its proximity and similar physical features to this monument, the Temple of Roma and Augustus signaled the divine status of its occupants, setting the stage to associate Augustus with those worshipped in the Erechtheion. The association illustrated that Augustus was no ordinary ruler; like these early kings he not only wielded power but would rise, as a god, to the heavens following his death. In addition, the mention of Megiste, the priestess of Athena polias, in the Temple of Roma and Augustus dedicatory inscription further links the two monuments.

Another temple dedicated to an apotheosized hero/king is the sanctuary of Pandion, located to the southeast of the Temple of Roma and Augustus (fig. 5.1). The sanctuary of Pandion and the Erechtheion were cult centers of individuals whose worship, like that of Augustus, was incorporated into the civic calendar. It appears that the designers of the Temple of Roma and Augustus were well aware that the area to the east of the Parthenon would be an appropriate place to honor and worship a king who achieved divine status and whose worship was to become part of civic life.

To the north/northeast of the Temple of Roma and Augustus stood the temple of Zeus and its sanctuary (fig. 5.1). The proximity of the new temple to the temple of the king of the gods and the city further calls attention to Augustus's and Rome's image as leaders of the city and world. It is noteworthy that Augustus was linked with Zeus in a number of cities (Day 1942, 136). Through associations created by the physical position between the Temple of Roma and Augustus, the Parthenon, the Erechtheion, and the sanctuaries of Zeus and Pandion, Augustus was placed among Athens's most ancestral figures, the temple's location corroborating his claim to authority.

The Temple of Roma and Augustus was a round temple, and the shape itself is significant. Circular (tholos) temples were used for various types of structures. Binder (1969) provides a useful collection of those found in the ancient world. The Temple of Roma and Augustus was once considered specifically parallel to the temple of Vesta in the Roman forum (Graindor 1927, 153–55). But recently scholars have viewed the Temple of Roma and Augustus as commemorative of Augustus's Parthian campaign, envisioning the acropolis as a whole monument for the celebration of defeats of eastern foes. Schmalz (1994, 32–35), Baldassarri (1995), and Rose (2005, 51–52) have argued that the temple's design was similar to a temple of Mars the Avenger that was intended to be built in Rome to celebrate Roman victory over the Parthians, but was only depicted on Roman coinage. The latter argument is convincing; but since the temple in Rome was never built, and the coins limited in their series and circulation, the Temple of Roma and Augustus ought to be considered in its own context and not in reference to other models. Furthermore, I would challenge those who assume designers were following a prescribed model, for Ionic columns were used in the Roma and Augustus temple (precisely reflecting the Erechtheion) rather than using the Corinthian columns depicted on coinage. The designers' aim was to integrate the monument into the acropolis site, forming relationships with surrounding monuments and space to create specific associations and meaning.

Whatever the motivation for its shape, the effects are dramatic. The design represents a unique form for a temple both on the acropolis and throughout Athens. Most important, the circular design causes viewers to perceive the other monuments mentioned earlier as radiating from the Temple of Roma and Augustus. Although the temple was the most recent construction among those I have mentioned, its shape and position demonstrate its authority and power, and that of those whose images it contained.

Visibility

Whereas the temple's entrance was on the east-west axis, there is a question of how the viewer's attention was directed (Schmalz 1994, 19). Was the entrance to the Roma and Augustus temple facing the Parthenon or was the entrance on the east side of the temple? An answer cannot be given with certainty. Both positions create interesting dynamics for viewers, as the Roma and Augustus temple could be viewed either in opposition to the Parthenon or superceding it, causing, in effect, visitors to the Parthenon to walk east of the Roma and Augustus temple and then to advance to the Parthenon. On whichever side the entrance was located, the temple caused visitors to approach the Parthenon differently and altered their experience. As Burden (1999, 69) aptly notes, "it was the last thing seen before entering and the first thing one saw upon leaving the venerable temple."

The height and location of the temple affected the visibility of the monument both on and off the acropolis. The Parthenon stood just over twenty meters in height. By contrast, the height of the Temple of Roma and Augustus (with its roof) was approximately ten meters. In ancient times, to access the plateau where the temple was situated (and also the entrance to the Parthenon), a causeway led directly from the Propylaia, up a ramp adjacent to the Parthenon's north side (fig. 5.1). One then had to veer to the right of the statue of Athena Promachos, which was directly in front of the Propylaia. The other side of the causeway was bounded by an elevated plateau, the site of the archaic temple of Athena, which was burnt by the Persians in 479 BC.[9] To reach the Temple of Roma and Augustus, visitors were channeled through this passage, for as one emerged from the Propylaia the Parthenon blocked sight of the temple. Although the temple was in a prominent location and space directly in front of the Parthenon's entrance, it was hidden from the view of those who visited until they had traveled far up the causeway. The temple was revealed only after one passed the Parthenon's northeast corner.

On the other hand, observation of the monument would have been apparent, perhaps even prominent, when the acropolis altar was being used. To spectators on the upper plateau east of the altar the temple would have been visible during the proceedings. It was also possibly visible from the area of the destroyed archaic temple and, though less apparent, to viewers who were located on the lower plateau west of the Erechtheion and the Promachos.

The temple's location in the center of the upper plateau masks it from view from the classical city over 100 meters below. Only structures built along the acropolis walls and the Parthenon, with its dramatic height, were visible. It would have been impossible to view the temple from such lower sites as the agora and along the Panathenaic way leading to the acropolis. It certainly would not have been visible from the west, even from elevated sites, due to the Propylaia, which would have blocked the lines of sight. Although the temple was visible from elevated sites on the east, those sites were not a significant part of the Athenian cityscape in the Augustan period. The question then arises: why build a temple in a site that is so visually restricted from the city below? Presumably (setting aside for the moment the financial costs of such an undertaking), the desire was not to usurp attention from the most visible marker of the acropolis, the Parthenon. Athens was identified by the monument, and the Augustan monument was not intended to trumpet the dominance of Rome over the city (unlike later cult temples in Ephesus or Pergamon, for example), but to acknowledge, simply and appropriately, the presence, authority, and divinity of the Roman emperor. The nuances of construction and restricted visibility demonstrate the careful balance that was struck between an important alteration of space and recognition of traditional monuments and identities.

Dedicatory Inscription

Another important element to the temple was the dedicatory inscription (figs. 5.2 and 5.3). I shall not provide a detailed history of the individuals mentioned in the inscription, who are important but have been adequately discussed by others (Graindor 1923; 1927, 169; Geagan 1992; 1997, 22–24; Schmalz 1994, 19–32; Hoff 1996, 190–92), but rather focus on the reception of the inscription by viewers. The inscription is in Greek, intended for an audience literate in Greek. This audience would consist of most visitors to the site (including many Roman visitors), but not all who saw the monument. Some visitors may have recognized the monument's inscription as Greek and nothing more. Others may have recognized only familiar formulaic portions of the inscription. In addition, the inscription was located atop the temple, and the letters are only a few inches in height. Although its legibility would have been enhanced by color in ancient times, its placement more than seven meters high shows that its specific message was less important than the fact that there was an inscription. The statues would have identified the temple, not the inscription.

Nonetheless, the contents of the inscription provide concrete historical information concerning the monument. Although much of the language is standard, the text illustrates some interesting features that highlight the monument's reception and Athenian attitudes to it. The inscription begins (as is typical) with the dedication of the Temple of Roma and Augustus from the people of the city, followed by the names of the Athenian civic officials serving to date the temple.[10] The dedication from the demos, the people of Athens, demonstrates public approval of the project. At minimum a majority of citizens voted to publicly dedicate the temple to Augustus. The mention of the hoplite general, Pammenes, is also important (Geagan 1967, 18–31; 1997, 21–22). Since others have discussed in depth what we know of his career, I wish to emphasize that this important civic magistrate is also the priest of Roma and Augustus. This integration of the priesthood into the existing civic political structure represents the temple's integration into the acropolis site and Athenian society.[11] As previously discussed, the mention of Megiste associates the temple with the Erechtheion and the acropolis site, of which Megiste was the chief priestess. Since we have so few monumental dedications on the acropolis, the priestess of Athena polias is not often found in our sources. Nevertheless, it may not be rash to envision her appearance in the inscription as more than a simple dating device. The decision to include the names of such high-level civic magistrates illustrates the willingness and desire these officials had to associate themselves and their positions with Rome. However, the mention of the archon in a dedicatory inscription is a standard dating device, since this was an annually chosen official (although we cannot firmly place his year in office).

The design and location of the monument demonstrate a conscious decision and awareness of their importance and impact. The Parthenon was not torn down, nor the acropolis razed, in order to build a great temple to Augustus; rather designers carefully incorporated Augustus and Roma into the site in a restrained and appropriate manner. Furthermore, the temple's use both of landscape and memory set the stage for the alteration of identity, both of the viewers and of the acropolis site itself. Although the acropolis was littered with dedicated statues, stelae, and other sculptural monuments, the Temple of Roma and Augustus was the first major temple addition to the site in centuries and marked a dramatic change from even the most ambitious sculptural programs. The decision to build a temple, and one in such a location and of such a style, differentiated Augustus from previous rulers and benefactors who were honored in the city.

Audience, Occasion, and Reception of the Temple

Who saw the Temple of Roma and Augustus, when did they see it, and how did they react to it? The audience obviously consisted of groups of Romans, Athenians, and other visitors to the site (see Habicht 1997b). To discuss the impact of a monument presents challenges, since assumptions and generalizations must be made about groups and their membership. Rather than focusing on individuals I discuss "community memory" (Alcock 2002, 15), the shared memory and experiences of specific groups. Although groups often overlap, and an individual can be part of more than one group, the term memory community is a useful term that allows us to understand better the nature of group identity.

Young Romans coming to Augustan Athens wanted to see the city that served as the literary and oratorical model for Rome. The appearance of a temple to Roma and the emperor on the acropolis would certainly have been recognized as a new foundation. It was traditional in the East for Roman leaders to be worshiped as, or associated with, gods, and Augustus had recently incorporated himself into the religious calendar of Rome (as well as in Athens), and referred to himself as the son of a god. Augustan festivals in Rome might have been paralleled at the acropolis temple in Athens. Although Augustus's worship outside of Rome would not have been surprising, its prominence abroad might have caused discomfort to some Romans. To Roman citizens, the temple may have seemed an ironic honor for the man who "restored" the Republic.[12] Because the statues, as well as other images throughout the city, referenced Rome, Athens became a location for Romans to see and interact with symbols of imperial power and authority (Alcock 2002, 53, 66ff.; Zanker 1988, 261–63). The revamped landscape of Augustan Athens aided this experience. The ancient agora had become the site for the collection of classical material including the addition of a Roman odeion (auditorium) and a classical temple possibly rededicated to Augustus's heirs (Shear 1981, 361–63; Thompson 1987, 6–9; Spawforth 1997, 186–88). The topography of the city was Romanized, specifically made Augustan, by the alterations to its civic spaces (Walker 1997, 75–78).

How did Athenians regard the new temple? This question entails an evaluation of who were "Athenians" after the Roman civil wars. During the Augustan age there is evidence for demographic shifts and greater urbanization (Alcock 1993, 60–64, 119–28; 2002, 48; Schmalz 1994, 4). Hence in Athens a "new" Athenian population was created. This would have resulted in new elites and increased competition for imperial favor, as well as residents whose unfamiliarity with the acropolis could be exploited through the Roma and Augustus temple. In addition to considering new and old residents of Athens, we can consider the division of Athenians into elite and non-elite groups.

For Athenians new to the city, the temple's position was presumably not seen as subversive to traditional Athenian history and culture, since new residents would have no memory of the site prior to the temple's existence and would not be disturbed or negatively impacted by the alteration of the acropolis. To longstanding residents of Athens, however, the location and presence of the new temple could not have failed to remind them of Rome's eminent presence on the sacred hill.

For elites, new and old, there was pressure to associate and gain favor with Rome. I have documented historical examples earlier, examined individuals and offices mentioned in the dedicatory inscription, and cited the studies of Daniel J. Geagan (1967, 1979a, 1979b, 1992, 1997), Christian Habicht (1997b), and Simone Follet (2002). Among our extant sources we have numerous examples of new elites appearing in the historical record. Due to their presence, one must imagine a community in which there was increased competition for imperial attention.

Non-elites present a group more difficult to quantify, since non-elite voices are rarely heard in historical sources. Although the dedicatory inscription provides evidence for public support for the project, one hesitates to rely on it as a source of widespread public approval. Nevertheless, the inscription is evidence that a vote was taken, and a majority of citizens did approve the project and had elected pro-Roman civic magistrates. The impact of the construction projects, specifically the Temple of Roma and Augustus, the Erechtheion, and later work in the agoras, would have been substantial for non-elites. Employment from these projects and related industry would have been extensive. Furthermore, the visual impact of a newly refurbished city must not be discounted. Roman support for these projects was critical, and their practical financial benefits were clear and may have overwhelmed sentimental and historical concerns. The Temple of Roma and Augustus may have been seen as fitting honor for the man who was responsible for the city's restoration.

We do know something of Athenian reaction to the temple relating to Augustus's visit to Athens in 22/21 BC. Augustus punished Athens by releasing Aegina (a nearby island territory) from its control; however, he also is said to have enjoyed participation in the Eleusinian Mysteries.[13] The historian Cassius Dio (57.7.2–4) reports that during this time a statue of Athena on the acropolis turned to the west and spat blood. This story has been literally interpreted to symbolize Athenians's displeasure with Rome (Hoff 1989, 269), although most scholars think it is an allegorical reference to some local uprising that occurred during Augustus's visit (Bowersock 1964, 120–21). While scholars debate which cult statue Dio refers to (Mansfield 1985, 174–76; Ridgeway 1992), I conjecture that Dio refers to the statue in the Parthenon, and the mythical story specifically refers to the sentiments felt by some Athenians to the erection of the Temple of Roma and Augustus. Those citizens who had sided against Augustus were still present in the city, which had lost the ability to sell honorific citizenships, in addition to suffering the loss of Aegina (Graindor 1927, 17; Day 1942, 134–36; Hoff 1989, 267–68). The building of a cult temple to Augustus on the most sacred site in the city must have been a provocation to a number of Athenians. The statue's "turn to the west" may have been symbolic of Athena's, and hence Athenians's displeasure that the new Roma and Augustus temple was located right in Athena's line of sight. Further evidence for dissension within the Athenian community is seen in the mention of a later civil disturbance in the city in ca. AD 13, when a Roman magistrate had to be sent to settle affairs (Graindor 1927, 41–45; Hoff 1989, 275; Spawforth 1997, 192). Thus, evidence exists of hostility to Rome among some Athenian citizens. Although we do not know which group or groups were responsible for these acts of resistance, whether elites, non-elites, or a combination of both, we may consider the problem in terms of practice and knowledge.

That is, how often, and on what occasions, did people actually go up to the acropolis? Priests of the temples (usually drawn from the elite class) had daily access to the acropolis. The site was also open to visitors and pilgrims to the temples. The Parthenon was still a major cult site, although its access was controlled. Letters from Roman youths to their friends and family inform us that they did visit the site. Pausanias (second century AD) writes that the site was open to tourists and travelers of all kinds, and this was presumably the case in the Augustan age as well.

How frequent were these visits? Religious and civic rituals took place on the acropolis, although major festivals occurred only a few days a year. Again, these events were probably restricted to the elites of the city. Even in the Panathenaia (Athens's major civic festival), only select officials and families were present on the acropolis, although other individuals were present along the Panathenaiac way to the acropolis. To summarize: although the acropolis site was open to all, it was frequented most often by the elite, and access was controlled. In the course of their daily lives, average citizens would not have seen, let alone visited, the monument. Massive crowds did not throng to the Temple of Roma and Augustus. In fact, a relatively limited portion of the population had contact with it, and these were Athenians who were responsible for sponsoring the temple and those Romans whose support they hoped to one day obtain. Yet every visitor to the site—Romans, elite and non-elite Greeks—were faced with a monumental Roman presence in Athens's most ancient and revered site.

Conclusion

The carefully positioned Temple of Roma and Augustus altered the perception of older and larger preexisting monuments. The temple drew the attention of visitors and loomed above them as they entered and viewed the Parthenon and religious rituals on the acropolis. It is hard to underestimate the impression and impact of the new forms of visual connection. First, images within the Temple of Roma and Augustus were associated with Greek images on the acropolis. Then, venerable constructions were now viewed along with the new Roman temple.

This admixture of Roman and Greek constructions was not new in their world, but it was new for the acropolis, where a symbol of Rome stood modestly but clearly on the peak of the acropolis.

Thus far I have focused on the initial construction and reception of the Temple of Roma and Augustus. Over time, the temple became just another part of the acropolis topography as Athens was subsumed into the Roman Empire. The temple's continued existence and use for the worship of later emperors demonstrates its "success." Although the memory of an acropolis without the Temple of Roma and Augustus might well have been preserved, it would have been difficult to "imagine away" the temple. The new temple created new memories, and it entailed the forgetting of old ones. After the temple's construction, the once-open space in front of the Parthenon had been irretrievably altered. The carefully chosen location and design allowed a small temple to radically restructure a sacred space. The new temple, subtly implying Roman presence and control, transformed the landscape of Athens's most important civic space and initiated a process of how future generations would imagine (sensu Anderson 1991) their pasts in their performance of civic and religious rites (Price 1984, 239–48). The temple encapsulates a site where past and present and the interests of rulers and locals come together and demonstrate both alliance and allegiance in the city's most important civic space.

The Temple of Roma and Augustus was a new development in the history of Athenian elites honoring Romans and seeking Roman patronage. From the second century BC on, many examples exist of Athenian rededications and honors given to Romans (Graindor 1927, 45–54; Day 1942, 171). Elite families not only wanted to increase Roman connections but also to hold religious/political offices and to secure Roman patronage for civil projects. The Temple of Roma and Augustus "worked" for Athenians, since, in spite of resistance, Augustus later authorized support for the construction of a new agora, and the city saw Roman sponsorship of other civic projects (Graindor 1927, 130; Day 1942, 138).

The placement of the Temple of Roma and Augustus conveyed a kind of prophecy that Rome was to be part of Athenian history. Associating and eventually assimilating Augustus to Athens's divine kings and earliest history was, of course, a sign of the presence, authority, and influence of Rome. New festivals and rituals involving Augustus, Roma, and the temple also required new roles for the older temples. By altering the landscape of the acropolis, the Temple of Roma and Augustus created not only a new present but also conveyed a message from the past: Rome was the logical culmination of Athenian history.

Acknowledgments

Research for this chapter was aided by a U.S. Department of State–funded Fulbright U.S. student program grant and a stay at the American School of Classical Studies, Athens. Thanks are due to its director, Steven Tracy, and to Glen R. Bugh for his helpful comments.

Notes

1. Recent exceptions are Alcock 2002, 1993; Baldassarri 1998; Hoff and Rotroff (eds.) 1997; Schmalz 1994; Geagan 1992, 1979a. The foundational studies of Graindor 1927, Day 1942, Binder 1969, Oliver 1983, and Hänlein-Schäfer 1985 must also be noted.

2. For general surveys on Athenian history in this period see Graindor 1927; Day 1942, 120–76; Habicht 1997a, 297–365.

3. Octavian was granted the title Augustus in 27 BC. The Temple of Roma and Augustus is definitively dated after 27, because the word *Sebastos*, equivalent to Augustus in Greek (Cassius Dio 53.16.8), was found inscribed on the temple (*Inscriptiones Graecae* [IG] II² 3173 [figs. 5.2 and 5.3]).

4. The Athenians even went so far as to erect statues of these "modern" tyrant slayers in the classical agora. Cassius Dio 47.20.4; Hoff 1989, 273; Camp 1986, 188.

5. Cassius Dio (48.39.2) and Seneca (*Suas.* 1.6) inform us that for this marriage Athens was required to provide a "dowry" to Antony of 1000 talents, further depleting the city's economic resources (Day 1942, 126–27, 133; Hoff 1989, 273). The episode exemplifies the degree to which Athens went to attract foreign favor.

6. Price 1984, 249ff. provides comparative examples; most applicable are Lesbos, Samos, Ephesus, Pergamon, and Miletus. Also see Mellor 1975, 145–54; Rose 2005, 51.

7. One should note a few inaccuracies with the generally excellent reconstruction in Rose 2005, 51. The terrain of the acropolis at the location of the temple slopes downward, and the actual side of entrance is unknown.

8. The decision to build the cult temple on the acropolis is of interest, for this breaks the pattern usually observed that cult shrines are typically built in administrative centers (Price 1984, 144–45; Alcock 1993, 180). However, an important exception to this occurs at Pergamon, where the altar to Augustus was located on the acropolis.

9. The site of the archaic temple was declared sacred and remained a memorial space (Diodorus Siculus 11.29.3; Hurwit 1999, 144).

10. Unfortunately, scholars have been unable to precisely date the terms of these officials.

11. It is important to remember that modern Western distinctions of religion and politics are inapplicable to the Greek and Roman world.

12. Early in his reign Roman citizens would not have been expected to worship Augustus, but rather Roma accompanied by his father, the deified Julius Caesar, whose worship was firmly established in Rome. Nonetheless Augustan imperial anniversaries became part of the civic calendar in Rome and abroad (Beard 1987).

13. The Mysteries were a cult ritual, details of which scholars know little, save it involved a journey from Athens to nearby Eleusis to honor the goddesses Demeter and Kore. The festivities were so enjoyable that during his next visit Augustus participated in the Mysteries again; although it was the wrong part of the year, the event had to be catered for him.

Bibliography

Alcock, Susan E. 1993. *Graecia Capta: The Landscapes of Roman Greece*. Cambridge: Cambridge University Press.

——— 2002. *Archaeologies of the Greek Past: Landscape, Monuments, and Memories*. Cambridge: Cambridge University Press.

Anderson, Benedict. 1991. *Imagined Communities: Reflections on the Origins and Spread of Nationalism*. Rev. ed. London: Verso.

Baldassarri, Paola. 1995. Augusto Soter: ipotesi sul monopteros dell'Acropoliateniese. *Ostraka* 4 (1): 69–84.

——— 1998. *Sebastoi Soteri: edilizia monumentale ad Atene durante il saeculum Augustum*. Archaeologica 124. Roma: G. Bretschneider.

Beard, Mary. 1987. A Complex of Times: No More Sheep on Romulus' Birthday. *Proceedings of the Cambridge Philological Society* 33:1–15.

Binder, Wolfgang. 1969. *Der Roma-Augustus Monopteros auf der Akropolis in Athen und sein typologischer Ort*. Stuttgart: Paul JLLG Photo-Offsetdruck.

Bowersock, Glen W. 1964. Augustus on Aegina. *Classical Quarterly* 14:120–21.

Burden, Jeffrey C. 1999. Athens Remade in the Age of Augustus: A Study of the Architects and Craftsmen at Work. Ph.D. diss., University of California, Berkeley.

Camp, John M. 1986. *The Athenian Agora*. London: Thames and Hudson.

Day, John. 1942. *An Economic History of Roman Athens under Roman Domination*. New York: Columbia University Press.

Follet, Simone. 2002. Les Italiens à Athènes (IIe siècle av. J.-C.–Ier siècle ap. J.-C.). In *Actes de la table ronde Ecole Normale Superieur Paris 14–16 Mai 1988*, eds. Christel Möller and Claire Hasenohr, 79–88. Bulletin de Correspondance Hellenique Supplement 41. Paris: École Francaise d'Athenes.

Geagan, Daniel J. 1967. *The Athenian Constitution after Sulla*. Hesperia supplement 12. Princeton: American School of Classical Studies, Athens.

——— 1979a. Roman Athens: Some Aspects of Life and Culture. I. 86 B.C.–A.D. 267, *Aufstieg und Niedergang der römischen Welt* II.7.1:371–437. Berlin: Walter de Gruyter.

———. 1979b. Tiberius Claudius Novius: The Hoplite Generalship and the *Epimeletia* of the Free City of Athens. *American Journal of Philology* 100:279–87.

———. 1992. A Family of Marathon and Social Mobility in Athens of the First Century B.C. *Phoenix* 46:29–44.

———. 1997. The Athenian Elite: Romanization, Resistance, and the Exercise of Power. In *The Romanization of Athens: Proceedings of an International Conference Held at Lincoln, Nebraska (April 1996)*, ed. Michael C. Hoff and Susan I. Rotroff, 19–32. Oxford: Oxbow Books.

Graindor, Paul. 1923. Étude sur Athènes sous Auguste: Les Athéniens à l'époque d'Auguste. *Musée Belge* 27:259–304.

———. 1927. *Athènes sous Auguste*. Cairo: Le Caire, Imprimerie nationale. Misr, Societe ananyme égyptienne.

Habicht, Christian. 1997a. *Athens from Alexander to Antony*. Cambridge: Harvard University Press.

———. 1997b. Roman Citizens in Athens (228–31 B.C.). In *The Romanization of Athens: Proceedings of an International Conference Held at Lincoln, Nebraska (April 1996)*, eds. Michael C. Hoff and Susan I. Rotroff, 9–17. Oxford: Oxbow Books.

Hänlein-Schäfer, Heidi. 1985. *Veneratio Augusti: eine Studie zu den Tempeln des ersten römischen Kaisers*. Roma: G. Bretschneider.

Hoff, Michael C. 1989. Civil Disobedience and Unrest in Augustan Athens. *Hesperia* 59:267–76.

———. 1996. The Politics and Architecture of the Athenian Imperial Cult. In *Subject and Ruler: The Cult of the Ruling Power in Classical Antiquity; Papers Presented at a Conference Held in the University of Alberta on April* 13–15, 1994, *to Celebrate the 65th Anniversary of Duncan Fishwick*, ed. Alastair Small, 185–200. Journal of Roman Archaeology supplement no. 17. Ann Arbor: Journal of Roman Archaeology.

———. 1997. *Laceratae Athenae:* Sulla's Siege of Athens in 87/6 B.C. and its aftermath. In *Romanization of Athens: proceedings of an International Conference Held at Lincoln, Nebraska (April 1996)*, eds. Michael C. Hoff and Susan I. Rotroff, 33–51. Oxford: Oxbow Books.

Hoff, Michael C., and Susan I. Rotroff, eds. 1997. *The Romanization of Athens: Proceedings of an International Conference Held at Lincoln, Nebraska (April 1996)*. Oxford: Oxbow Books.

Hurwit, Jeffrey M. 1999. *The Athenian Acropolis: History, Mythology, and Archaeology from the Neolithic Era to the Present*. Cambridge: Cambridge University Press.

Kawerau, Georg. 1888. Der Temple der Roma und Augustus auf der Akropolis von Athen. *Antike Denkmaler* 1:13.

Lawrence, Arnold W. 1996. *Greek Architecture*. 5th ed., revised by Richard A. Tomlinson. New Haven: Yale University Press.

Mansfield, John M. 1985. The Robe of Athena and the Panathenaic Peplos. Ph.D. diss., University of California, Berkeley.

Mellor, Ronald. 1975. *Thea Rhōmē: The Worship of the Goddess Roma in the Greek World*. Hypomnemata XLII. Göttingen: Vandenhoeck and Ruprecht.

——— 1981. The Goddess Roma. *Aufstieg und Niedergang der römischen Welt* No. 17.2:950–1030. Berlin: Walter de Gruyter.

Oliver, James H. 1983. *The Civic Tradition and Roman Athens*. Baltimore: Johns Hopkins University Press.

Price, Simon R. F. 1984. *Rituals and Power: The Roman Imperial Cult in Asia Minor*. Cambridge: Cambridge University Press.

Ridgway, Brunilde S. 1992. Images of Athena on the Akropolis. In *Goddess and Polis: The Panathenaic Festival in Ancient Athens*, ed. Jennifer Neils, 118–42. Princeton: Princeton University Press.

Rose, Charles B. 2005. The Parthians in Augustan Rome. *American Journal of Archaeology* 109:21–75.

Schama, Simon. 1995. *Landscape and Memory*. New York: A. A. Knopf.

Schmalz, Geoffrey C. R. 1994. Public Building and Civic Identity in Augustan and Julio-Claudian Athens. Ph.D. diss., University of Michigan, Ann Arbor.

——— 1996. Athens, Augustus, and the Settlement of 21 B.C. *Greek, Roman and Byzantine Studies* 37 (4): 381–98.

Shear, Theodore L. 1981. Athens from City State to Provincial Town. *Hesperia* 50:356–77.

——— 1997. The Athenian Agora: Excavations of 1989–93. *Hesperia* 66:495–548.

Sinopoli, Carla. 2003. Echoes of Empire: Vijayanagara and Historical Memory, Vijayanagara as Historical Memory. In *Archaeologies of Memory*, eds. Ruth M. Van Dyke and Susan E. Alcock, 17–33. Malden, Mass.: Blackwell.

Spawforth, Antony. 1997. Early Reception of the Imperial Cult in Athens: Problems and Ambiguities. In *The Romanization of Athens: Proceedings of an International Conference Held at Lincoln, Nebraska (April 1996)*, eds. Michael C. Hoff and Susan I. Rotroff, 183–99. Oxford: Oxbow Books.

Stevens, Gorham P. 1958. *Restoration of Classical Buildings*. Princeton: American School of Classical Studies, Athens.

Thompson, Homer A. 1987. Impact of Roman Architects and Architecture on Athens 170 B.C.–A.D. 170. In *Roman Architecture in the Greek World*, eds. Sarah Macready and Frederick H. Thompson, 1–17. Society of Antiquaries London Occasional Papers NS #10. London: Thames and Hudson.

Travlos, John. 1971. *Pictorial Dictionary of Ancient Athens*. New York: Praeger.

Walker, Susan. 1997. Athens under Augustus. In *The Romanization of Athens: Proceedings of an International Conference Held at Lincoln, Nebraska (April 1996)*, eds. Michael C. Hoff and Susan I. Rotroff, 67–80. Oxford: Oxbow Books.

Zanker, Paul. 1988. *The Power of Images in the Age of Augustus*. Trans. Alan Shapiro. Ann Arbor: University of Michigan Press.

6 Inscribing the Napatan Landscape
ARCHITECTURE AND ROYAL IDENTITY

Lindsay Ambridge

When kings of Nubia conquered Egypt in the eighth century BC, they carried with them an identity and a past that had been subject to the vagaries of war and colonial domination. They confronted their competing pasts—and their diverse audience—with a visual language of architecture and landscape that sought to manipulate social memory and negotiate between multiple pasts and the present. I present in this chapter the evidence for these multiple pasts, emphasizing the visible architectural features on the landscape that caused them to be remembered. Beginning with the massive mud-brick architecture of the Kerma Period and following with the temple complexes of colonized Nubia, the landscape was lastingly configured by an ever-shifting cultural and political context. The primary case study will focus on the period of reassertion of indigenous Nubian control—the Napatan Period—through the lens of mortuary architecture. One site in particular, the cemetery of Kurru, reveals that the appropriation of a symbol charged with layers of meaning—in this case, the pyramid form—can be used to reconcile conflicting identities and histories. I focus on an explicitly elite form of architectural expression and do not pretend to speak to the differing means of identity construction and memory practice that occurred below the level of royalty. Here, the analysis emphasizes royal identity—just one of many that existed in a heterogeneous society replete with the varying memory communities that result from a long and eventful history.

Historical Background

The complex terminology associated with the study of Nubian cultures illustrates the ambiguity that historically characterized the scholarship of this region. "Nubia" refers to that region of Africa situated between the first and sixth Nile cataracts, in modern southern Egypt and Sudan (fig. 6.1).

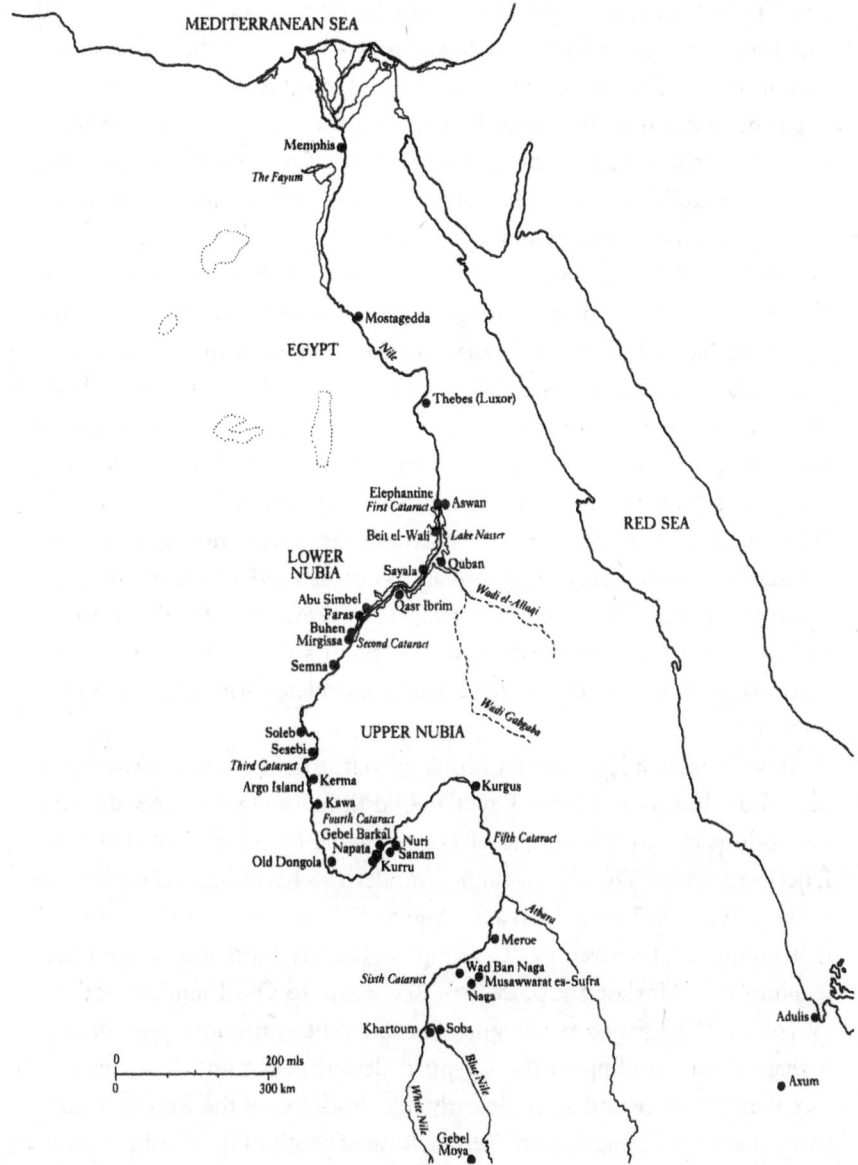

FIGURE 6.1 Map of Egypt and Nubia (Quirke and Spencer 1992, 203)

In antiquity, it lay directly south of the ancient Egyptian kingdom. Despite expansion southward in several periods, the land of Egypt (*Kemet*),[1] as the Egyptians perceived it, ended in the area of the first cataract. The Egyptians conceived of Nubia as divided into two distinct areas, Lower Nubia and Upper Nubia, to which they assigned different names. This mirrored the division of Egypt itself, which was always viewed as the "two lands," even in times of strong central unification. However, the conceptual and linguistic division of the Nubian landscape was not merely a projection of the Egyptian mindset; the archaeological evidence indicates that there were indeed differences in the material culture and developmental trajectory of these two regions (Kendall 1997, 12–13).

To set Nubian chronology within an Egyptian framework is to yield to the tradition of subordinating the archaeology and history of the region to that of Egypt (see Emery 1965, in which Nubian history is completely structured according to Egyptian history). However, the history of these two regions is intertwined to such a degree that it is necessary to understand how the history of each informs the other. Additionally, it was not until the first half of the first millennium BC that Nubians left their own written records. Even then, these were not written in an indigenous Nubian language; instead, Nubians used Egyptian language and hieroglyphs. Thus, the supporting textual evidence for the previous two millennia must be drawn from Egyptian sources. For this reason, chronological references to Nubia will be correlated with dynastic Egypt (table 6.1).

It is the ancient Egyptian terminology that structures our knowledge of the culture history of Nubia. Egyptian Old Kingdom (2686–2160 BC) rock inscriptions classify the people of Lower Nubia by the names of Wawat, Irtjet, and Setju.[2] The corresponding modern archaeological classification of the cultures of Lower Nubia is "A-group" in the late fourth–mid-third millennium BC, followed by "C-group" in the late third–mid-second millennium BC. (Morkot 2000, 38, 47). According to Old Kingdom autobiographies, the Egyptians recognized a different entity in Upper Nubia, perhaps corresponding to the Egyptian designation Yam.[3] It is this culture that is now regarded as the early manifestation of the Kerma culture (named after the capital city of Kerma, located south of the third cataract). It is from the Classic Kerma Period that our historical narrative will begin. Though the Kerma culture is not the focus of this chapter, it represents the first indigenous state-level polity in Upper Nubia, and thus it was one of the primary sources of identity and social memory that the later Upper Nubians, of the Napatan period, could draw upon.

TABLE 6.1 Comparative Timeline

Egypt	Nubia
Old Kingdom 2686–2160 BC	C-group culture in Lower Nubia; Early Kerma Period in Upper Nubia
Middle Kingdom 2055–1650 BC	Egypt controls Lower Nubia; Middle Kerma Period, Upper Nubia
Second Intermediate Period 1650–1550 BC	Egypt withdraws from Nubia; Classic Kerma Period; Kerma controls Lower Nubia
New Kingdom 1550–1069 BC	Egypt regains Lower Nubia; destruction of Kerma ca. 1460 BC; period of colonized Nubia ("wretched Kush")
Third Intermediate Period 1069–664 BC	Lack of evidence from Nubia until rise of Napatan rulers in 8th c. BC

	25th Dynasty (Napata controls Egypt) 747–656 BC
	  –Piye
	  –Shabaqa
	  –Shebitqo
	  –Taharqa
	  –Tanwetamani

Late Period 664–332 BC	Napatan Kingdom Continues within Nubia until 250 BC
Ptolemaic-Roman Period 332 BC–AD 395	Meroitic Kingdom 250 BC–AD 350

Source: Shaw 2000; Kendall 1997

Upon the reunification of Egypt in the Middle Kingdom (2055–1650 BC), Egyptian kings conquered all of Lower Nubia. It is in this period, the Middle Kingdom, that the Egyptian sources no longer use the name Yam when referring to Upper Nubia. Instead, the texts refer to an "ominous, nebulous power in the same region called *Kush* (italics added)" (Kendall 1997, 17). The Egyptians' perception of this threat was manifested in the construction of several forts midway between the second and third cataracts, pushing the Egyptian military presence farther south than it had been in the Old Kingdom.[4] Kush, at this time, lay outside the Egyptian sphere of influence and can be considered synonymous with the kingdom of Kerma. However, the term *Kush* often refers generically to the entire region of Nubia for both this and later periods. I avoid the use of this ambiguous term in this chapter. For the three periods discussed here, the following terms will be employed: Kerma Period (corresponding to the Egyptian Middle Kingdom, Second Intermediate Period, and early New Kingdom); colonized Nubia (corresponding to the New Kingdom); and Napatan Period (corresponding to the Third Intermediate and Late Period).[5]

Throughout the Middle Kingdom, Kerma loomed, unconquered, to the south of Egypt's fortresses. When Egyptian centralization disintegrated in the Second Intermediate Period, the power vacuum in Nubia allowed Kerma to flourish, resulting in the Classic Kerma Period (1700–1550 BC). With the rise of the New Kingdom, Egypt again reconquered Lower Nubia. Egyptian expansion continued throughout the New Kingdom—Kerma was quashed by the third king of the New Kingdom, Thutmose I, and Egyptian control extended deep into Upper Nubia, to the fourth cataract (Trigger 1976, 108). This is the period referred to here as colonized Nubia, which included both Upper and Lower Nubia. With the end of the New Kingdom, Egypt was forced to withdraw from Nubia, and a powerful family of rulers arose in the area of the fourth cataract, in a region called Napata. Their rise to power corresponds to the Egyptian Third Intermediate Period (1069–664 BC), with their conquest of Egypt occurring toward the end of this period, ca. 730 BC. The span of time in which the Napatan kings ruled Egypt is the twenty-fifth dynasty in Egyptian chronology (ca. 730–656 BC). After losing control of Egypt, the twenty-fifth dynasty ended, the Napatan kings withdrew into Nubia, and the Napatan kingdom continued for another three centuries but was contained within Nubian borders. Egypt moved on to the twenty-sixth dynasty, a return of native Egyptian kings.

Competing "Pasts" for the Napatan Period: The Kingdom of Kerma and Colonized Nubia

Following the historical outline of the previous section, I now briefly consider the context from which the Napatan rulers emerged, beginning with the kingdom of Kerma, which represents the earlier source of memory and tradition from which these rulers could draw. Kerman monumental architecture demonstrates two very significant points: first, Upper Nubia had an indigenous cultural tradition distinctly different from that of Egypt, and second, the architecture remained a highly visible and imposing reminder of the Kerma past. Following the destruction of Kerma, the period of colonization by the Egyptians was the later cultural milieu from which the Napatan kings arose. With colonial domination a new form of elite architecture emerged in Nubia, adding another layer of meaning to the symbolically charged landscape.

Historically, the rise of complexity in Nubia was thought to be directly dependent on influence from Egypt, both culturally and economically. When Harvard archaeologist George Reisner excavated Kerma remains between 1913 and 1916, he interpreted them as remnants of an Egyptian outpost (Reisner 1923, 24–25). His theory was not completely unfounded, as there was indeed Egyptian material culture present, primarily statuary, inscribed stone vessels, and small faience objects. However, Reisner disregarded the overwhelmingly un-Egyptian nature of the architecture and burials as evidence for an indigenous culture. Though Reisner's reluctance to ascribe to this culture an origin indigenous to the area of the third cataract was likely influenced by the intellectual biases of the early twentieth century, this general attitude of the derivative nature of Nubian cultures still hovers in the academic arena.[6] An archaeologist of sub-Saharan Africa wrote in the late 1980s: "Egyptian commercial and colonial involvement in Nubia had already elicited an indigenous Nubian response by the latter part of the Second Intermediate Period" (Connah 1987, 37). In fact, the Kerma culture originated earlier than Graham

Connah claims. Palace foundations and stratified cemeteries existed in the Early Kerma Period, ca. 2500–2050 BC (Kendall 1997, 39–40), and textual sources from Egypt suggest a state society in Upper Nubia ca. 2000 BC (O'Connor 1993b, 13).

The Kerma kingdom controlled a territory that stretched from the southern boundaries of the Egyptian empire (midway between the second and third cataracts) to the fourth or fifth cataracts (Bonnet 1996, 45). The city of Kerma itself was located just south of the third cataract, surrounded by a mud-brick enclosure wall with four fortified entrances (Bonnet 1996, 47). A religious complex stood in the center of the city, comprising small chapels, a small palace, storage magazines, and workshops (Bonnet 1996, 48; Bonnet 1986, 13–16). The central monument of this quarter, which still dominates the landscape today, is known as the Western Deffufa (fig. 6.2). A massive mud-brick structure, it represents a long history of architectural development; Bonnet's team recognized twelve building phases (Bonnet 1992, 613–14). Its façade is vaguely reminiscent of an Egyptian temple pylon, though the similarity with Egyptian form ends there. In contrast to

FIGURE 6.2 The mud-brick Western Deffufa at Kerma (courtesy of Peter Lacovara)

Egyptian temples, the deffufa (interpreted as a temple; see Bonnet 1996, 47) is entered from the side and is mostly solid mud brick with the exception of a staircase that leads to a small internal chamber and another staircase that leads to the roof (O'Connor 1993a, 51). Reisner discovered remains of Egyptian stone and faience vessels, as well as Hyksos seals, in the vicinity of the Western Deffufa (Reisner 1923).[7] At the time of Reisner's excavation in 1916, it stood at a height of 19.3 meters; its counterpart, the Eastern Deffufa, located in the elite cemetery associated with the city, stood at 11 meters. According to Charles Bonnet (1996, 48), the Western Deffufa would originally have stood at approximately 25 meters in height.

To the southwest of this ritual quarter stood a structure distinguished by its unique architecture: a large round hut, built of mud brick and wooden posts, with a conical roof. Its vast interior room led Bonnet (1992, 616) to interpret it as a royal audience hall that had no architectural parallel in Egypt or central Africa in this early period. The overall town layout, "organic" in its unplanned appearance, does not resemble the fortified Egyptian towns located in the region of the second cataract (Bonnet 1992, 616). Thus, the most visible statements of the cultural heritage of Kerma, particularly in the case of the well-preserved deffufas, are distinctly indigenous to Upper Nubia.

By the early 1990s, the capital city of Kerma was the only settlement of this period that had been excavated (Bonnet 1992, 623), and the geographic extent of Kerman settlement was unclear. However, a subsequent survey project in the northern Dongola Reach (an area in the northern half of the stretch of land between the third and fourth cataracts) has shed some light on this issue. Population densities reached their peak during the Kerma period, with large permanent settlements occurring in the agriculturally rich areas south of the capital city (Welsby 2001, 572, 589).

Another aspect of monumental architecture is the burial tumuli of the kings of Kerma. Both royalty and non-royalty were buried in round earthen tumuli throughout Kerma's history. In the Classic Kerma Period, the three largest reached a diameter of ninety meters and one to two meters in height (fig. 6.3). The exterior was paved in mud brick and encircled with black stones. In the interior was a corridor that bisected the length of the mound and contained hundreds of human sacrifices (Reisner 1923). Larger tumuli were accompanied by mud-brick funerary chapels,

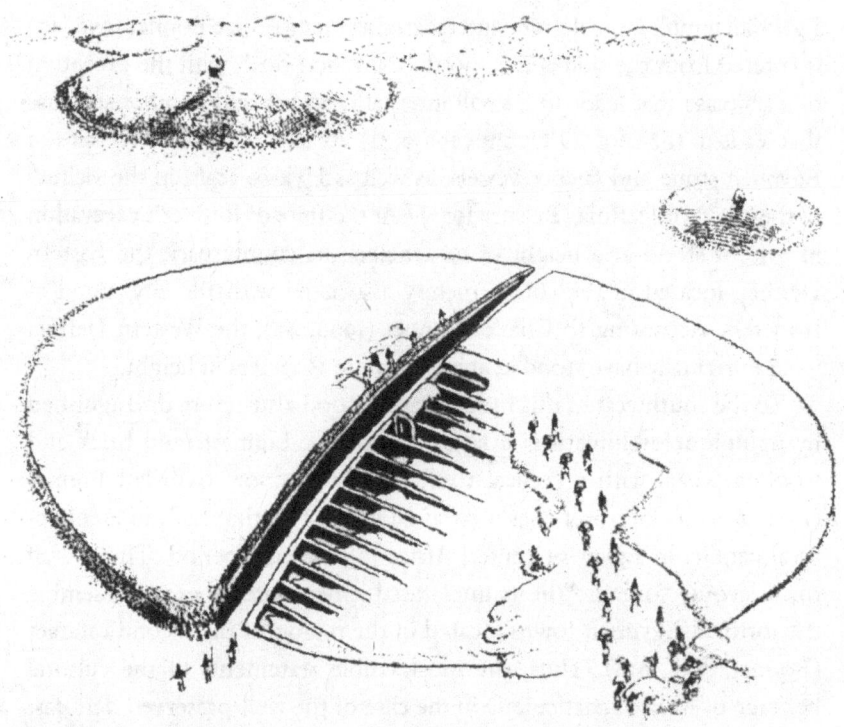

FIGURE 6.3 Reconstruction of a royal tumulus at Kerma (O'Connor 1971)

the interior decorated with faience, gold leaf, and painted motifs of animals and boats (Bonnet 1992: 623). The kings of Kerma were familiar with Egyptian burial customs, as evidenced by the few fragments of Egyptian-style coffins and motifs (such as the winged sun-disk), but overall, the burials were distinctly un-Egyptian (O'Connor 1993a: 57). Remains of tumuli of comparable style, though considerably smaller, were discovered further south by the Dongola Reach survey (Welsby 2001: 583).

As I stated initially, the constructed landscape of the Kerma Period demonstrates the unique characteristics of Upper Nubian culture. With regard to an Egyptian influence on this region, David O'Connor states: "Nubian selection of Egyptian cultural traits was always voluntary and partial.... Egyptian influence is seen only in very limited ways, indicating that Nubians were resistant or indifferent to Egyptian culture as a whole" (O'Connor 1993a, 56). Additionally, the preceding discussion emphasized the deffufas and the tumuli because of their visibility on the landscape. Though exhibiting destruction layers, the mud-brick edifices of the deffufas survived to the heights of 19.3 and 11 meters. The visibility of the tumuli after the fall of Kerma is harder to determine; Egyptian sources indicate that the cemetery was desecrated by the Egyptian conquerors. In modern times, the circular tumuli and their monolithic capstones are visible on the surface, though they are perhaps not discernible from a great distance.[8] However, the presence in the cemetery of the Eastern Deffufa would have drawn attention to this area as one of Kerman activity.

With the reunification of Egypt and the start of the New Kingdom in 1550 BC, the Egyptians regained control over Lower Nubia. Perhaps in retaliation for Kerma's alliance with the Hyksos enemy in the north, the pharaohs of the eighteenth dynasty pushed farther into Nubia than in previous periods. Additionally, the desire to control gold mines and trade with the interior of Africa was likely a motivating factor in Egypt's expansion into Nubia. The third king of the eighteenth dynasty, Tuthmose I, reached as far as Kurgus, north of the fourth cataract. Though Kerma was sacked, uprisings continued until the reign of Tuthmose III, who finally subjugated Upper Nubia ca. 1460 BC. After this point, Egypt controlled Lower and Upper Nubia as far as Kurgus, until the end of the New Kingdom in 1070 BC. Egyptian domination seems not to have extended as far as the fifth and sixth cataracts (O'Connor 1993a, 58–60; Smith 2003, 136; Trigger 1976, 108–10). This was the period of colonized Nubia, which constitutes the second well-defined (archaeologically and textually, at least) "past" to which the later Napatan kings had access.

The phrase "colonized Nubia" implies a monolithic entity that is, in fact, quite far from the likely reality of the situation. Lower Nubia was subject to an intense strategy of acculturation by the Egyptians. The architecture, graves, and material culture from New Kingdom sites in Lower Nubia are overwhelmingly Egyptian in nature. The position "viceroy of Kush" was established—a post held by an Egyptian who reported directly to the pharaoh. Two deputies, one each for Lower and Upper Nubia, served the viceroy; it was possible for Egyptianized Nubians to rise to these positions (Smith 2003, 84–86; Trigger 1976, 114–17). In Upper Nubia, the situation differed. O'Connor cites the lack of archaeological data for the colonization of Upper Nubia but hypothesizes that the Nubians of this region also came to dominate various levels of the administration, if slightly less Egyptianized than their Lower Nubian counterparts (1993a, 65). Beginning in 1997, the Dongola Reach Project of UCLA conducted a survey to address this dearth of evidence. As a result of this project, Stuart Tyson Smith maintains that there are only three sites south of the third cataract that are distinctly Egyptian in nature: Tombos, Gebel Barkal, and Kawa. He suggests that Egyptian policy upriver of the third cataract was one of "hegemonic domination," rather than concentrated acculturation (Smith 2003, 87–94).

Despite the lack of direct Egyptian colonization in this region, one of Egypt's most important building projects—and one that is very significant for the rise of the Napatan kings—was Gebel Barkal, located at the fourth cataract. Gebel Barkal is a small mountain of sandstone that rises up from the flat desert surrounding it on all sides. Aside from its conspicuousness in the landscape, there was one feature in particular that caught the Egyptians' attention: at one end of the formation is a freestanding spur of rock that resembled, to the Egyptians, the uraeus.[9] They declared it the origin of a ram-headed manifestation of the most important state god, Amen—also the god of Thebes, the religious capital of New Kingdom Egypt. At the foot of the mountain, Thutmose III built a temple to Amen, which was enlarged and modified by successive kings into the nineteenth dynasty. Gebel Barkal became conceptually linked to the main Amen temple at Karnak (Thebes), and thus to the ideological core of Egyptian kingship (Haynes 1992, 36–37; Kendall 1999, 325–27).

There are several aspects of colonized Nubia that are significant to the question of later Napatan identity and social memory. The Nubian identities forged during Egyptian domination would influence the decisions made by the rulers who arose in Napata two centuries after colonial rule ended. Smith argues for an ethnic duality among the Nubians: that which was self-defined and that imposed by the dominating power (Smith 2003, preface). He also argues *against* the inevitability of cultural assimilation—an idea that is central to this chapter's discussion of Napatan royal identity as presented in monumental architecture. The presence of non-royal, Egyptian pyramid tombs at sites as far south as Tombos are significant to understanding the Napatan appropriation of this symbol.

It is equally important to note the continuity of indigenous, Kerma elements in the landscape of colonized Nubia. Despite the havoc wreaked at the city of Kerma by the Egyptians, indigenous traditions continue in the material culture during the New Kingdom, and a Kerma settlement was situated across the Nile from the Egyptian colonial settlement at Tombos (Smith 2003, 95, 195–97). Thus, in this section I have demonstrated that the Napatan rulers were a part of a complex cultural history, both indigenous and colonial. In the words of Jan Assmann: "The state of Napata thus had two very different pasts to draw on, an older and more properly Nubian one, centered in Kerma, and a younger, Egyptian one, which in the New Kingdom . . . Egyptianized the country with temples and myths" (Assmann 2002, 319).

Imitation or Negotiation? Perceptions of the Napatan Twenty-Fifth Dynasty

The history of Nubia between the end of the New Kingdom in 1070 BC and the rise of the Napatan rulers in the early eighth century BC is cloudy; there are sparse Egyptian textual references to viceroys of Nubia during the early Third Intermediate Period (Taylor 2000, 352; Török 1997, 144), but it is unlikely that these officials held much sway in Upper Nubia after the decline of centralized administration in Egypt. The clearest archaeological evidence for the emergence of rulers of Upper Nubia comes from the cemetery of Kurru, located several miles downstream of the fourth cataract and the site of Gebel Barkal (Napata in the Egyptian sources). The earliest tombs could date to the eleventh century BC (Török 1995, 208), though there is no real consensus on this issue.[10] The earliest definitive date for a Napatan king is 760 BC, during the reign of Kashta. Kashta controlled both Upper and Lower Nubia to the very border of Egypt at Aswan, and it was under his successor Piye that the Napatan kings expanded their control into Egypt and became its twenty-fifth dynasty (Taylor 2000, 353).

As demonstrated by the evidence presented in the preceding sections, the cultural and political landscape out of which the Napatan kings emerged was not a clean slate, so to speak. Monuments of the Kerma kingdom were still visible on the Upper Nubian landscape, and Kerma traditions had persisted into the period of colonial domination, and perhaps beyond. The colonial past was also not forgotten; Egyptian funerary monuments and the temples of Gebel Barkal were visible features (though Assmann [2002, 319] maintains that they were in disrepair). Egyptian influence may also have persisted in Lower Nubia into the eighth century. Given these two disparate traditions—indigenous kingdom and subordination to Egypt—any construction of Napatan identity would have been a negotiation of these overlapping categories.

However, several scholars have tended to oversimplify the Nubian colonial experience and/or devalue Napatan culture as merely derivative of Egyptian culture. In his classic work *Nubia under the Pharaohs*, Bruce Trigger speculates as to whether, after the end of colonial rule, "Nubia as a whole returned to an essentially tribal way of life. The Dongola reach may not have had to regress greatly if, as some believe, the Egyptianization of that region was superficial by comparison with what had taken place north of the Third Cataract" (1976, 140). This establishes a simplistic equation between Egyptian and Nubian identity—Egypt and sophistication on one side, with "regression" and tribal organization on the other. Given the evidence of the resources commanded by the Kerma rulers, it can be argued that it was not a tribal structure that Upper Nubia had left behind and to which it would return. Additionally, the implication that Upper Nubians would simply regress to their previous state (whatever that may have been), or statically maintain Egyptian customs, without evaluating or being affected by their colonial experience, is an underestimation of Nubian involvement in constructing their own identity.

Regarding the nature of Napatan cultural expression, there are a variety of scholarly responses, from condescension to consciously and carefully appreciative evaluations of the indigenous contribution. Few, however, go very far beneath the surface to think about why, and for whom, the Napatan kings constructed their public image. For Connah, the legacy of Napatan culture was "little more than a diluted and provincial imitation of that of pharaonic Egypt" (1987, 40). In a recent encyclopedia entry, the general impression of Napatan kings is one in which they "copied styles and symbols of the earlier Egyptian pharaohs" (Leclant 1999, 426). In a similar vein, Joyce Haynes speaks of the "Kushite reverence for ancient traditions" (1992, 27). The latter two interpretations are based on the largely Egyptian style of Napatan temples, statuary, reliefs, and inscriptions, and thus indeed speak to one level of Napatan royal identity. However, they also gloss over the complexity of meaning involved in the choices made by the kings of the twenty-fifth dynasty and also the complexity of the audience they addressed. David O'Connor and Andrew Reid have recently stated that, although elements of Napatan culture were distinctly Nubian, "its strongly Egyptian aspects are also a historical reality" (2003, 17). A significant question that follows from this—a question central to this chapter—is how the Napatan rulers utilized, manipulated, and integrated these Egyptian aspects within their own cultural context.

In the remainder of this chapter I demonstrate that the Napatan appropriation of traditional Egyptian symbols can be seen as an act of identity negotiation, rather than a passive, inevitable imitation of a more sophisticated culture. Before proceeding, we must establish the basis on which a distinction can be made between negotiating and imitating. The former involves actively remembering, manipulating, or erasing the past, whereas the latter refers to maintaining the status quo or "inevitably" evolving out of what came before. Crucial to this distinction is the element of *choice*. A study by Carla Sinopoli (2003) of fifteenth- to sixteenth-century AD Vijayanagara architecture in southern India illustrates this idea. Emerging in an area with a diverse history and ruling over a diverse subject population, the rulers of the Vijayanagara Empire were exposed to several different regional styles of temple architecture. For reasons of legitimacy and expression of imperial ambition, the kings drew on an architectural style from a distant region when there were other choices closer at hand. Such a perspective frees interpretation of culture change from notions of simple and unthinking imitation. Susan Alcock (2002, 44) also investigates "the varieties of memory communities and of commemorative choices" available to the inhabitants of Roman Greece. Provided that the ruling elite are able, economically and politically, to construct monuments based on, or reinterpreting, past models, then the motivations behind these choices can be investigated.

The Cemetery of Kurru: Linking Pasts and Present

The subject chosen here for an investigation of the construction of Napatan royal identity in the twenty-fifth dynasty is the cemetery of

Kurru, located in the heart of the region termed Napata.[11] I have chosen it for three primary reasons. First, the prominence of royal mortuary monuments on the landscape makes them accessible, at least visually, to a wide range of the population. These monuments were consciously constructed to convey a message, via a visual language, of royal identity to an audience wider than just the royal family. The task, then, is to examine the nature of the visual language and the range of messages it conveyed.

Second, given the expenditure of resources and planning involved in mortuary monuments in both Egypt and Nubia, their conception and construction was begun during the life of the individual buried within them. Although it is true that rarely does anyone bury him- or herself, the monuments at Kurru convey a notion of identity fostered by the actual people buried within them (Smith 2003, 193–94).

Third, the necropolis at Kurru has rarely inspired any critical analysis of Napatan identity and the construction of social memory. Perhaps part of the reluctance to investigate the changing visual language of the pyramids is a product of the time depth that informs the modern perspective. By the eighth and seventh centuries BC, pyramids seem, to us, like a cliché—a tired symbol of past glory. The Napatan appropriation of this Egyptian symbol led earlier scholars to quickly conclude that "the intimate contact with the sophisticated culture of Egypt, acquired by conquest, led to the Egyptianizing of their burial practices and funerary beliefs" (Dunham 1958, 107). Little to no attention was given to the relationship between the pyramids and their tumuli and mastaba predecessors, all of which occupy the same landscape and sacred space. Later scholars, such as O'Connor (1993a), emphasized the indigenous aspects of the Kurru monuments; however, in so doing, the subtle connections with the Egyptian models become submerged (a point that will be returned to in the section to follow). A notable exception to this trend is László Török (1995, 1997, 2002), who has analyzed the Kurru pyramids in relation to a formation of Napatan power ideology. He recognizes the "intricate patterns of interaction of Egyptian influences and indigenous traditions" (Török 1995, 204) in the development of this ideology. I acknowledge the stimulus of his analysis and seek to expand on the complexities and varieties of messages carried via the visual language of monuments. Crucial to the analysis that follows are the spatial relationships between the components of the Kurru landscape and their connection with past landscapes.

Description of the Site

The site of Kurru (fig. 6.4) consists of two main plateaus, the north and the south, separated by a wadi. The earliest burials are located on the highest ground of the north plateau. They consist of six tumuli (tum. 1, tum. 4, tum. 5, tum. 2, tum. 3, and tum. 6, in chronological order).[12] The excavator described the first five as circular gravel mounds, with no traces of chapels or enclosure walls (Dunham 1950).[13] Tumulus 6, the last of the series, was innovative in its masonry casing, horseshoe-shaped enclosure wall, and mud-brick chapel on the east face. It also contained the first evidence of a funerary bed in the burial chamber. After this tumulus, the sequence changes to mastaba tombs.[14] Kurru (Ku.) 14, 13, 11, 10, 23, 21, and 9 are the seven mastabas of this sequence, in chronological order (Török 1995, 211). Interestingly, Ku. 14 contains a circular tumulus within its outer rectangular frame, illustrating the transition from tumulus to mastaba. Ku. 14 also illustrates a change from the mud-brick chapel of Tum. 6 to a stone chapel. The mastabas of this series are all surrounded by a rectangular stone enclosure wall with a forecourt, and are arranged in a row from the northeast to southwest, at a lower elevation than the tumuli situated to the west. Another transitional tomb, Ku. 8, follows this series. Ku. 8 belonged to Kashta, the first Napatan king to claim the title "king of Upper and Lower Egypt" (though it was his son, Piye, who actually conquered Lower Egyptian territory). Kashta's tomb was also a mastaba, but probably incorporated a small pyramid atop the mastaba foundation.[15] Additionally, the southeastern enclosure wall of his tomb runs inward in order to avoid invading the space of an older mastaba.

The four remaining royal tombs of the period under discussion are pyramids: Piye's (Ku. 17), Shabaqa's (Ku. 15), Shebitqo's (Ku. 18), and Tanwetamani's (Ku. 16). These pyramids were surrounded by enclosure walls and a forecourt, and had a chapel against their east face. All but Shebitqo's were situated to the east of the row of mastabas. The burial chambers contained Egyptian funerary equipment, such as *shabti* (servant) figures, amulets, objects with representations of Egyptian gods and

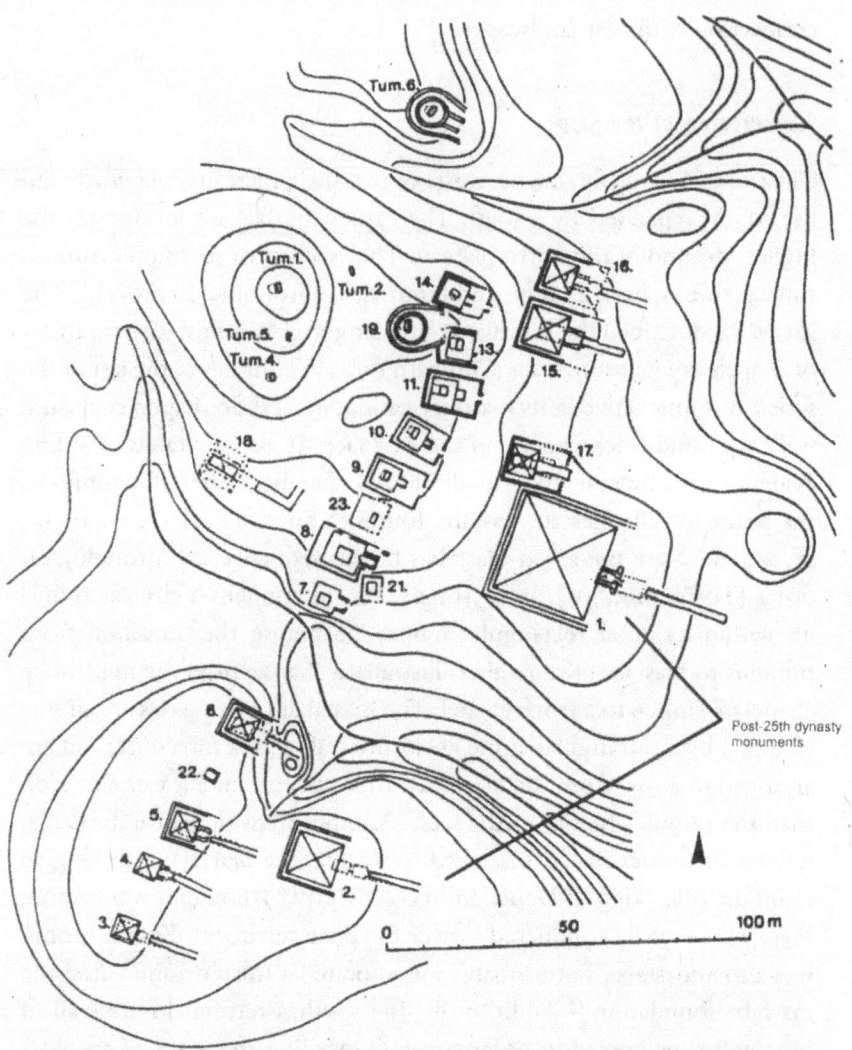

FIGURE 6.4 Plan of the royal cemetery at Kurru with numbered tumuli and pyramids. Note that Ku. 1 and Ku. 2 are later monuments and were not part of the twenty-fifth dynasty landscape. Map reprinted by permission of the publishers from *The Royal Cemeteries of Kush, Volume I: El Kurru*, by Dows Dunham, Cambridge, Mass: Harvard University Press, Copyright 1950 by the President and Fellows of Harvard College.

goddesses, and objects with hieroglyphic inscriptions. The presence of canopic jars (containers for internal organs) suggests that the kings were mummified, but the presence of funerary beds is a distinctly Nubian burial practice dating back to the kingdom of Kerma.

Conclusion

The cemetery must be analyzed on a regional scale. Why would a family of kings who claimed legitimate sovereignty over all of Egypt choose to be buried within Nubia? Why the specific site of Kurru? The cemetery of Kurru—eternal resting place of the divine king—can be seen as a visual statement of the Napatan place of origin. This statement may seem unspectacular when applied to the earlier tumulus and mastaba burials, since they represent rulers who originated in Upper, or southern, Nubia, and who did not yet control Egyptian territory. However, after the expansionist ambitions of Kashta and the increasing sphere of Nubian influence under Piye, it is significant that the twenty-fifth dynasty kings chose to retain their burial place at Kurru, within Upper Nubia. This does not necessarily imply that these kings were expressing solely Nubian identity. As discussed earlier, the site of Gebel Barkal was an important cult center of the Egyptian god Amen in colonized Nubia, and the Napatan kings explicitly legitimized their rule through their worship of Amen and the presence of his primordial cult center in the heartland of their kingdom. In this case, the strategy used by the Egyptian colonizers to incorporate Nubia ideologically into the empire enabled the Napatan kings to claim legitimacy as rulers of all of Egypt. Thus, the proximity of the royal burial ground to Gebel Barkal would have expressed, simultaneously, a Nubian origin and a legitimacy acceptable to Egyptians (and, by this point, to most Nubians as well, who would likely have incorporated the ram-headed Amen into their indigenous system of religious belief). It should also be noted that King Piye chose not to rule from within Egypt, instead returning to his capital at Napata. However, the subsequent rise of local rulers in the Egyptian delta (the ephemeral twenty-fourth dynasty), forced Piye's successors to maintain a greater presence in the Egyptian city of Memphis (Taylor 2000, 353–55).

In considering the choice of Kurru as a royal burial ground, one may usefully compare the New Kingdom pharaoh Akhenaten's establishment of his capital city of Amarna on land that was free from strong associations with previous regimes, utilizing the "empty past of the ideational landscape" (Richards 1999, 98). Considering that the Napatan rulers—both the earliest ones and those of the twenty-fifth dynasty who chose to remain there—had two pasts to draw from, it is significant that they did not choose a site specifically associated with one of those pasts. In other words, Kurru is neither Kerma nor Gebel Barkal. It is a site with a local, indigenous past imbued with significance for the Napatan royal line. The deffufas of Kerma would still have dominated the landscape of the third cataract region, a reminder of a powerful indigenous past. Yet the Napatan rulers chose not to return to the site of the cemetery and the Eastern Deffufa at Kerma.

Similarly, though the proximity to Gebel Barkal was likely an element in the ideological significance of Kurru, the early rulers of Napata, as well as those who comprised the Egyptian twenty-fifth dynasty, did not choose to be buried at Gebel Barkal itself. This is particularly significant when one considers that later Napatan rulers (three-and-a-half centuries after Napata lost control of Egypt) established a pyramid cemetery at Gebel Barkal for approximately three generations (Török 1997, 395). By the time Piye asserted his influence as far north as the Egyptian delta, it is possible that as many as fourteen generations (Török 1995, 208) of Napatan rulers had been buried in Kurru. Piye built the first royal Nubian pyramid and remained at Kurru, a landscape uniquely associated with the Napatan line. Though he did not establish a new cemetery in the grand settings of either Kerma or Gebel Barkal, the development and form of the monuments at Kurru represented a "negotiation" of the two pasts of Upper Nubia and their role in establishing Napatan identity. This issue will be addressed, but first we must take a closer look at the internal spatial arrangement of the tombs at Kurru and their development over time.

The earliest burials are located on the highest ground, which would have been the most prestigious area of the funerary landscape. Yet, as the style of the tomb changed over time and as many were added to the site, the newer burials were careful not to disturb the older ones. As mentioned, the enclosure wall of Kashta's tomb (Ku. 8) was built such that it would not interfere with the space of an earlier mastaba (Ku. 21). Though the tombs tend to cluster by type, becoming larger toward the east, the location of Shebitqo's pyramid (Ku. 18) indicates that the boundaries of the earlier tumuli and mastaba were respected. Ku. 18 is located to the west of the row of mastaba tombs, and south of the tumuli; thus, it is physically set apart from the other twenty-fifth-dynasty pyramids, yet clearly designed with an awareness of the spatial boundaries of the previous tombs and unobtrusive upon them. It is also clear that the four twenty-fifth-dynasty royal pyramids, and their associated queens' pyramids on the southern plateau, were not intended to dominate the landscape to the exclusion of the previous monuments. The ground plan of the pyramid and its enclosure wall is only slightly larger than the mastaba complexes in the previous series. This evidence indicates that the successive Napatan kings of the twenty-fifth dynasty integrated their funerary monuments into the total landscape at Kurru, without obliterating, destroying, or significantly overshadowing the tombs of their predecessors (remember that Ku. 1 and 2 on the site plan were much later additions after the twenty-fifth dynasty). This indicates not only a tradition of respecting and remembering an indigenous family line over a long period of time, but also actively situating twenty-fifth-dynasty tombs, both literally and symbolically, within the context of indigenous tradition.

The form and development of the Kurru tombs make references to the two pasts of Upper Nubia. The circular gravel mound evoked the funerary monuments of both the kingdom of Kerma in Upper Nubia and the C-group tombs of Lower Nubia prior to the Egyptian colonization in the New Kingdom. Though Trigger (1976, 144) maintains that the tumuli probably do not represent a conscious return to forms of a previous kingdom, the Kerma culture continued into the period of colonized Nubia, and the tumuli in the cemetery at Kerma were probably still prominent on the landscape at the third cataract, as I have noted earlier. There is a possibility that the early Napatan rulers were harkening back to the traditions of an early indigenous power, though this can only remain as speculation. However, it can also be said that the Egyptian funerary monuments of the period of colonial domination were also visible on the landscape, and the early Napatans were choosing *not* to utilize these forms.

The switch from mastaba to pyramid tomb can not simply be perceived as an evocation of a traditional Egyptian symbol of royalty and power. By the time of the twenty-fifth dynasty, the meaning and use of the pyramid form had undergone many transformations, both within Egypt proper and into the territory of colonized Nubia. To make a mental leap from the Kurru pyramids to the classic pyramid forms of the Egyptian Old Kingdom is to overlook the changing meaning and accessibility of the pyramid—a change of which the Napatans would have been aware. Additionally, viewing the Kurru pyramids in the light of the Giza pyramids gives rise to the overly simplistic explanation that the Kurru examples are derivative, a pale imitation of a glorious past. As I will demonstrate, the pyramid symbol carried a much more complex layering of meaning.

By the time the eighteenth dynasty and the New Kingdom were well established in Egypt, pyramids were no longer built by royalty and, in fact, were no longer the exclusive prerogative of royalty. The New Kingdom saw the rise in popularity of private pyramids, especially in the area of Thebes and colonized Nubia (Lehner 1997, 192–93). Figure 6.5 illustrates a Theban private pyramid tomb of the type that was common in the New Kingdom, and which Nubian elite would have seen when they traveled to Egypt for the annual tribute ceremony for the pharaoh.

FIGURE 6.5 Reconstruction of a private pyramid tomb from the Theban area (Lehner 1997, 192)

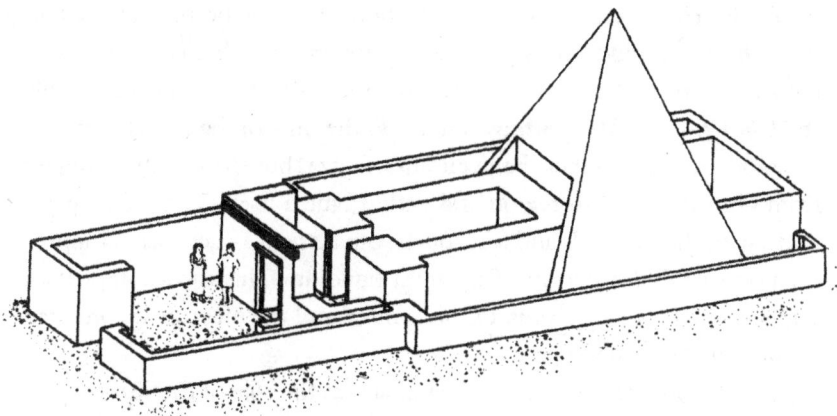

FIGURE 6.6 Reconstruction of the pyramid tomb of Siamun from Tombos (Smith 2003, 140)

Additionally, because the young princes of Nubia were transported to Egypt to receive an education in order to acculturate them into Egyptian values and behavior, the Nubian elite of colonized Nubia knew well that the pyramid form was no longer a royal prerogative and symbol of power. The New Kingdom style of private pyramid, incorporating a forecourt and chapel, was also built in the colonial cemeteries within Nubia. Figure 6.6 illustrates the pyramid of Siamun, an Egyptian official of the New Kingdom buried at Tombos, a site located at the third cataract in Upper Nubia (Smith 2003, 139–42). The Nubians would have been familiar with the pyramid as a symbol of the private elite and, more specifically, the colonizing elite.

O'Connor attempts to place the development of the Kurru pyramids within an indigenous framework: "The introduction of the pyramid, under Piye, is surely Egyptian-inspired, probably by the sight of the great pyramids in the Memphite region . . . but the change is still sensitive to the indigenous Nubian tradition of royal tombs, for the Kurru pyramids, like the [Kurru] mastabas (and unlike their Egyptian prototypes), are quite small—the average diameter is 13.50 meters. The pyramids have rectilinear enclosures and single-cell chapels, derived from the mastabas and not the Egyptian pyramids" (O'Connor 1993a, 69).

This view attempts to move away from previous interpretations, in which the Napatan rulers were thought to be merely copying the Memphite pyramids. However, O'Connor's reaction seems to be based in somewhat the same mind-set as previous interpretations, that is, in assuming a connection (or "inspiration") between the Kurru pyramids and only the *Old Kingdom Memphite* pyramids. By the time of the Napatan rulers, the model was no longer the pyramids of Giza, but the private examples from both the Theban region and within Nubia itself. The Kurru pyramids, with their chapels and forecourts, can be seen as a conscious appropriation of this *later* form of pyramid building. This carries important implications for the meaning of this symbol and the message it conveyed in the Napatan context.

Török (1997, 122; 2002, 50–51) emphasizes the role of the Kurru pyramids in the "power-ideology" and myth of the Napatan state, suggesting that Egyptian mortuary religion offered an ideology of political and dynastic continuity that was needed at the time of the Napatan control of Egypt. Though this interpretation may reveal one level of the meaning of the pyramid symbol, it assumes that the meaning of the symbol had remained relatively unchanged since its Old Kingdom form. As mentioned earlier, pyramids no longer signified royal power, simply and directly. In fact, they no longer signified royalty exclusively. The Kurru monuments, with their small size and integration into a landscape of previous, non-pyramid structures, neither dominate the landscape nor give the impression of absolute royal power and continuity as did the Old Kingdom examples. I suggest that the Kurru pyramids represent an appropriation of the colonized past—a past that would have been visible on the landscape and perhaps still contained within the collective memory of Nubians. When Kashta and his successors entered Egypt triumphantly, they would have been bombarded with images of their colonized past: the subordination of "wretched Kushites" depicted on almost every major temple complex in the Theban area, including complexes to which the Napatan kings made their own additions (such as Karnak and Medinat Habu). The Napatan kings did not attempt to obliterate these reminders of their subordination; rather, they appropriated a common symbol of the elite colonizers and incorporated it into a mortuary landscape that also included indigenous traditions, without masking their indigenous culture history in the process. Kurru represents the intentional visibility of two pasts, in which the indigenous tradition is juxtaposed with the new prerogative of the Napatan conquerors. The pyramids themselves negotiated between the idea of a "glorious" Egyptian past, to which the Napatan kings were the heirs, and the realities of former colonial domination, since the Kurru pyramids follow most closely, both temporally and stylistically, on the private pyramid forms of the colonizers—New Kingdom Egypt.

I have illustrated in this chapter the competing pasts of Upper Nubia and how the reconciliation of those pasts manifested in royal architecture. The continuity of the pyramid form in Nubia lends weight to the argument that there are many levels of meaning embedded in the visual language of architecture. Although power and dynastic continuity could be one way of interpreting the meaning of the Kurru landscape, the continuity of pyramid building in Nubia long after the Napatan withdrawal from Egypt, and even long after the gradual fading of pharaonic civilization, indicates that there are multiple layers of meaning—especially given that in Nubia, too, pyramids became accessible to non-royalty.

The audience for the mortuary display at Kurru, located far outside the boundaries of Egypt, would have been primarily Upper Nubians. Due to architectural reminders, the once-powerful Kerma kingdom and the subsequent period of Egyptian colonial domination would have been rooted in the collective memory of this population. The visual language of architecture and landscape was employed to manipulate this social memory and to forge new royal identities.

Notes

1. Italics indicate an ancient Egyptian word, so as to differentiate from those commonly used terms (such as Kerma) that are in fact modern names.

2. The exact territorial boundaries corresponding to these ancient designations are not fully agreed upon in the scholarly literature. Contrary to Kendall (1997), O'Connor (1993a) interprets *Wawat* as encompassing all of Lower Nubia, placing Setju and Irtjet in Upper Nubia, while Yam would refer to a territory farther south. Morkot (2000) maintains the likelihood of Yam referring to the Kerma region in Upper Nubia. The modern terms *lower* and *upper* are defined in reference to the Nile cataracts: Lower Nubia encompasses the area between the first and second cataracts, whereas Upper Nubia refers to the area between the second and sixth cataracts.

3. The sixth-dynasty autobiography of Weni mentions Yam in Nubia; also, the sixth-dynasty official Harkhuf notes in his autobiography that Yam was the destination of his three expeditions to Nubia (see Lichtheim 1973, 18–27).

4. For forts at the second cataract, see Emery, Smith, and Millard 1979 and Vercoutter 1970–76. For those midway between the second and third cataracts, see Zabkar and Zabkar 1982, Dunham and Janssen 1960, and Dunham 1967.

5. See table 6.1.

6. See Trigger 1982, 224 for a note on the strong racial element in Reisner's interpretation of Nubian history.

7. The Hyksos were the Asiatic rulers of Lower Egypt during the Second Intermediate Period, when they attempted to form an alliance with the kingdom of Kerma and place pressure on the Upper Egyptian rulers from both directions.

8. As indicated by a 1982 photograph in Kendall 1997, 22.

9. Uraeus refers to the image of the rearing cobra that was a symbol of kingship; it was worn on the forehead in conjunction with a crown or headdress.

10. Dunham (1958) and O'Connor (1993a) cite mid-ninth century BC.

11. The capital of the kingdom, thought to have been near the cemeteries of Kurru and Nuri, has not yet been identified (Shinnie 1996, 100); thus the term *Napata* refers to the area encompassing Gebel Barkal, Kurru, and Nuri.

12. The chronological order is given in Török 1995, 208–9.

13. All further description in this chapter relies on Dunham (1950) unless otherwise noted.

14. The term *mastaba* is Arabic for "bench," and refers to a grave with a rectangular superstructure—a type known from as early as the Egyptian Early Dynastic Period.

15. See O'Connor (1993a, 117) for his argument against Kendall's claim that the previous mastabas also had pyramid tops.

Bibliography

Adams, William Y. 1984. *Nubia: Corridor to Africa*. Princeton: Princeton University Press.

Alcock, Susan E. 2002. *Archaeologies of the Greek Past: Landscape, Monuments, and Memories*. Cambridge: Cambridge University Press.

Assmann, Jan. 2002. *The Mind of Egypt: History and Meaning in the Time of the Pharaohs*. Trans. Andrew Jenkins. New York: Metropolitan Books. First published 1996 by Carl Hanser Verlag.

Bonnet, Charles. 1986. *Kerma: Territoire et Métropole*. Quatre leçons au Collège de France. Cairo: Institut Français d'Archéolgie Orientale du Caire.

——— 1992. Excavations at the Nubian Royal Town of Kerma: 1975–91. *Antiquity* 66 (252): 611–25.

——— 1996. Habitat et Palais dans l'Ancienne Nubie. *Haus und Palast im Alten Ägypten*, ed. Manfred Bietak. Wien: Verlag der Österreichischen Akademie der Wissenschaften.

Connah, Graham. 1987. *African Civilizations: Precolonial Cities and States in Tropical Africa: An Archaeological Perspective*. Cambridge: Cambridge University Press.

Dunham, Dows. 1950. *The Royal Cemeteries of Kush*. Cambridge, Mass.: Harvard University Press.
——— 1958. *The Egyptian Department and Its Excavations*. Boston: Museum of Fine Arts.
——— 1967. *Second Cataract Forts II: Uronarti, Shalfak, Mirgissa*. Boston: Museum of Fine Arts.
Dunham, Dows, and J. Janssen. 1960. *Second Cataract Forts I: Semna, Kumma*. Boston: Museum of Fine Arts.
Emery, Walter B. 1965. *Egypt in Nubia*. London: Hutchinson & Co.
Emery, Walter B., H. S. Smith, and A. Millard. 1979. *The Fortress of Buhen: The Archaeological Report*. London: Egypt Exploration Society.
Haynes, Joyce L. 1992. *Nubia: Ancient Kingdoms of Africa*. Boston: Museum of Fine Arts.
Kendall, Timothy. 1997. *Kerma and the Kingdom of Kush, 2500–1500 B.C.* Washington, D.C.: Smithsonian Institution, National Museum of African Art.
——— 1999. Gebel Barkal. *The Encyclopedia of the Archaeology of Ancient Egypt*, ed. Kathryn Bard, 325–28. New York: Routledge.
Knapp, A. Bernard, and Wendy Ashmore. 1999. Archaeological Landscapes: Constructed, Conceptualized, Ideational. In *Archaeologies of Landscape*, eds. Wendy Ashmore and A. Bernard Knapp, 1–30. Malden, Mass.: Blackwell.
Leclant, Jean. 1999. Kushites. In *The Encyclopedia of the Archaeology of Ancient Egypt*, ed. Kathryn Bard, 423–28. New York: Routledge.
Lehner, Mark. 1997. *The Complete Pyramids*. London: Thames and Hudson.
Lichtheim, Miriam. 1973. *Ancient Egyptian Literature, Volume I: The Old and Middle Kingdoms*. Berkeley: University of California Press.
Morkot, Robert. 2000. *The Black Pharaohs: Egypt's Nubian Rulers*. London: Rubicon Press.
O'Connor, David. 1971. Ancient Egypt and Black Africa: Early Contacts. *Expedition* 14.
——— 1993a. *Ancient Nubia: Egypt's Rival in Africa*. Philadelphia: The University Museum of Archaeology and Anthropology, University of Pennsylvania.
——— 1993b. Chiefs or Kings? Rethinking Early Nubian Politics. *Expedition* 35 (2): 4–14.
O'Connor, David, and Andrew Reid, eds. 2003. Introduction: Locating Ancient Egypt in Africa; Modern Theories, Past Realities. In *Ancient Egypt in Africa*. London: Institute of Archaeology Press, University College London.
Quirke, Stephen, and Jeffrey Spencer, eds. 1992. *The British Museum Book of Ancient Egypt*, 203. London: Thames and Hudson.
Reisner, George. 1923. *Excavations at Kerma, I-V.* Harvard African Studies, vols. 5–6. Cambridge, Mass.: Harvard University Press.
Richards, Janet. 1999. Conceptual Landscapes in the Egyptian Nile Valley. In *Archaeologies of Landscape*, eds. Wendy Ashmore and A. Bernard Knapp, 83–100. Malden, Mass.: Blackwell.
Shaw, Ian, ed. 2000. *The Oxford History of Ancient Egypt*. Oxford: Oxford University Press.

Shinnie, P. L. 1996. *Ancient Nubia*. London and New York: Kegan Paul International.

Siliotti, Alberto. 1996. *Guide to the Valley of the Kings*. Vercelli, Italy: White Star.

Sinopoli, Carla. 2003. Echoes of Empire: Vijayanagara and Historical Memory, Vijayanagara as Historical Memory. In *Archaeologies of Memory*, eds. Ruth M. Van Dyke and Susan E. Alcock, 17–33. Malden, Mass.: Blackwell.

Smith, Stuart Tyson. 2003. *Wretched Kush: Ethnic Identities and Boundaries in Egypt's Nubian Empire*. New York: Routledge.

Taylor, John. 2000. The Third Intermediate Period. In *The Oxford History of Ancient Egypt*, ed. Ian Shaw, 330–68. Oxford: Oxford University Press.

Török, László. 1995. The Emergence of the Kingdom of Kush and Her Myth of the State in the First Millennium B.C. *Cahiers de Recherches de l'Institut de Papyrologie et d'Egyptologie de Lille* 17:203–28.

—— 1997. *The Kingdom of Kush: Handbook of the Napatan-Meroitic Civilization*. Leiden, Netherlands: Brill.

—— 2002. *The Image of the Ordered World in Ancient Nubian Art: The Construction of the Kushite Mind, 800 B.C.–A.D. 300*. Leiden, Netherlands: Brill.

Trigger, Bruce G. 1976. *Nubia under the Pharaohs*. London: Thames and Hudson.

—— 1982. Reisner to Adams: Paradigms of Nubian Cultural History. In *Nubian Studies: Proceedings of the Symposium for Nubian Studies*, ed. J. M. Plumley, 223–26. Warminster: Aris & Phillips.

Vercoutter, Jean. 1970–76. *Mirgissa*. 3 vols. Paris: Direction général des relations culturelles, scientifiques et techniques.

Welsby, Derek. 2001. *Life on the Desert Edge: Seven Thousand Years of Settlement in the Northern Dongola Reach, Sudan*. 2 vols. BAR International Series 980. Oxford: Archaeopress.

Zabkar, Louis, and Joan Zabkar. 1982. Semna South: A Preliminary Report on the 1966–68 Excavations of the University of Chicago Oriental Institute Expedition to Sudanese Nubia. *Journal of the American Research Center in Egypt* 19:7–50.

7 Negotiated Pasts and the Memorialized Present in Ancient India
CHALUKYAS OF VATAPI

Hemanth Kadambi

Between the fall of the northern Gupta Empire and the rise of the Chola state in the south is a period usually referred to as the Early Medieval (ca. AD fifth century to ca. tenth century) in Indian history. This period is characterized by what some scholars believe was a feudal society (Sharma 1965; Jha 2000). Although "feudalism" in Indian history is debated (Mukhia 1981, 2000), there is consensus on one front: many competing kingdoms with lofty claims to the legacy of the erstwhile powerful Gupta Empire rose for the first time.

Generally, most scholarly works on this period gloss over dynamic interactions among polities (interpolity and intrapolity) in their landscape (Yazdani 1960; Shastry 1960). A significant part of those interactions stems from complex relationships with the past and their contemporary local manifestations. Recent studies of the perception of the past in the past have shown that archaeologists encounter materials that inform on people's attitudes toward their pasts and how those were utilized for claims, counterclaims, and active denial of those pasts (Van Dyke and Alcock 2003). Such studies, I believe, help build a holistic and dynamic picture of interactions among past societies. There is enormous potential to undertake an explicit investigation of the perception of the past in the past in studies of Indian history (Sinopoli 2003). This chapter is an attempt to do so and seeks to explore one vector of perception—the formation and transformation of identities—of the past in the past in a regional landscape.

I show the process of identity formation through the workings of multiple, mutable memories in the Malaprabha Valley, North Karnataka, between the mid-sixth and mid-eighth centuries AD. By *identity* I do not mean a single entity that can be comprehensively defined and pinpointed in the archaeological record. People live with multiple identities, hence

I do not talk of political identity or social identity alone, for these flow into each other, and their material manifestations may reveal either one or both or more.

The Chalukyas of Vatapi (mid-sixth–mid-eighth centuries AD) make a compelling case for the issues taken up in this chapter. This dynasty built more temples than any other dynasty at this time, and so the Malaprabha Valley is called the cradle of Indian temple architecture. The Chalukyas left behind a political and cultural legacy that was uniquely local and simultaneously reflective of a regional trend. This regional trend is documented in many ways, including the rivalry and wars between the Chalukyas and their southern neighbors, the Pallavas of Kanchi; in the emergence of new languages such as Kannada and Telugu (both around the fifth century AD); and the evolution of scripts that were hitherto unknown.

In the same vein, historians of South India see the Chalukyas of Vatapi as progenitors of administrative apparatuses and architectural styles that were emulated by subsequent dynastic houses in North Karnataka until the advent of the Vijayanagara Empire in the fourteenth century (Shastry 1960; Dikshit 1981; Ramesh 1984). It may be pertinent here to give a brief overview of the Chalukyas who are the subject of this chapter's inquiry.

Political Geography during the Reign of the Chalukyas of Vatapi

The Chalukyan sites addressed in this chapter lie in the semiarid climatic zone in North Karnataka State along the seasonal Malaprabha River (fig. 7.1). These sites are Vatapi (Badami), Mahakuta, Pattadakal, and Aihole, all major centers of art and urban activity during the reign of the Chalukyas. Rolling sandstone hills overlying Precambrian metamorphic rocks and covered with thin soil cover provided raw materials for stone architecture, as well as minerals for mining activities (Sundara 1975). Situated at an elevation of 300–600 meters above sea level, the region received between 600–1000 mm of annual rainfall, and dry farming, along with pastoral activities, were the main subsistence. At its height, the Chalukyan polity stretched from the Narmada River in the north to the Tungabhadra River in the south, encompassing an area of approximately 55,000

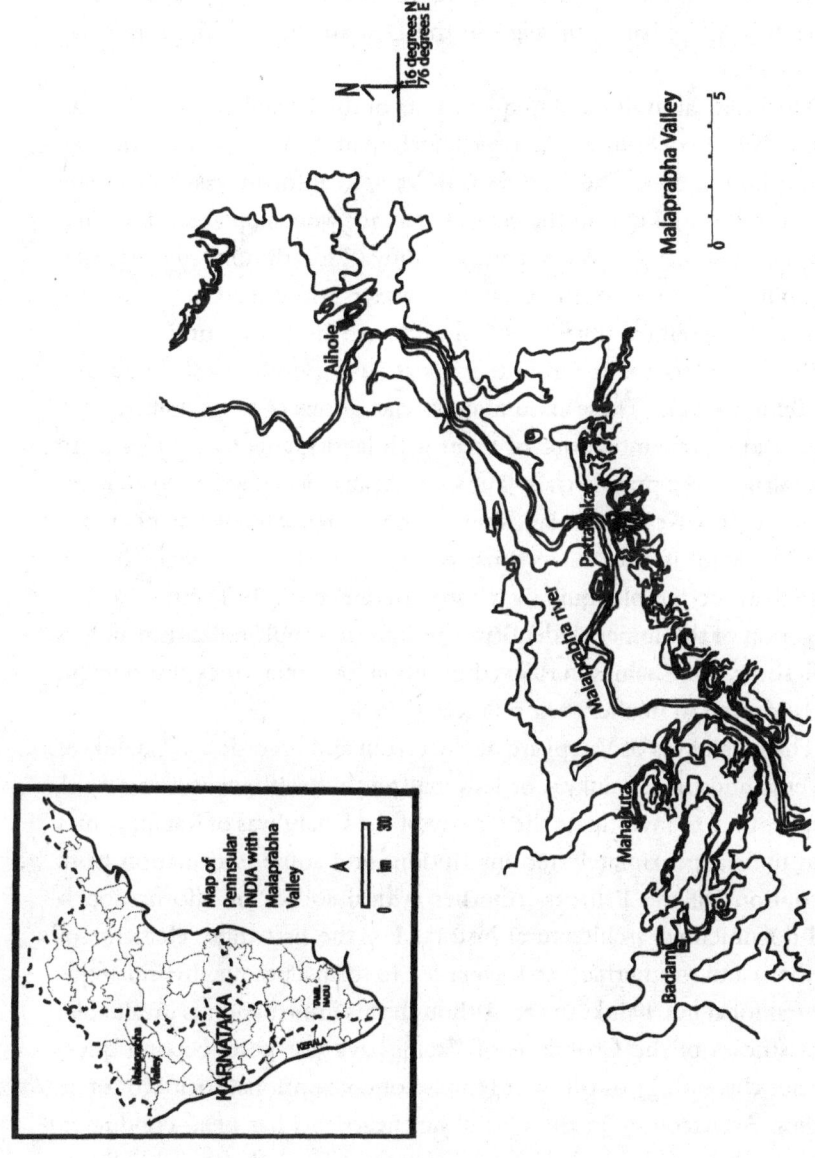

FIGURE 7.1 Malaprabha Valley (Michell 1979, 27)

square kilometers. Polekesi I of the Chalukya family supposedly defeated his Kadamba overlords and established the capital at Vatapi by building a fort on top of the sandstone cliff, ca. AD 543. (Ramesh 1984, 40). This ushered in the Chalukyan reign in the Deccan that lasted around two hundred years.

The political rivalry and frequent wars of the Chalukyas with the Pallavas of Kanchi of South India is well documented in many inscriptions of both ruling houses. The Chalukyas of Vatapi had many vassals—among them the Rashtrakutas in the central Deccan, who supplanted the Chalukyas around AD 750. A comparative study of inscriptions suggests that the political fortunes of the Chalukyas waxed and waned in accordance with the geopolitical situation of entire South India. Inscriptions of the Chalukyan rulers are in Sanskrit language, using both old Kannada and old Telugu scripts. These abound in proclamations of kings' military victories and commemorations of them with land grants to temples or to *Brahmanas*—the priestly class. The Chalukyan rulers negotiated an identity for themselves in the landscape around their capital Vatapi (today called Badami) in the Malaprabha river valley and memorialized it with more than 100 temples built over a span of one-and-a-half centuries. The formation of this imperial identity went beyond simple militarism and, as I will show, the Chalukyan rulers drew upon local memories enshrined in the landscape to further their political agenda.

The Chalukyas of Vatapi are distinct from and precede the Chalukyas of Vengi and the Chalukyas of Kalyana (tenth–twelfth centuries AD). A major source to investigate the history of the Chalukyas of Vatapi comes from their approximately 180 inscriptions and some information from inscriptions of the Pallavas. Another critical source of information is well-documented architectural history. For the first time, elements of northern and southern art styles merged to form a unique, hybrid architectural form in Chalukyan art. Although this information is invaluable, most studies of the Chalukyas of Vatapi have not gone beyond questions of chronology of rulers or temples or conventional socioeconomic studies. Archaeology in the Chalukyan heartland has been conducted but is not well published. However, apparent from the available information, pre-Chalukyan times in the Malaprabha Valley impinged on the Chalukyas' sixth-century building activity. The fragmentary nature of archaeological evidence does not preclude us from finding useful information about the Malaprabha Valley. Archaeological explorations in this area for many decades have brought to light sites from the lower Paleolithic up to the Early Historic (ca. 300 BC–ca. AD 300) and Early Medieval periods (ca. AD 300–ca. 900). Much of this information is in the form of short notices in annual reports, and the majority of sites have not been excavated or even explored systematically. Some significant works on the lower Paleolithic (Joshi 1955) and Megalithic phases in this region (Sundara 1975) are critical, and I have culled data from the latter for this chapter. Archaeological evidence from pre-Chalukyan times cited in this chapter are from published records of the Megalithic Phase of South India (ca. 1500 BC–ca. AD 300), alternatively called the Iron Age and the Early Historic Period (ca. 300 BC–ca. AD 300). In addition to the published materials, I have used my own field observations in an attempt to investigate the creation and transformation of Chalukyan identity.

I argue that the Chalukya ruling house settled a region that was considered sacred, in part owing to the presence of vast numbers of mortuary monuments. Having settled, they undertook the task of memorializing their landscape, as had been done before them by various groups of people whose roles still need to be recovered. The practice of invoking some pasts while denying others is suggested in their records. Such synchronic processes of active legitimization and selective use of social memory helped the Chalukyas negotiate a space for their sovereign rule for more than two centuries. Moreover, Chalukyan art styles were kept alive by deliberate archaisms in the architecture of subsequent decades by the Rashtrakuta dynasty. Only five centuries later, in the inscriptions of the Later Chalukyas (tenth century–mid-twelfth century AD), we encounter genealogies of the Chalukya family of Vatapi for the first time. This implies a strong impetus to recall a past.

This chapter does not present the perception of the ordinary people who lived and died under the Chalukyan reign. Although contemporary literature provides some accounts of "commoner" attitudes toward life, these are generally broad and not nuanced enough to make a parallel study of the transformations of those attitudes commensurate with the changing identities of the Chalukyan rulers. Undertaking systematic archaeological investigations may provide useful information to understand perspectives of nonroyalty.

Chalukyas of Vatapi: Reuse of a Sacred Landscape

The Chalukyan centers of Aihole and Pattadakal have dolmens and chamber tombs, as well as an incredible number of temples of the Chalukyan phase and some from the pre-Chalukyan phase. Their locations near ores of iron or gold and near sources of water can be explained in connection with resource-mobilization strategies. S. Settar (1979, 32) writes that "it is interesting to note the coincidence of the location of these two artistic traditions—Megalithic and Chalukyan—which demonstrates as it were, the attempts of the people of different millennia to bridge the gap of several centuries." Settar, however, believes the link is "indistinct" while affirming that megalithic building activity dominated the area for centuries only to be replaced by the building tradition of the Chalukyas of the imperial house in the sixth century AD.

The Chalukyas settled a region that was already sacred. Sacred places have long-term, yet mutable, memories (Alcock 2002; Bradley 1998, 2000) and, as will be shown, the Chalukyas inscribed in their natural landscape memories that were embodied in stone architecture. These memories may constitute a general reuse of a memorial landscape. Through this picture I hope to clarify Settar's statement about the "indistinct" links between the Chalukyan and megalithic sites.

Megaliths and Early Chalukyan Memory

Aihole's temples and clusters of dolmens (figs. 7.2 and 7.3) are in close proximity to each other on the right bank of the Malaprabha River. Nevertheless, Aihole is primarily known for its clusters of structural temples and cave temples dating back to the sixth–eighth centuries AD.[1] The 133 megaliths extend over 21.43 hectares around and in the vicinity of Aihole (Moorti 1994, 114). The megaliths at the sites of Aihole, Guledagudda, Pattadakal, Akkaragal, Khayddigere, and Chilapur are designated as the Aihole group (Sundara 1975).

At least four architectural types of tombs in the Aihole group exist, possibly because of different groups of people having different funerary practices (Sundara 1975); the four types perhaps were chronologically separated. Alternatively, a group may have adopted distinct modes of

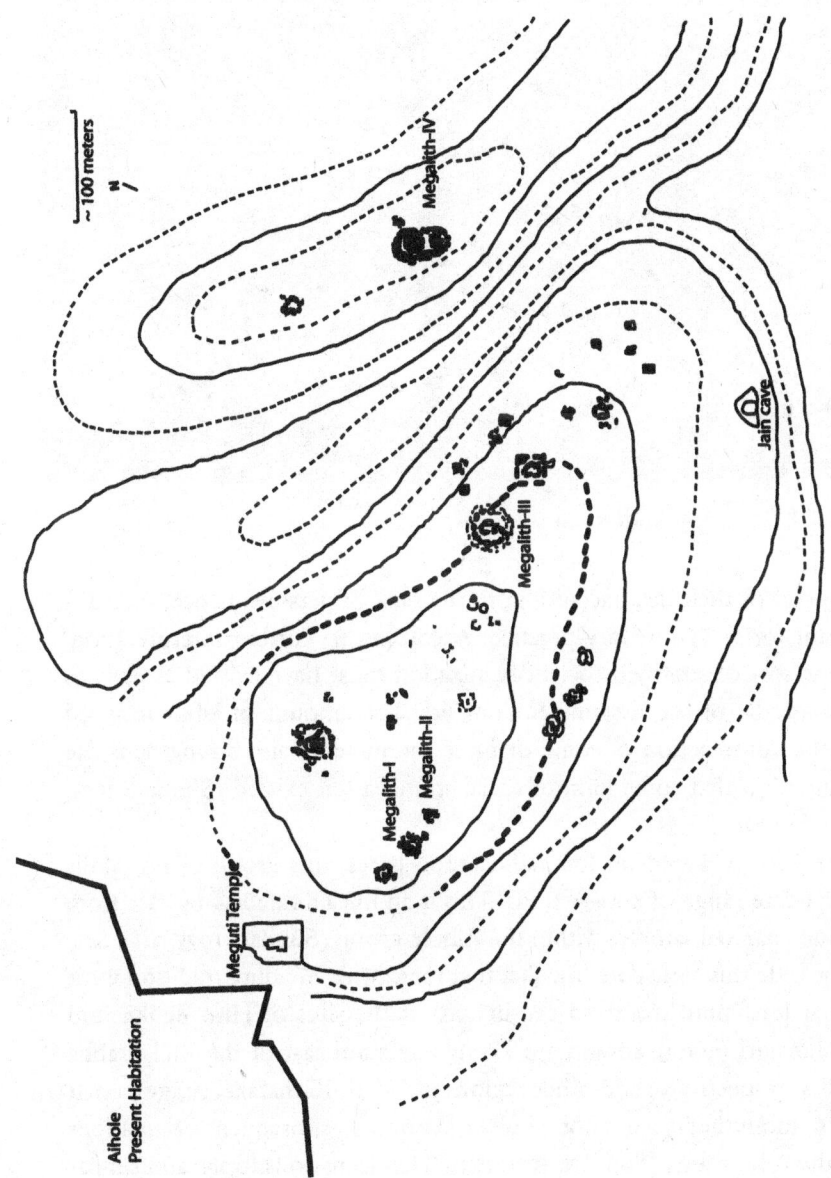

FIGURE 7.2 Aihole site plan (Sundara 1975, 241)

FIGURE 7.3 Aihole dolmen

disposal of their dead according to the rank of persons; hence, four different forms of funerary practice. According to current interpretation, some sort of stratified social organization must have existed as early as the middle of the first millennium BC. The amount of labor invested in the construction of some of these monuments also strengthens the suggestion that some kind of social stratification existed (Sundara 1975; Reddy 1994).

Although based on few radiocarbon dates, this group of megaliths has a date range of 800–600 BC. This is an uncalibrated C-14 date from wood charcoal samples within the Aihole group (Sundara 1975, 215). Setting aside this early date, the fact that megalithic building tradition went on at least until the third century AD at the sites of Hire Benkal and Brahmagiri (about 80 and 150 kilometers southeast of the Malaprabha Valley, respectively) and other regions in North Karnataka, suggests that these monuments were not wholly unknown to subsequent occupations in the Aihole area (Sundara 1975, 215). This scenario is likely, and similar to the recently proposed scenario that populations at Niligiri Hills in the southern Indian state of Tamil Nadu used and reused "Megalithic" monuments well into the twentieth century (Zagarell 1997).

FIGURE 7.4 Dolmen-like Ravulaphadi Cave, early seventh century AD, Aihole

An important piece of evidence to clarify the nature of the "indistinct link" between the megaliths and the subsequent cave and temple constructions at Aihole is the architectural similarity between the megalithic capstone placement and construction of the ceiling of an early cave at Aihole (fig. 7.4) and Bankanaveri. According to C. R. Bolon,

> The cave's front wall of masonry blocks "supports" visually a "capstone"–like portion of the boulder in which the cave is excavated. The boulder has a natural fold in the rock at the ceiling level while the crest of the boulder is centered over the cave like a natural *sikhara* (tower). These elements of the boulder's shape may have determined the choice of the outcropping of the hill for excavation. No doubt the fold in the rock formation facilitated excavation and determined the ceiling line. Beyond the physical similarity to a sacred architectural form, there may have been religious reasons for the choice of a temple excavation site resembling a dolmen. (Bolon 1981, 34)

The dolmens were considered sacred, and the Chalukyas kept the memory of these mortuary features alive, as seen in the architectural style of the caves. We may consider these acts of erecting dolmens as inscribing and transforming memories in the Malaprabha landscape. Chalukyan religious architecture in the natural landscape at Aihole, Pattadakal, Badami, and other sites further commemorated a sacredness that was associated with the region for centuries. The selection of suitable locales by the Chalukyas, and continued building activity in the same landscape as the megaliths, suggests they made a meaningful choice—one of self-legitimization and that constituted a reuse of a sacred landscape.

Evidence from Pre-Chalukyan Excavations at Temples in Aihole and Pattadakal

To strengthen the argument that the Chalukyas initiated acts of remembrance in order to legitimize their presence in this sacred landscape, I draw upon information from two partial excavations. These excavations were carried out under the precincts of standing temples of the Chalukyan Period and hence complete exposures were not possible.

Brick Temple in the Sangameshwara Temple Complex at Pattadakal

Dr. S. R. Rao, excavating between 1969 and 1971, found a major portion of a brick structure underlying the foundations of the hall of the Sangameshwara temple (fig. 7.5). The plan of this structure revealed a pillared hall and a detached rectangular cell or room on the east.[2] The overall dimension of the hall, the western extremity of which is still unexposed, is fourteen meters from east to west and fifteen meters from north to south. Traces of a flight of steps can be seen on the eastern side, and remains of two brick walls enclosing one of the bays at the western end of the nave are also visible. Four rows of pillars dividing the hall into two side aisles and a nave are clearly seen. The base of each pillar is one meter square, but the bases along the periphery are not attached to the walls. Obviously the peripheral wall, perhaps only a parapet, did not support the roof. Perhaps the superstructure was made of timber. It is not entirely clear how the sanctum was placed, but if it did not join the rear wall then it would have closely resembled the plan of another temple, the Gaudergudi at Aihole, dating to the Chalukyan

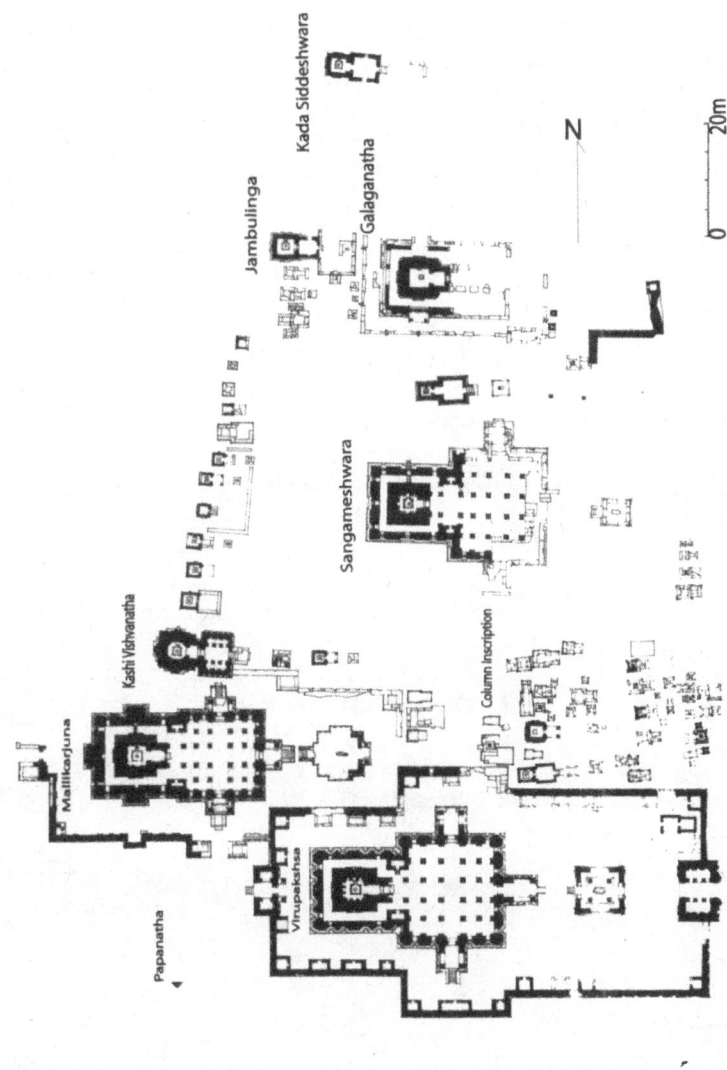

FIGURE 7.5 Pattadakal site plan (Meister and Dhaky 1986, 24)

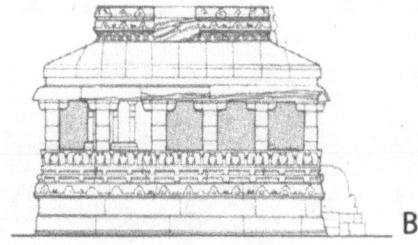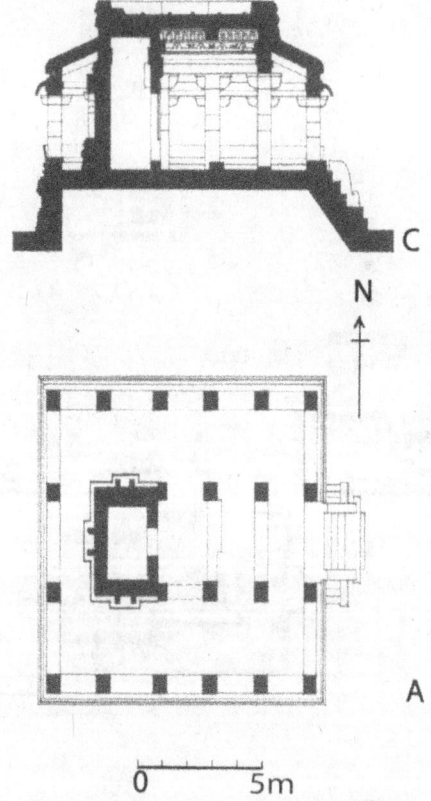

FIGURE 7.6 Gaudergudi, Aihole (Meister and Dhaky 1986, 47)

Period (fig. 7.6). Rao (1978) confidently asserted that the underlying brick temple dated to the third century AD based on ceramic sequence, and that it was a precursor to the earliest of the Chalukyan temples.[3] Furthermore, evidence of pre-Chalukya occupation in the area comes from a mound cutting that revealed second- to third-century ceramics and is 150 meters away from the site of this brick temple and the Sangameshwara temple.

Brick Temple under the Ambiger-gudi Temple at Aihole

A brick wall, discovered while exposing the buried plinth of the Ambiger-gudi temple, lay under the rear wall of the sanctum of the stone Ambiger-gudi temple. Between the brick wall below and the stone temple above was a layer, probably of sediment, with typical red-ware bowls of the first through third centuries AD. The excavator, Rao, believed the Ambiger-gudi temple was built into the brick temple of which a single cell, most certainly, and sanctum sanctorum are partly traceable. Though the evidence for the cell's plan is not definitive, Rao suggested the brick temples of the third century AD must have "served as models" for the early stone temple constructions of the Chalukyas (Rao 1978, 272–75).

Evidence from the excavations of brick temples at Pattadakal and Aihole have not been systematically published, and I have not succeeded in locating the ceramic materials in question. In the absence of much-needed information, any suggestions of what the evidence may constitute for my purpose here must be tentative. Perhaps the preceding examples can be seen as acts of emulation and borrowing from either contemporaneous groups of people or as the active recalling of memories. Whatever the ultimate strategy (perhaps both), the Chalukyas sought to establish their firm presence from the sixth and seventh centuries AD with stone architecture that has left an indelible mark on the landscape.

Curiously, the Chalukyan inscriptions are silent on the issue of previous occupation in the area of their temples. If we are to believe their inscriptions, these areas were unoccupied in immediate pre-Chalukyan times. We know from historical records, however, that this area came under the sway of the Kadambas of Banavasi (Ramesh 1984).

Mutable Memories, Lasting Control: Evidence from Art History and Local History

The inscriptions of the Chalukyas tell us that they followed the dominant Brahmanical faith of the times and adopted its symbolic and religious icons. I suggest, however, that this is only part of the story; there is evidence that local religious identities played into considerations of political supremacy. From ethnoarchaeological, art historical, and local historical data, I show that the Chalukyas sought actively to incorporate local diversity into their monumentalized Brahmanical practices.

This process of incorporation is not unique to the Chalukyan enterprise. The history of South Asian politicoreligious context is filled with examples of such incorporation (Jaiswal 1967; Thapar 2003). However, in specific cases there is an interesting dynamic to such incorporation. Looking at such a process highlights the specific features of the Chalukyan reign, one that could not have survived without subsuming and elaborating on local identities. In other words, the Chalukyan rulers actively negotiated their religious and political identity with local, diverse interests.

The Yellamma Cult and the Chalukyas

The site of Yellamma-gudi at Saundatti, about fifty kilometers west of Badami, is associated with the fertility goddess Yellamma, or Ellama. Today this place is a center for a major annual pilgrimage for 400,000 devotees of the goddess. She is associated with God Parasurama's mother, Renuka, the wife of sage Jamadagni (*Gazetteer of Belgaum* 1987, 956–57). Her temple is situated atop the hill, near megalithic tombs. G. D. Sontheimer's (1989) work shows that Yellamma is one of the Saptamatrka, or seven divine mothers, who nourished the rulers on earth, and Yelmakkaltai, or the mother of seven children. Her cult is popular among the pastoralist groups of the Dhangars and Kurumbas of southern Maharashtra and North Karnataka even today (Sontheimer 1989, 55).[4]

Archaeological evidence shows that the Yellamma temple precincts at Saundatti date back to either early Rashtrakuta or Late Chalukyan times (mid-eighth–mid-eleventh centuries AD; *Gazetteer of Belgaum* 1987). The

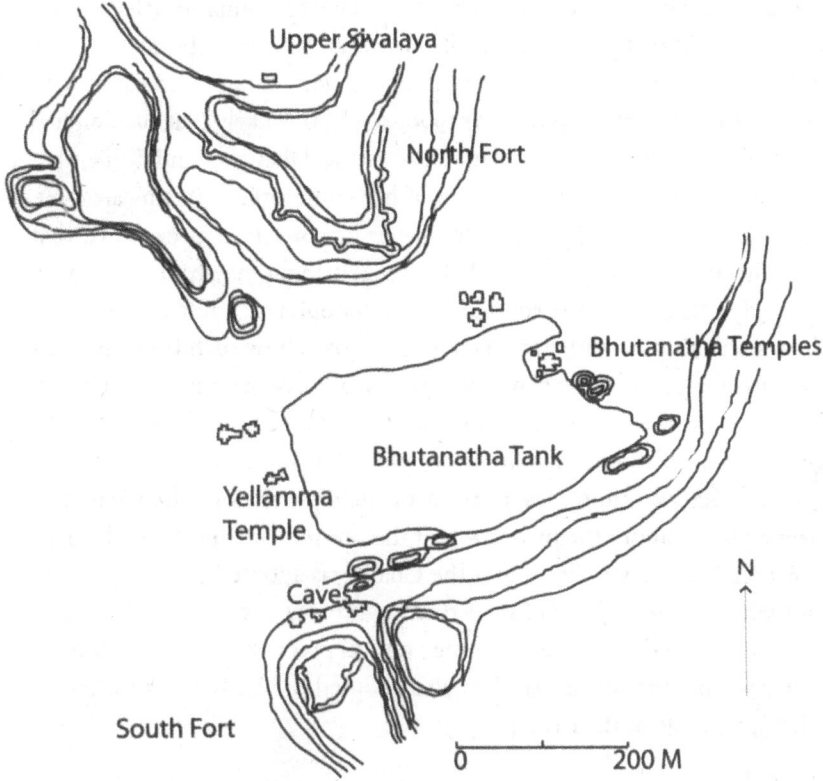

FIGURE 7.7 Badami site plan (Michell 1979, 47)

megalithic tombs of a preceding period are also located in the same area on the hill. Scattered sherds of early historic red ware (ca. third century BC–ca. third century AD) and the megalithic black and red ware have been found around this area (Sundara 1975). It is likely that the Yellamma fertility cult was popular among the locals when the Chalukya rulers wrested control of this region from their political forebears, the Kadambas of Banavasi. The Yogeswara temple (Yellamma temple on fig. 7.7), which faces east and stands opposite the Bhutanatha temples bordering the lake, is seen at Badami. This temple may also be a seat of the pastoral fertility goddess, Yellamma.

While I was conducting fieldwork at Badami, a local informant said that the temple was dedicated to Yellamma, consort of Lord Bhutanatha (Shiva), whose own temple stands on the opposite end of the Bhutanatha tank. The temples face each other. The Yellamma temple belongs to the period of the Chalukyas of Vatapi, a claim corroborated by the district *Gazetteer*, which also mentions that the temple is affiliated with Yogeshwara (*Gazetteer of Bijapur* 1996, 484).[5] It is likely that Badami had accorded to Yellamma a similar status as the Dhangars and Kurumbas had, although there is no evidence of her cultic origins in this area yet. A monument, especially a temple, in her honor serves as evidence that even during the reign of the Chalukyas Yellamma may have been worshipped in Badami by the ruling house, although this is not evident from their inscriptions. Sontheimer (1989) has shown how such belief systems have generated their own mythologies and consequently their perversions and even architectural expression on the ground. The Saundatti Yellamma-gudi and the Yellamma temple at Badami do point to this process. Besides, we know that in most of their inscriptions the Chalukyas claimed to be under the protection of the seven divine mothers, the Saptamatrka. This may indicate that the Chalukyas adopted the seven divine mothers and thereby established their legitimacy over the local population. One should remember that the political precursors to the Chalukyas in this region, the Kadambas, had also adopted the Saptamatrka as legitimizing symbols of their rule.

Lajja-Gauri in Chalukyan Art

The worship and varied iconographic representations of another fertility goddess—Lajja-Gauri—were also prevalent during the reign of the Chalukyas, although their inscriptions are curiously silent on this. Lajja-Gauri, or "Shameless Gauri," is a name for the consort of Lord Shiva (Bolon 1997, 1). She is commonly depicted in a sitting posture, spreading her upright bent knees, always supine, with pudendum displayed and generally headless or lotus-headed. Her hands, held high above, usually carry some creepers (fig. 7.8). This goddess is seen in ca. fourth-century AD *itihasa-purana*, or mythological literature of India (Bolon 1997; Thapar 2003). She is identified with other goddesses of the Brahmanical pantheon, such as Renuka, the wife of sage Jamadagni just as Yellamma is identified with the same.[6]

Based on sculptural evidence for her worship in the Chalukyan heartland, the cult of Lajja-Gauri flourished during Chalukyan times. Twelve

Pasts and Present in Ancient India 171

FIGURE 7.8 Lajja-Gauri

large stone images, all of them three to four feet high and carved in relief, are located in the Malaprabha Valley near Badami, in Mahakuta, near Pattadakal and Aihole (Bolon 1997, 24).[7] According to Bolon, "the goddess Lajja-Gauri was especially important to the people ruled by the early Chalukya kings during the last two decades of the seventh century as is apparent from the number, size and quality of her images made at this time" (Bolon 1997, 24).

An inscription belonging to the time of King Vinayaditya (mid-seventh century AD) indicates that the king levied taxes on childless couples, thereby bringing to light possible coercive measures of control exercised by the Chalukyan authority (*Indian Antiquary* 19, 145). He apparently started the practice of building Lajja-Gauri shrines in order to propitiate the fertility goddess so as to ensure a regular supply of soldiers for the army (Bolon 1997, 32).

That the king built Lajja-Gauri shrines may indicate the complicated interplay between local identity and Chalukyan royalty and their interrelations in the landscape. Moreover, this interrelation highlights the multivocal ritual space prevalent in the valley. Along with the elaborate iconography of Brahmanical deities—including Varaha (boar-faced incarnation of Lord Visnu); Narasimha (man-lion incarnation of Lord Visnu); Nataraja (Shiva as cosmic dancer); Trivikrama (incarnation of Lord Visnu as the giant strider); Mahisasuramardhini (goddess Parvati, who destroyed Mahisa, the evil bull); Ganesa (elephant-headed god and son of Shiva); and Kartikeya (family deity of the Chalukyan rulers and son of Shiva) among others—in temples, we also find the presence of Yellamma and Lajja-Gauri.

Bolon argues that the Chalukyan rulers forged a local identity that gave legitimacy to their reign. Most Chalukya rulers after Pulakeshin II (died ca. AD 642) had their name suffix as "-aditya." If this were the sanskritised version of their names then we may say these names mean "of aditi" or the offspring of Aditi, the mother of the gods. Stella Kramrisch identified the "naked woman spreading her legs and displaying her pudenda" as Aditi Uttanapad (Kramrisch 1956, 259–70). Aditi is seen as a fertility goddess akin to Yellamma and Lajja-Gauri. The correlation of use of the suffix "-aditya" by all the later Chalukya kings, with Aditi, the mother of the gods, indicates a strong local affiliation of the ruling house at Badami and Pattadakal.

The Chalukyas were defeated by the Pallavas, their southern rivals, who are known to have occupied the region from ca. AD 642–ca. AD 655. After this thirteen-year period of turmoil, the Chalukyan fortunes were restored at Vatapi and Pattadakal in ca. AD 655. by Vikramaditya I. From this period on we see increased temple dedications to the Shiva pantheon and the Saivite (affiliated to Shiva) suffix "-aditya" in the names of rulers. This is perhaps not a coincidence as much as an active political strategy employed to gain loyalty from a region that was now predominantly Saivite. This move constitutes a transformation of Chalukyan identity from what existed earlier. Susan Alcock (2002) has argued that times of distress and turmoil can lead to resignification of relationships with the past. Indeed, a similar situation seems to have occurred around the mid- to late-seventh century AD under the Chalukyan reign, when a change in the ritual affiliation of the Chalukyan rulers was felt strongly and memorialized in names like Vikramaditya, Vijayaditya, and Vinayaditya, with the suffix "-aditya" affiliated with the Saivite religious sect, whereas earlier rulers in this dynasty took on names like Jayasimha, Pulakeshin, and Kirtivarman, of the Vaishnavite sect.

Apart from trying to identify with the local religiopolitical themes, the Chalukyas sought legitimacy to reign in two other ways. First, like their political forebears—the Kadambas of Banavasi—the Chalukyas of Vatapi laid claims to the lineage of Manavya (a mythical sage) and called themselves the children of Hariti (the divine mother) in their inscriptions (*Indian Antiquary* 8, 46; *Indian Antiquary* 11, 67). In the absence of any known real kinship links with the Kadambas, K. V. Ramesh (1984, 25) and others, including myself, believe this appropriation of lineage memory served in the best interest of the Chalukyas to legitimize their presence in the Malaprabha Valley. Second, repeated reference to a Chalukyan ancestor having performed important Vedic sacrifices (precursor to some aspects of Hinduism) in the past gave the dynasty an air of authority over that past. Although Vedic religion was practiced in some form along with puranic Hindu rituals (which began around the fourth century AD), the former was being relegated to the realm of the remembered. Anyone who articulated that remembrance (namely Brahmanas and kings who had performed Vedic sacrifices) had a hold over a hoary past, one that laid the foundations for the present. Recognition of that past in the form of land grants to Vedic Brahmanas ensured an otherworldly merit (good karma) as well as this-worldly legitimacy. Presumably the population under the Chalukyas must have admired and revered the achievements of the Chalukyas of Vatapi and legitimized their sovereignty.

Military victories of the Chalukyas of Vatapi also helped legitimize their reign. Their grandiose titles (in Sanskrit), such as Satyasraya ("He in whom truth resides") and Prithvivallabha ("Lord of the Earth"), were coveted and adopted by Chalukyas of another dynasty, four centuries later.

Remembering the Chalukyas of Vatapi

In this last section I briefly present architectural and genealogical data of the Chalukyas to show how this dynasty left an indelible mark on the Malaprabha landscape. The Chalukyas suffered major military reversals in the mid-eighth century AD. Their vassals, the Rashtrakutas, defeated the Chalukyas and took over their territory, ca. AD 750, although stray references to land grants by Kirtivarman II (the last ruler) and his descendants lasted until ca. AD 760 (Michell 2002, 5).

With the disappearance of the Chalukyas of Vatapi from the building scene, the Rashtrakutas took the lead and consciously imitated the earlier Chalukyan styles (Michell 2002, 16; Meister and Dhaky 1986, 134–35). This is seen at temples two and three, among the Kunti group of four temples at Aihole. The Kunti group of temples are generally believed to have been built by the Chalukyas of Vatapi and are all dedicated to the worship of Lord Vishnu.

The west-facing Temple Three has its sanctum sanctorum (fig. 7.9) placed within a hall and drawn toward the back wall as in the Chalukyan temples one and four. The plain wall of the hall, one-third the depth of the hall on the south side, is another archaic feature. The heavy, sloping roof of the hall, the raised platform together with the *hara* (cloistered parapet in the superstructure) above the nave, are also local characteristics. M. W. Meister and M. A. Dhaky (1986, 134–35) believe the *kaksasanas* (plural for a kind of seat) with the *purnaghata* (decorative motif of the vase of plenty) seem to be from the late Chalukya phase at Aihole. Despite these traits, some distinctly Rashtrakuta traits—its four nave pillars, the dwarf pillars along the kaksasanas, and the style of the sanctum sanctorum door frame—securely establish the temple to post-Chalukya building activity. The dwarf pillars present a new technique for embellishment, and a conspicuous purnaghata on the door frame is of Rashtrakuta style. The temple is dated to around the third quarter of the ninth century AD.

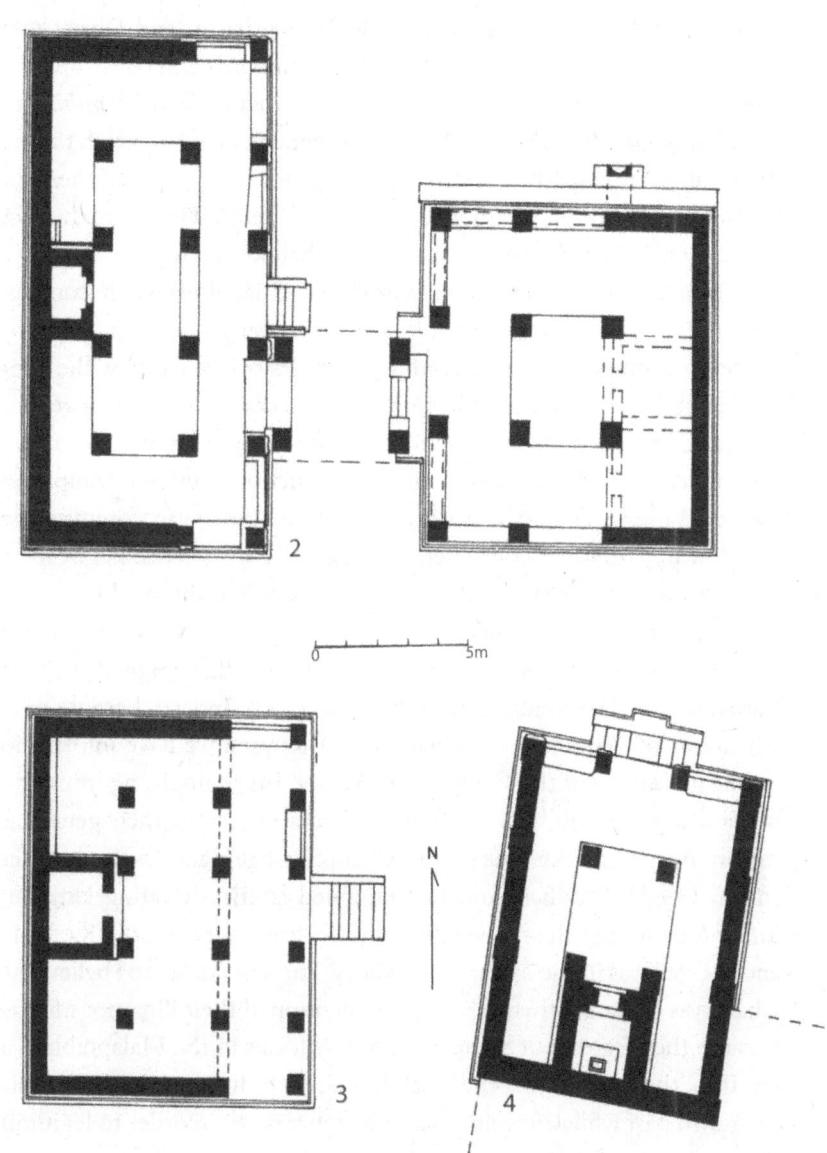

FIGURE 7.9 Plan of Kunti group of temples, Aihole (Meister and Dhaky 1986, 136)

The east-facing rectangular Temple Two (Meister and Dhaky 1986) (fig. 7.9) resembles Temple One, built during the second phase of building activity by the Chalukyas (ca. AD 700–ca. 750). Its *adhishtana* (molded base) is like Temple One, and its general features match those of the Chalukyan Lad Khan temple at Aihole (fig. 7.10). Its peripheral pillars in front, however, resemble the pillars of Temple Three and therefore date closer to Temple Three than to the Chalukyan temples.

Although a few more examples can be cited at Aihole where construction under the Rashtrakutas took place at a later phase (first quarter of the tenth century AD), the preceding examples suffice to show the adoption of conscious archaisms in temple construction—an act of remembering. One can argue that the Rashtrakutas sought legitimacy for their acceptance around Aihole in temple construction activity by employing the very same skilled artisans who worked for Chalukyan-commissioned temples. Regardless, a continued existence of a style in the landscape by the political successors of the Chalukyas at Aihole is discernible.

Memories of the Chalukyas of Vatapi were actively recalled, as seen from the inscriptions of their namesake dynasty that reigned in North Karnataka from the tenth to twelfth centuries AD. Indeed, because of the Chalukyas of Vengi and the Chalukyas of Kalyana we have information on the genealogy of the Chalukyas of Vatapi. Intriguingly, no inscription of the Badami Chalukyas yields any information about their genealogy. According to Ramesh (1984), the Chalukyas belonged to the northern Indian city of Ayodhya[8] and had migrated south, defeating kings and finally establishing themselves in the buffer zone between the Kadambas and the Pallavas in the Malaprabha Valley. Ramesh (1984, 20) believes the Chalukyas of Vatapi themselves never mentioned their illustrious lineage because they feared not being accepted by locals in the Malaprabha Valley. If so, then we see that the Chalukyas seem to have consciously denied their own past while affirming claims to other pasts, in order to legitimize their present political enterprise.

The records of the Eastern Chalukyas of Vengi and Western Chalukyas of Kalyana have elaborate mythical stories explicating the origin of the dynasty, recalling as many as fifty-nine kings at Ayodhya before Vijayaditya, who set out to conquer *daksinapatha* (the south). According to one version, Vijayaditya's son, Visnuvardhana, performed penance at the Chalukya hill and conquered the Pallava ruler who killed his father,

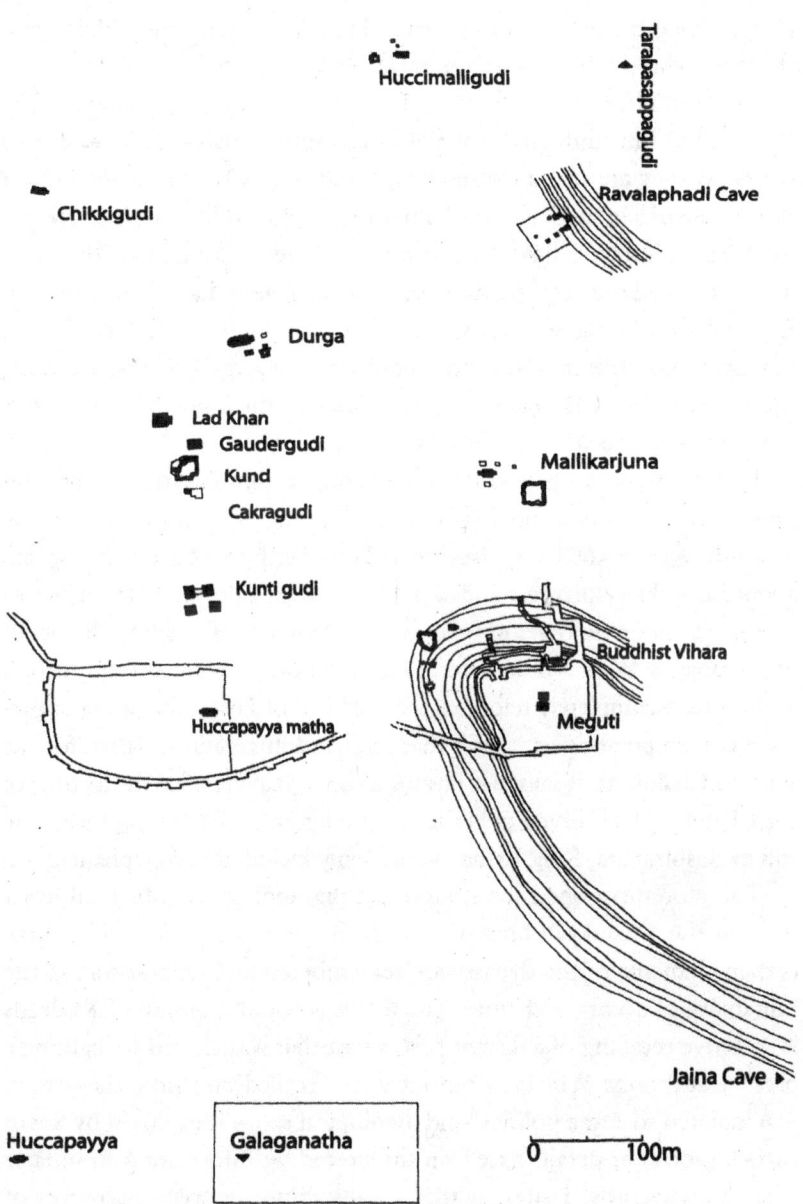

FIGURE 7.10 Plan of Aihole (Meister and Dhaky 1986, 19)

then married the daughter of his rival. He begot a son named Polekesi I, the ruler who established his capital at Vatapi ca. AD 543.

The founders of the lineage, Jayasimha (Vijayaditya) and his son Ranaraga (Visnuvardhana) may have been subordinates of the Kadamba rulers, as they are not mentioned with lofty titles such as Satyasraya or Prithvivallabha in the Kalyana Chalukya inscriptions. Jayasimha is referred to twice in Vatapi Chalukya inscriptions. The inscription of the Chalukyan ruler Mangalesa, ca. AD 599, refers to Jayasimha as King (*nripah*) Jayasimhavallabhendra, who was born in the family of Chalikyas. The next reference to him is from the Aihole pillar inscription of Mangalesa's successor, Polekesi II, dated to ca. AD 634–35, which proclaims a victorious campaign executed by King Jayasimha.

Not until 400 years later does the name Jayasimha surface again, this time in the Nilagunda copper plates inscription of Vikramaditya VI in the eleventh century AD. Two verses are dedicated to him. One of them speaks about his military prowess and says that he was endowed with virtues of past kings (*adi-raja-charitah*). He is also praised for alleviating the plight of his subjects. What is more interesting about this inscription is the second verse, which completely relocates the memory of Jayasimha in the immediate contemporary past, a past that mattered in creating a space for the Kalyana Chalukyas. It says that Jayasimha once again revived the fortune of the Chalukyas by burning either 105 or 500 kings, and defeating Indra, the son of Rashtrakuta, King Krsna, whose army included 800 elephants.

The aforementioned inscription is enlightening regarding information on the Chalukyan lineage and, more significantly, for seeing how certain elements of the dynasty are remembered and demonstrating the mutability of events over time. The fictive account of Jayasimha's deeds is an active recalling of a distant past, a past that was altered to legitimize present authority. Which memories were recalled and how these were manipulated to suit a political and ideological setup is explored by Susan Alcock (2002) in detail. Based on the preceding information from later Chalukyan records, I suggest that royalty chose between narratives of multiple pasts and altered some of the choices precisely because they were more mutable than others. In the case of the later Chalukyas, the memory of Jayasimha and the Chalukyan genealogy were excellent choices to manipulate because these were the lesser-known facets from the records of the Chalukyas of Vatapi.

Conclusion

The chief aim of this chapter has been to describe the complex process of identity formation in South India during the Early Medieval Period. I argue that the Chalukyas of Vatapi established their reign in the Malaprabha Valley through a negotiation of religious and political status, in addition to successful military campaigns. Their identity as sovereigns was formed and simultaneously transformed by this process of negotiation in the sacred landscape of the Malaprabha Valley. I take negotiation to be a synchronous temporal and spatial process. Temporality here refers to the ability to recall an ancient past (as seen in the adoption of the Vedic religious symbolism) in the present and thereby to perpetuate an aura of sacredness. Spatiality considers how the material reconfiguration of that ancient past has the ability to "memorialize the present," that is, make the present into a seamless culmination of the past. An example is the land grants given to Vedic Brahmanas in distant areas, thus extending the Chalukyan legitimacy farther afield. The construction of temples on or in the vicinity of other and perhaps earlier temples and mortuary megaliths is another example. I also argue that the construction of the Yellamma temple recalled a widely worshipped pastoral deity, and this worship was apparently transposed into the worship of Lajja-Gauri during Chalukyan times.

To consider how subsequent dynasties in the area viewed the Chalukyas of Vatapi is to further substantiate that the past was important for acquiring legitimacy. I suggest that conscious archaisms in temple construction were an act of remembering, and I demonstrate that memories are seldom straightforward or remain unchanged. In fact, "memories" were ignored or tampered with, as I show in the case of the missing genealogy of the Chalukyas of Vatapi in their own inscriptions. However, four centuries later, we find a lengthy and illustrious genealogy of the Vatapi Chalukyas in the inscriptions of a dynasty with the same name. The latter situation occurred at a time of political volatility, necessitating an illustrious past to legitimize present (hoped-for) stability.

Finally, I hope to have clarified that understanding the past "in its own terms" is a different and significant way to comprehend processes underlying changes in past societies. Clearly, more focused research of this nature is required for the Chalukyas—undertaking intensive and extensive documentation of material culture of their times and integrating this documentation with the vast corpus of historical research. With this chapter, I hope to have taken a step in this direction.

Acknowledgments

I would like to thank Norman Yoffee and my fellow seminarians for an excellent and insightful IML seminar. I owe many thanks to Carla Sinopoli and Norman Yoffee for critically reading and assisting me in editing this chapter. I also place on record my gratitude to the anonymous reviewers of this chapter whose suggestions helped tighten the arguments. Many thanks to the publishers for their excellent work in fine-tuning this chapter. However, any failings herein are wholly mine.

Notes

1. Chronology for the Chalukyas comes from several inscriptions that mention the Saka era where Saka year 1 equals AD 78; dates also come from relative stylistic analyses of the numerous temples in the landscape.

2. See plan of Gaudergudi. I have not seen an illustration of the excavation under discussion.

3. This conclusion is not challenged seriously by anyone. However, Rao's dates for this temple and the occupation mound nearby do not agree with Sundara's (1984) later ascription. Nevertheless, this debate does not hinder my argument.

4. For instance, among the seven mother goddesses worshipped by the Dhangars (a pastoral community in southern Maharashtra moving into North Karnataka with their herds of sheep and goats), one of them is dongarci-Yallavva—goddess Yallavva of the hill that is the hill of Saundatti (Samvadatti) in the Belgaum district, Karnataka State (Sontheimer 1989, 40) The terms *-amma* and *-avva* mean "mother."

5. J. F. Fleet seemed to think that the temple was originally dedicated to the Jaina faith, first appropriated by the Brahmanas and then by the pastoral cult (Fleet, 1877).

6. Sage Jamadagni is the father of Parasurama, who is believed to be an incarnation of Lord Visnu, of the Hindu pantheon. Parasurama beheaded his mother, Renuka, on orders from his father, as she had committed an impure act. Due to Parasurama's pleading for his mother's life, sage Jamadagni decrees that Renuka be worshipped by all childless women in the hope of having worthy sons such as Parasurama himself.

7. The images are located at Naganathakolla near Badami, Mahakuta, Chikka Mahakuta, Siddhanakolla near Pattadakal, Bhadranayakana Jalihal, again near Pattadakal, and Bala Brahma temple at Alampur in Andhra Pradesh.

8. This is the same city where it is believed Lord Rama was born. In the sixth century AD, a majority of the narratives of the epic story of Rama did not deify him. By the tenth century, however, there are definite signs of deification of Rama, the perfect human being, in literature and architecture. The accounts that Ramesh bases

his argument on belong to tenth-century AD religious and popular literature; hence it is likely that historical events of the time are reflected in fictive claims.

Bibliography

Alcock, Susan E. 2002. *Archaeologies of the Greek Past: Landscape, Monuments, and Memories*. Cambridge: Cambridge University Press.

Bolon, Carol Radcliffe. 1981. Early Chalukyan Sculpture. Ph.D. diss., University of Pennsylvania.

——— 1997. *Forms of the Goddess Lajja-Gauri in India Art*. Delhi: Motilal Banarsidass Publishers.

Bradley, Richard. 1998. *The Significance of Monuments: On the Shaping of Human Experience in Neolithic and Bronze Age Europe*. London and New York: Routledge.

——— 2000. *An Archaeology of Natural Places*. London and New York: Routledge.

Dikshit, D. P. 1981. *Political History of the Chalukyas of Badami*. Delhi: Manager of Publications.

Fleet, J. F. 1877. Sanskrit and Old Canarese Inscriptions. *Indian Antiquary* 6:139.

Gazetteer of Belgaum. 1987. Vol 17. Karnataka, Bangalore: Printed by the Director of Print., Stationery and Publications at the Govt. Press.

Gazetteer of Bijapur. 1996. Vol 2. Karnataka, Bangalore: Printed by the Director of Print., Stationery and Publications at the Govt. Press.

Indian Antiquary (Bombay). 1879. Vol. 8.

——— 1882. Vol. 11.

——— 1892. Vol. 19.

Jaiswal, S. 1967. *Origin and Development of Vaisnavism*. Delhi: Oxford University Press.

Jha, D. N., ed. 2000. *The Feudal Order: State, Society and Ideology in Early Medieval India*. Delhi: Manohar.

Joshi, R. V. 1955. *Pleistocene Studies in the Malaprabha Basin*. Poona: Deccan College Post-Graduate and Research Institute, Poona and the Karnatak University, Dharwar.

Kramrisch, Stella. 1956. An Image of Aditi-Uttanapad. *Artibus Asiae* 19:259–70.

Meister, M. W., and M. A. Dhaky. 1986. *Encyclopaedia of Indian Temple Architecture: Upper Dravidadesa*. Vol. 1, Part 3. Delhi: Oxford University Press.

Michell, George. 1979. Malaprabha Valley. Figures on page 1 and page 47. In Praise of Badami, Aihole Mahakuta and Pattadakal. *Marg* (Bombay) 32 (1).

——— 2002. *Pattadakal: Monumental Legacy*. Oxford: Oxford University Press.

Moorti, U. S. 1994. *The Megalithic Culture of South India: Socio-Economic Perspectives*. Varanasi, India: Ganga Kaveri Publishing House.

Mukhia, H. 1981. Was There Feudalism in Indian History? *Journal of Peasant Studies* 8 (3): 273–310.

———, ed. 2000. *The Feudalism Debate*. Delhi: Manohar.

Ramesh, K. V. 1984. *Chalukyas of Vatapi*. Delhi: Agam Kala Prakashan.
Rao, S. R. 1972. A Note on the Chronology of the Early Chalukyan Temples. *Lalit Kala* 15:9–15.
—— 1978. *The Chalukyas of Badami*. Seminar papers. Ed. M. S. Nagaraja Rao. Bangalore: The Mythic Society.
Reddy, E. Shivanagi. 1994. Evolution of Building Technology in Early Andhra Pradesh (Up to the Fourteenth Century A.D.). Ph.D. thesis, Central University, Hyderabad.
Settar, S. 1979. In Praise of Badami, Aihole, Mahakuta and Pattadakal. Special Issue. *Marg* (Bombay) 32 (1).
Sharma, R. S. 1965. *Indian Feudalism*. Calcutta: University of Calcutta.
Shastry, N. K. 1960. *History of South India*. Delhi: Oxford University Press.
Sinopoli, Carla. 2003. Echoes of Empire: Vijayanagara and Historical Memory, Vijayanagara as Historical Memory. In *Archaeologies of Memory*, eds. Ruth M. Van Dyke and Susan E. Alcock, 17–33. Malden, Mass.: Blackwell.
Sontheimer, G. D. 1989. *Pastoral Deities in Western India*. New Delhi: Oxford University Press.
Sundara, A. 1975. *Early Chamber Tombs of South India*. Delhi: University Publishers (India).
—— 1979. Some Early Chalukyan Temples: Notes on Further Traces and Additions. *Quarterly Journal of the Mythic Society* 1–2. Bangalore: The Mythic Society.
—— 1984. Early Kadamba Temple Architecture: Recent Notices. *Quarterly Journal of the Mythic Society* 75 (3): 260–69.
Thapar, Romila. 2003. *A History of India*. New Delhi: Permanent Black.
Van Dyke, Ruth M., and Susan E. Alcock, eds. 2003. *Archaeologies of Memory*. Malden, Mass.: Blackwell.
Yazdani, G. 1960. *Early History of the Deccan*. London: Oxford University Press.
Zagarell, Allen. 1997. The Megalithic Graves of the Niligiri Mountains and Moyar Ditch. In *Blue Mountains Revisited: Cultural Studies on the Nilgiri Hills*, ed. Paul Hockings. Delhi: Oxford University Press.

8 Creating, Transforming, Rejecting, and Reinterpreting Ancient Maya Urban Landscapes
INSIGHTS FROM LAGARTERA AND MARGARITA

Laura P. Villamil

Scholars have long focused on ancient cities—their origins, patterns of growth and decline, and diversity in form and function—to understand the development of urban society as well as the evolution of social complexity (Blanton 1976; Childe 1950, 1957; Smith, M. 2003; Wheatley 1972). During the Classic Period (AD 250–800) the ancient Maya built hundreds of major civic-ceremonial centers, the material remains of which reveal the complexity of the society that thrived in them (fig. 8.1). Recent studies (e.g., Ashmore and Sabloff 2002; de Montmollin 1988; Houk 1996, 2003) have examined the ideological and sociopolitical factors responsible for the layout and composition of ancient Maya cities. These approaches have contributed to our understanding of the nature of ancient Maya centers and their regional role by exploring how ancient Maya elites used the built environment to *communicate* their power and authority, and thus how elites manipulated the built environment as a political strategy at local and regional levels.

For example, de Montmollin (1988) has argued that at the site of Tenam Rosario—a regional capital in Chiapas, Mexico—elites designed the built environment to reproduce spatially the polity's hierarchical and territorial organization in microcosm. De Montmollin maintains that this was an elite strategy aimed at politically integrating the capital and its territory. Other scholars have examined recurrent patterns in plaza and site plans, at both local and regional scales (e.g., Andrews 1975; Ashmore 1992; Becker 2003, 2004; Houk 2003). For instance, Wendy Ashmore (1986, 1989, 1991, 1992; Ashmore and Sabloff 2000, 2002) has suggested that some of these recurrent spatial patterns reflect site planning templates based on Maya cosmological principles. According to Ashmore, elites employed these site planning principles in order to (1) express and thus legitimate their power and authority, and (2) profess affiliation with elites from other important sites by emulating their building projects.

FIGURE 8.1 Map of the Yucatán Peninsula showing the location of Lagartera, Margarita, and other ancient Maya sites

Houk (1996, 2003) has added that these site planning principles can supply information on regional political histories.

What these studies do not address, however, is (1) how the built environment actually shapes, reinforces, and transforms social relations, and consequently how it *becomes* a source of power; (2) what role other social groups (that is, non-royal elites, commoners) played in shaping the built environment of Maya centers; and (3) how the built environment varied through time and between sites. Highlighting variability in the built environment and understanding the sources of this variability can give us additional insights into the nature, development, and regional role of Maya major centers. It may allow us to discover interesting patterns of social interaction that characterized these ancient cities and the various social strategies employed by the people who built and lived in them, as well as how these patterns and strategies changed through time and varied from site to site as Maya society evolved.

In this chapter I focus on the spatial and temporal variability evident in the material remains of two ancient Maya cities, Lagartera and Margarita, located in central Quintana Roo, Mexico. Spatial variability refers to the built environment and includes differences in layout, composition, and scale, whereas temporal variability focuses on the unique developmental trajectory of each center as well as how patterns in the built environment changed through time.

I focus on these two dimensions of variability—spatial and temporal—because, as I will discuss in more detail, the spaces created within and around these centers were fundamental in shaping, reinforcing, and transforming social relations. Cities were not fixed entities, passive settings supporting the theater of social life. They were constantly being transformed by the dynamic interaction between social groups at all scales, local to regional. In turn, the spaces created by these patterns of social interaction further shaped the nature of social relations. From this perspective, I explore how the ancient Maya created, transformed, and reinterpreted the urban landscapes at Lagartera and Margarita. I argue that the built environments of these two sites were the material manifestation of various (and cumulative) social and political strategies that shaped society throughout its long-term development.

The Spatial Dimension of Social Life

Increasingly, space (encompassing both the built environment and natural landscapes) is being recognized as a social construct (with cultural meaning), and as a dynamic dimension of social life that shapes, constrains, and reinforces social action (e.g., Lawrence and Low 1990; Ashmore and Knapp 1999; Smith, A. 2003; Tilley 1994). Because it is an integral part of social life, space is a key arena where social relations are played out. As Soja (1996, 46) points out, "all social relations become real and concrete, a part of our lived social existence, only when they are spatially 'inscribed'—that is, *concretely* represented—in the social production of social space." Therefore, exploring the cultural value (that is, ideological, political, religious, and/or economic) assigned to both human-made and natural spaces allows us to examine diversity in social strategies and how these further shape social interaction.

Social interaction occurs in time and space, it "takes place." Rules of behavior—the proper way to conduct oneself socially—have a spatial dimension. Because all social structures are, by definition, recurrent patterns of behavior, they often leave a material imprint. Because of this, the organization of society in space is a material product that results in patterns in the built environment. It is this concrete, material dimension of social space that becomes instrumental in producing and reinforcing social differences and inequalities, as well as in promoting social integration and group cohesion.

The Spatial Construction of Society

The built environment is an effective tool for shaping, reinforcing, and transforming social relations. Rapoport (1990) argues that the main purpose of the built environment—including buildings, platforms, walls, pathways, monuments—is to evoke particular behaviors in specific contexts by offering culturally specific cues that define the setting, as well as the rules of how and when to act. But this quality of the built environment goes beyond simply defining the activities or functions of buildings and other spaces. The built environment can also be used to communicate more abstract messages, such as group identity, social distinctions, or the nature of the social order (Lawrence and Low 1990; Moore 1996).

One way in which the built environment can shape social interaction is by defining patterns of behavior that create and reinforce social differences. These range from age and gender differences within the household to relationships of subordination and domination at the regional level. Individuals or groups with the necessary (ideological, economic, social) resources can create and/or manipulate spaces that define social boundaries. These are physical spaces that include and exclude social groups by allowing or restricting access, directing movement, and even prescribing appropriate modes of behavior. The built environment can evoke the social hierarchies and power differences present in society.

It becomes an effective disciplinary technology since "discipline proceeds from the distribution of individuals in space" (Foucault 1977, 141). The built environment allows people not only to take their place in society, but also to put others in their place. Therefore, the built environment can become a valuable social resource. As such, it is subject to competition over its construction (who can and cannot build certain types of buildings or spaces and where) and use (who has access to those spaces). Because of this, the built environment becomes the material manifestation of social and political strategies. Since the built environment is an instrument that helps establish social differences and unequal power relations, it is also a source of social power and prestige. Therefore, its control and manipulation is also a source of social conflict.

Creating social differences, whether ephemeral or permanent, by restricting access to specific spaces is common to all hierarchical societies. Even in societies where social distinctions are not institutionalized, men's and women's spaces are often clearly demarcated. Space can be used to create and reinforce gender differences within the household (for example, when women's and men's activity areas are clearly defined and often differentially valued), between the household and community (when there is a marked domestic/female vs. public/male dichotomy), and in the community (when women are restricted from entering certain socially valued spaces, such as men's houses). Beyond gender, social differences can be established through ritual initiation and reinforced by differential access to sacred spaces (for example, the "Made People" of the Northern Tiwa Pueblo, who increasingly restricted access to kivas [Fowles 2004; Ortiz 1969]).

In complex societies, the built environment can be used as the material means by which social distinctions and power relations are defined, institutionalized, and subsequently reproduced in society. "Power . . . is contextualized and made concrete, like all social relations, in the (social) production of (social) space" (Soja 1996, 86–87). Emerging elites with the necessary resources (charisma, ancestral claim, prestige, wealth, and/or moral authority) can use their influence and/or authority to define, control, and restrict access to socially valued spaces. One way to do this is by commissioning the construction of monumental buildings and spaces—by appropriating resources and the labor of others—that embody new social, religious, and political messages.

Trigger (1990) argues that the ubiquity and grandeur of monumental architecture in early civilizations are effective and enduring means to convey messages of social distinctions because they evoke the conspicuous consumption of human labor:

> Monumental architecture and personal luxury goods become symbols of power because they are seen as embodiments of large amounts of human energy and hence symbolize the ability of those for whom they were made to control such energy to an unusual degree. Furthermore, by participating in erecting monuments that glorify the power of the upper classes, peasant labourers are made to acknowledge their subordinate status and their sense of their own inferiority is reinforced. (125)

The result was the creation of dominant spaces that carried specific meanings or messages of exclusivity and social differentiation. Since the built environment affects patterns of behavior by directing the movement of people through space, it also becomes a powerful instrument of social control.

For example, in some ancient societies emerging elites coopted widely shared ritual practices and their associated spaces, appropriating labor and resources to build those socially charged spaces, and *regulated or restricted their access* to generate and institutionalize social differences. Swenson proposes that in the early complex societies of the Andes the manipulation of ritual violence (sacrifice), and the resulting "architectural patterns of ritual exclusivity" (2003, 263), were effective mechanisms for generating and institutionalizing social inequality. The spaces created within the ceremonial cores of major centers, where such rituals of violence took place, became "a source of great power . . . fiercely guarded and controlled by elite members of the population" (2003, 284).

In addition to shaping social relations by defining social distinctions, the built environment also reinforces these relations by reproducing specific modes of social interaction over generations. The built environment can be used to reproduce forms of social inequality because its perceived permanence allows the social distinctions it defines to appear timeless, natural, the "way things have always been." As Blanton (1989, 413) notes, "As a communications media [sic], monumental architecture is actually relatively efficient. The initial costs of construction may be great, but once built a massive building or plaza can be seen by thousands of people over great lengths of time, broadcasting continuously for even thousands of years." Because of this quality, the built environment can become instrumental in maintaining the social order. One way in which the built environment can be manipulated to re-create or maintain the social order is to control socially valued spaces (sacred places, monuments) over generations by building continually in the same locale (a common practice in the Maya area and in Mesoamerica in general). Another way is to emulate similar valued spaces, copying the building projects of predecessors, or those from faraway places that hold some special meaning and thus confer status. Some places become sources of power in themselves, and their control gives social currency to those who have control and access to them.

The built environment can also be used to transform society (e.g., Castells 1983). Another characteristic of the built environment is that it is malleable, modifiable, and subject to reinterpretation. Even though the built environment may be *perceived* as permanent and immutable, it can be modified and transformed. Although those with the resources to construct and maintain the most visible remains of the built environment are often the dominant elites, which means that what we often find is the remains of dominant spaces, elites were not the only ones responsible for the spatial form of ancient settlements. Other social groups were not passive recipients of elite conceptions of spatial order but actively participated in its making. Focusing on variability makes us aware that other social groups may have had their own social strategies and patterns of social interaction that were mapped onto the built environment. By examining how spatial patterns changed through time, we may be able to identify how space was negotiated between various social groups. This often takes the form of increased access to previously inaccessible spaces, such as areas near sacred precincts, increased number and elaboration of residences, and even emulation of elite patterns of spatial behavior.

Over time, people can begin identifying aspects of the built environment with a specific social order that reinforced particular modes of social interaction, or with specific social groups. Because of this, we may also be able to identify in the built environment significant social transformations, such as when a social group challenges or destroys the spaces associated with other groups. This transformation often takes the form of destruction or vandalism associated with war or conquest. However, we can also see similar phenomena manifested in less dramatic ways, such as when a group does not adhere to the spatial conventions of former times. The formality of previous spatial form is redefined (for example, from a formal ceremonial space to residential space), or even more actively modified (by looting, scavenging of materials, or razing). In the archaeological record of ancient settlements we can identify this less catastrophic, but no less socially significant, transformation of the built environment. Such transformations can be the material manifestation of a different social strategy: one that rejects a former social order and seeks to establish a new one.

Thus, exploring variability in the built environment of major centers in the Maya area and understanding the sources of this variability may allow us to recognize the process by which different social and political strategies were materialized in the urban landscape; how spatial strategies may have shaped, constrained, and reinforced social relations; and how these spatial strategies changed through time and varied from site to site.

Lagartera and Margarita

The sites of Lagartera and Margarita are located in the southern edge of the northern Maya lowlands, in the interior of present-day Quintana Roo, Mexico (fig. 8.1). Lagartera is approximately ninety kilometers northwest of the city of Chetumal, and Margarita is twenty-six kilometers south of Lagartera. I designed a program of archaeological research at these two sites specifically to investigate the sociopolitical factors responsible for their different layouts (Villamil and Sherman 2005; Villamil 2005). During a previous survey of south-central Quintana Roo, Peter Harrison (1981, 272–73) noted the existence of two recurring site layouts in this region of the Maya lowlands: sites consisting of a single core of monumental architecture versus sites consisting of multiple dispersed complexes. Lagartera and Margarita were among the sites reported as possible examples of each of these site plans. During an initial reconnaissance of the region in 1998, I confirmed that Lagartera consists of one contiguous monumental core, characteristic of the single-nucleus pattern. In contrast, Margarita is composed of multiple spatially dispersed complexes of monumental architecture, characteristic of the multiple-nuclei pattern.

In order to transcend the simple single-nucleus versus multiple-nuclei dichotomy, subsequent field research under my direction included detailed documentation of the layout, composition, and scale of the built environments at Lagartera and each of Margarita's complexes. Spatial data was obtained through survey and mapping, and chronological data, obtained through excavations, were used to identify patterns in the built environments and to reconstruct the history of occupation of each site. Comparing the layout, composition, temporal development, and regional context of Lagartera and Margarita revealed additional dimensions of variability that suggest the built environments at these two sites were the result of distinct sociopolitical strategies that changed through time.

Lagartera

During the 2002 field season, we intensively surveyed approximately fifty hectares around the single monumental core of Lagartera. In the course of this survey, we mapped 101 monumental structures in detail, as well as 115 additional cultural features, including residential mounds, house foundations, and walls.

Lagartera is characterized by the enormous volume of its civic-ceremonial architecture and by an emphasis on formal open spaces (fig. 8.2). The eastern third of the site core is dominated by the Ciudadela, a massive agglomeration of raised plazas covering six hectares and reaching fifteen meters in height. On these monumental platforms we find a series of open plazas, enclosed courtyards, temple platforms up to twenty-seven meters in height (structures 18 and 27), and range structures—long rectangular buildings that likely functioned as administrative buildings. The central third of the site core is a compact cluster of adjoining open plazas and patios. It includes the Main Plaza (Group 1) formed by four range structures averaging eighty meters in length and ten meters in height. To the west of the Main Plaza is an open plaza dominated by Structure 48, a temple platform eighteen meters high; to the north is the Acropolis, a massive platform supporting several buildings and an open plaza on its summit. In this central area we also find a series of residential patio groups as well as a ballcourt. Interestingly, the residential constructions are found only in this central part of the site and, in comparison with the elaborate and extensive residential zones at Margarita, they are modest

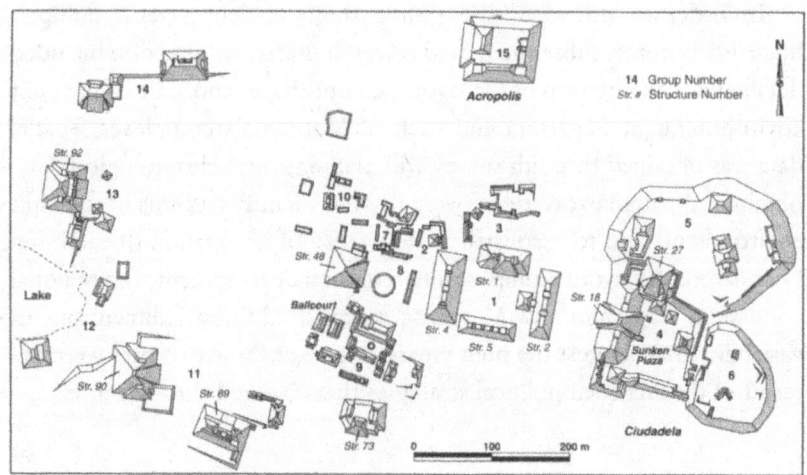

FIGURE 8.2 Lagartera, Quintana Roo, Mexico

in size and extent. The western third of the site is formed by an arc of freestanding monumental structures enclosing an extensive open area. It includes the largest temple at the site, Structure 90 (thirty-eight meters high), in addition to three triadic structures—platforms supporting three temples that enclose a raised courtyard (structures 92, 89, and 73).

Excavations throughout the core of Lagartera allowed us to reconstruct the temporal development of the site. Details on the nature of these and other chronological details are described elsewhere (Villamil and Sherman 2005; Villamil 2005). Below I summarize the broadest temporal trends.

The initial occupation of Lagartera dates to the Middle Preclassic Period (ca. 600–400 BC). The limited distribution and small number of unmixed cultural deposits dating to this period indicate that the settlement at this time may have been no larger than a small farming village. During the Late Preclassic Period (400 BC–AD 250), however, Lagartera's monumental core underwent significant growth. At this time we have the first evidence of monumental construction, including the deposition of great amounts of fill to level plazas and patios, as well as the construction of overlying floors. These activities signal the initial building phases of associated civic-ceremonial structures. The distribution of ceramic material indicates that many of the primary civic-ceremonial spaces—and therefore the locus of ritual, royal, and administrative activity—were already being defined by the Late Preclassic. This also suggests that Lagartera was becoming a central place of some regional importance by this time.

Lagartera continued to grow through the Early Classic (AD 250–550), reaching its peak of construction by the end of this period. Existing structures, plazas, and patios were enlarged while new buildings appeared. The data indicate that the bulk of the Ciudadela complex was built at this time. Excavations in this complex support the idea that the Ciudadela was built during a single substantial construction effort in the early part of the Early Classic. Although it is quite probable that future excavations in the Ciudadela will expose earlier (and even later) stages of construction, our data at present point to a primarily Early Classic occupation.

During the Early Classic there is evidence of strong connections between Lagartera and sites in the northern Petén in Guatemala, most likely with the city of Tikal. Lagartera participated in the northern Petén ceramic sphere (Tzakol), evidenced by the presence of Early Classic Petén gloss wares. Another connection is the shared stylistic conventions by Tikal and Lagartera as seen on Stela 1 from Lagartera (Villamil 2005). The posture and regalia of the ruler depicted on this fragmentary monument are similar to those seen on some of the earliest stelae at Tikal. It was during the Early Classic expansion of Tikal's influence that the practice of erecting commemorative stelae became widespread. At this point little can be said about similarities or differences in architectural style, as exposed architecture is absent at Lagartera.

Given its scale, and the emphasis on monumental civic-ceremonial architecture and spaces at Lagartera, it seems likely that Lagartera was one of the primary regional centers in central Quintana Roo during the Early Classic. In terms of monumentality and extent, there are only two other comparable centers in the region: Chacchoben and Chichmuul (fig. 8.1). Chacchoben, located fifty kilometers southeast of Lagartera and the only other site in this part of central Quintana Roo that has been investigated in recent years, is reported to have had a major Early Classic occupation (Romero 2000). Although Chacchoben is comparable to Lagartera in architectural composition and scale, also being characterized by large temples and massive platform groups, its extent is approximately half that of Lagartera. Chichmuul, thirty kilometers to the east of Lagartera, has not been investigated since it was initially registered and partially mapped by Peter Harrison (1981). Although Chichmuul appears to rival Lagartera in terms of architectural monumentality, its extent is unknown. Robert Fry's (1973) ceramic analyses suggest a major occupation at Chichmuul during the Early Classic, with construction continuing into the Late Classic (AD 550–800). This contrasts with the temporal pattern found at Lagartera.

Beyond scale, Lagartera's regional importance can be inferred from the prominence of special-purpose architectural groups (large temples and range structures, massive platforms, and the ballcourt), large open plazas for public ceremonies, and the presence of carved monuments. Lagartera's massive constructions attest to the ability of an elite class to extract and concentrate great amounts of labor and resources. The Early Classic Stela 1 indicates that Lagartera had a king in office at this time. These different lines of evidence point to the development, during the Early Classic Period, of a strong centralized authority structure, perhaps with the aid, under the auspices of, or even under the direct subordination of, the expanding Tikal state.

During the Late Classic, most sites in the Maya lowlands experienced expansion, continuous monumental construction, and a significant increase in population. In contrast, our evidence indicates there was a sharp decline in monumental construction and occupation at Lagartera during this period. Occupation and construction activity during the Late Classic appear to have been restricted to the core residential area and to the Main Plaza (Groups 1, 2, 3, and 9). This pattern contrasts sharply with the Early Classic apogee.

However, until we obtain data from the residential areas around the monumental core, it will not be possible to judge whether this pattern of decline extends to the surrounding hinterland. Even if the surrounding habitation areas were still occupied and thriving, such a dramatic decline in construction in the monumental core—which, after all, was the locus of administration and other kinds of elite activity—suggests a major change, weakening, or perhaps even a collapse of the authority structure (ruler and supporting elites) that sustained Lagartera as a regional center during the Early Classic. It may not be a coincidence that it is during the Early to Late Classic transition that sites in the Petén, primarily Tikal, also experience a temporary decline, the so-called Middle Classic Hiatus, thought to be the result of a combination of warfare, conquest, and adverse environmental circumstances (Chase and Chase 2000; Robichaux 2000; Willey 1974).

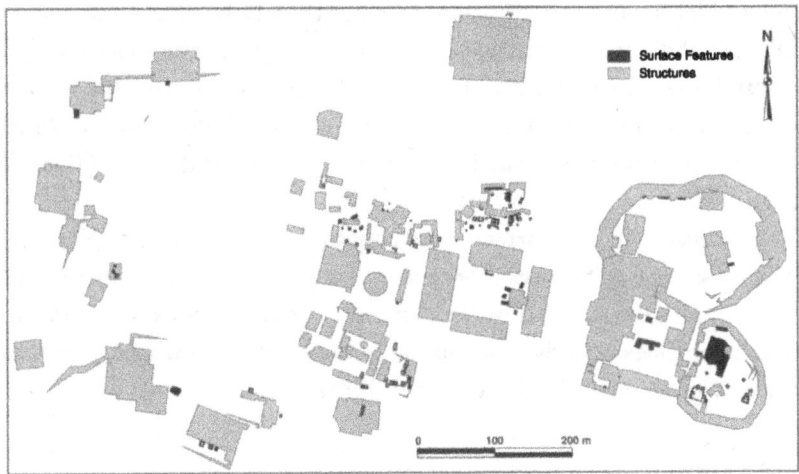

FIGURE 8.3 Lagartera, distribution of surface features interpreted as evidence for a Terminal Classic reoccupation of the site

At Lagartera, the Terminal Classic (AD 800–1000) is difficult to characterize. Ceramically, it marks the last occupation of the core of the site. Terminal Classic deposits appear in the uppermost levels of many of the excavation units, but these deposits postdate final floor construction episodes. The distribution of Terminal Classic material coincides with the presence of modest architectural features, such as small circular or apsidal house foundations, very low rectangular platforms, and low walls that appear to be house-lot boundaries. These features were constructed using building materials obtained from nearby structures (fig. 8.3). This suggests a pattern of widespread reoccupation of the site core without major construction, perhaps consisting of a squatter population building perishable structures.

That this is a reoccupation of the site, and not just the last episode in an unbroken sequence of continuous occupation, is implied by the dramatic departure from the previous formal spatial arrangement of public and ceremonial buildings, plazas, and patios at the site. This indicates not only a completely different spatial organization; the nature of this reoccupation appears to have been primarily residential and occurred *after* the site appears to have been abandoned.

This reoccupation is a widespread pattern found at most sites in the southern interior of Quintana Roo. Peter Harrison (1979) was the first one to identify this reoccupation, naming it the Lobil phase, and assigning it to the Late Postclassic (after AD 1250). Subsequent archaeological research in southern Quintana Roo revealed that it was probably a much earlier occupation, Terminal Classic, given that no Postclassic material was found directly associated with similar features at that site (Villamil 1995).

Our research at Lagartera and Margarita supports the interpretation that these surface features represent a Terminal Classic reoccupation of the site. This is suggested by the patterning of Terminal Classic material, which coincides with the distribution of these small residences, as well as the lack of ceramics that postdate the Terminal Classic.

Margarita

Margarita is a multiple-nuclei center, composed of four complexes of civic-ceremonial and elaborate residential architecture: a central complex (Complex A) surrounded by complexes to the east (Complex B), south (Complex C), and north (Complex D; not mapped) (fig. 8.4).

The investigations at Margarita during 2000 focused primarily on the central, eastern, and southern complexes. In these zones we intensively surveyed a total of forty-two hectares, locating and mapping in detail 242 monumental structures and 389 additional cultural features—including low residential mounds, house foundations, walls, wells, and quarries. There is ample evidence of dense household remains in the areas between the major architectural complexes. However, these intermediate regions have yet to be surveyed.

For the purposes of this chapter I will focus primarily on Complex A (for a more detailed description of all of Margarita's complexes see Villamil and Sherman 2005; Villamil 2005). Complex A is the most extensive of Margarita's complexes (fig. 8.5). It is dominated by three main plazas (groups 2, 4, and 5) defined by large range structures. One of these plazas (Group 4) contains a smaller nested quadrangle group that may have been the residential compound of the city's most elite family. Some 250 meters south of the main plazas lies the Acropolis, the only truly monumental construction in Complex A. The Acropolis comprises a massive platform measuring approximately one hundred meters by eighty meters at its base and rising to a height of eight meters. On its summit another large platform, seven meters

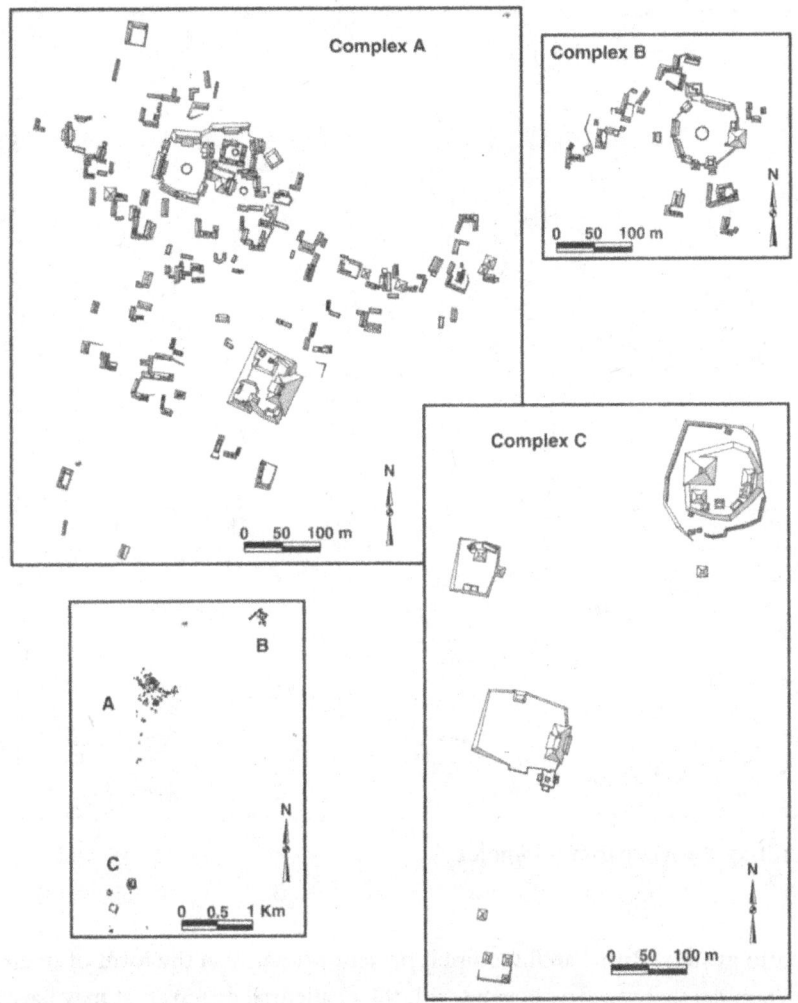

FIGURE 8.4 Margarita, Quintana Roo, Mexico, complexes A, B, and C

high, supporting three additional buildings on its summit, dominates the eastern half of the main platform. The western half of the Acropolis has an open plaza with two sunken patios, with additional buildings to the north and south of the central raised plaza.

What distinguishes Margarita's Complex A, however, is a dense concentration of elaborate residential groups and a relative absence of monumental ceremonial architecture and associated spaces. The vast majority of structures constitute small and relatively private household

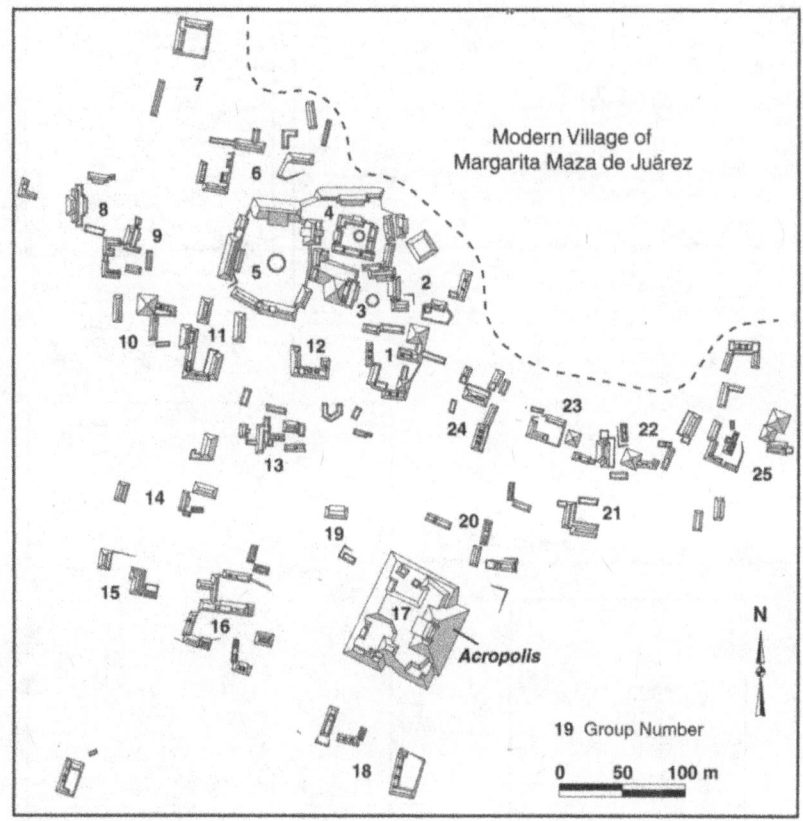

FIGURE 8.5 Margarita, Complex A

patio groups. Ritual architecture is present primarily in the form of small pyramidal structures associated with the residential groups that may have served as ancestral shrines.

Similar to the pattern found at Lagartera, the initial occupation of Margarita's Complex A occurred during the Middle Preclassic. Unlike the pattern found at Lagartera, however, redeposited Middle Preclassic material was relatively rare in later deposits. We interpret the scarcity of Middle Preclassic material as indicating a very small occupation. Complex A at this time was probably a hamlet consisting of no more than a few households.

The first evidence for the formal construction of plazas and monumental platforms in Complex A is associated with Late Preclassic material.

This material was found in plaza fill deposits sealed by one or more Late Preclassic plaza floors. These units concentrate primarily around the central plazas. In addition, three other areas show considerable Late Preclassic activity: the Acropolis, whose main platform may have been built in its entirety during this period; a small plaza (Group 25) associated with two small pyramidal structures, located on the east edge of the site; and another small plaza (Group 8) on the west edge of the site. This distribution suggests that a small core of public space, and at least some of the associated public architecture, was established by the Late Preclassic. At this time, Margarita's Complex A might have become a relatively minor civic-ceremonial center.

This trend continues into the Early Classic, where we have evidence for continuing plaza construction. This construction activity, however, is concentrated primarily in the same areas where we saw construction during the previous period. We found no evidence for any significant growth in settlement.

In contrast to Lagartera, it is during the Late Classic that Margarita's Complex A grows to its present extent and likely reaches its peak of construction and maximum population. Most excavations yielded Late Classic material, including new areas that were occupied for the first time during this period. In addition, construction continued in the main plazas. The Late Classic pattern of occupation appears to have continued through the transition into the Terminal Classic. However, most of the deposits associated with Terminal Classic ceramics are primarily surface deposits and, as was the case with Lagartera, postdate the final plaza and patio floor constructions. However, we identified a floor dating to the Terminal Classic as the final construction episode of a patio associated with a small pyramidal structure on the east edge of the site (Group 22). In addition, we uncovered two Terminal Classic burials that had been placed within the patio of a western residential group (Group 9).

As was the case with Lagartera, there is ample evidence for a subsequent reoccupation of Margarita's Complex A. In Margarita's case, this reoccupation appears to have been much more intense and covered a larger area (fig. 8.6). In Margarita's Complex A we recorded approximately 300 simple house foundations, low platforms, and a system of walls distributed throughout the survey area.

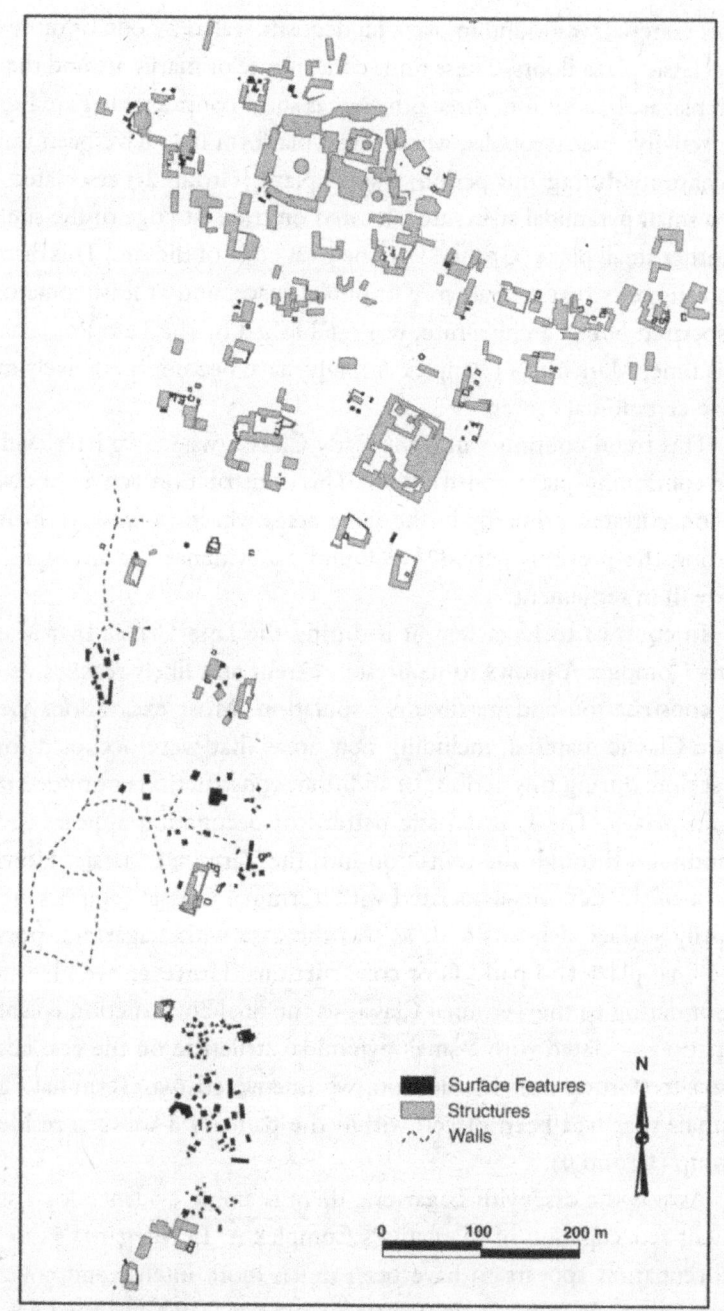

FIGURE 8.6 Margarita, Complex A, distribution of surface features interpreted as evidence for a Terminal Classic reoccupation of the site

Divergent Urban Patterns as Materialized Sociopolitical Strategies

Investigations of the spatial organization and developmental histories of Lagartera and Margarita brought to light two additional dimensions of variability, one spatial and the other temporal. In the spatial dimension, beyond the simple single-nucleus versus multiple-nuclei dichotomy, the two sites differ considerably in the details of their internal architectural composition and spatial organization. The emphasis of Lagartera's built environment is on monumental civic-ceremonial architecture, reflected both in architecture and in formal open spaces, as well as the limited residential areas within the site core. In contrast, Margarita is notable for the number and density of its elaborate residential groups and the much reduced emphasis on public architecture and ceremonial spaces.

In addition, the spatial differences between Lagartera and Margarita have a significant temporal dimension. Our investigations revealed that although Margarita and Lagartera were roughly contemporaneous, with occupation spanning from the Middle Preclassic to the Terminal Classic, each site's distinct spatial pattern was the product of divergent developmental trajectories. Lagartera emerged as an important center earlier, growing considerably during the Late Preclassic, reaching its peak during the Early Classic, and declining soon thereafter. In contrast, Margarita's growth was very gradual during the Late Preclassic and Early Classic, intensifying only during the Late Classic. By the end of the Late Classic both sites appeared to have been mostly abandoned. However, also at both sites, we have evidence of a minor—and relatively brief—reoccupation during the Terminal Classic.

Based on these two case studies, I suggest that the distinct spatial patterns resulted from changing sociopolitical strategies intended to shape interactions between social groups within the context of the formation, maturation, and collapse of a regional polity in central Quintana Roo. One strategy, represented by the built environment at Lagartera, was adopted in the Late Preclassic (400 BC–AD 250) and Early Classic (AD 250–550) period of state formation. A second strategy, which emerged during the Late Classic (AD 550–800) as the state matured and the sociopolitical system was restructured, was materialized in the built environment at Margarita. Finally, a third strategy is exemplified by the pattern of reoccupation at both sites, which followed the collapse of the regional sociopolitical system during the Terminal Classic to Postclassic transition (AD 900–1100).

The Late Preclassic to Early Classic Strategy: Creating Social Difference

During the Late Preclassic and Early Classic the emphasis was placed on the construction of monumental architecture and formal civic-ceremonial spaces. During these periods, the core of Lagartera comprised large, open ceremonial spaces (paved plazas surrounded by imposing temples and range structures) as well as highly inaccessible monumental complexes (limited-access plazas and courtyard groups) that may have been the exclusive domains of emerging elites. Residential architecture *within* the monumental core was minimal, and access to it may have been highly restricted. In the Late Preclassic and Early Classic, population aggregation was not emphasized. Based on this evidence, I argue that a built environment was created that emphasized difference and thus helped to define, and eventually to institutionalize, social distinctions. This strategy was used as a means of legitimizing the emergence of a new social order centered on the institution of divine kingship and its links to the supernatural.

Lagartera grew dramatically during the Late Preclassic, reaching its peak of construction in the Early Classic. It was during this period that states were established in the Maya lowlands for the first time. The formation of these states involved a shift from a kin-based social structure (typically found in pre-state societies) to one characterized by social stratification—extreme social distinctions and hierarchy, class differentiation, and social inequality. To support this process of sociopolitical transformation, an ideology that justified the new social order emerged. As Van Buren and Richards (2000, 4) note,

> Ideologies of order and hierarchy within that order were of fundamental importance to early states in which large populations were organized by novel means, and rulers attempted to maintain control during periods of rapid political and economic change. Civic order resulted from the creation of new institutions, the imposition of laws, and the use of coercion, but worldly order was generated by incorporating

society into a broader, more perfectly ordered cosmological whole. Elites played a critical role in this endeavor as they occupied the point of articulation between society, the gods, and the privileged dead.

For the ancient Maya, and other Mesoamerican groups, this manifested in the development of an ideology of separate descent (Marcus 1992). While emerging elites claimed divine and celestial origins, commoners were considered to be descendants of ancestors made of earth or clay. In this way, elites not only established themselves as intermediaries between the supernatural and society, but they also sanctified their right to rule (Marcus 1992, 224–25). As mediators between the supernatural and society, elites, and rulers in particular, became responsible for the maintenance of the cosmic order as well as the well-being of their subjects—conditions that further legitimized divine kingship and social inequality (Houston and Stuart 1996; Webster 2002a, 434).

Ruling elites elaborated widely shared ritual practices such as ancestor veneration (Lucero 2003; McAnany 1995, 1998) and used their religious authority to commission the construction of monumental temples and ceremonial spaces for the performance of rituals that maintained the cosmic and social order (Freidel and Schele 1988). Stephen Houston and David Stuart (1996, 294) suggest that temples, considered "god houses," and the gods themselves, were "possessed" or owned by rulers. They add that rulers not only incorporated references to deities in their personal names, but they also assumed their identities through ritual impersonation. This further reinforced rulers' connection with the supernatural. Elite status was also reinforced by privileged access to special food and drink, objects of personal ornamentation and clothing, as well as distinct mortuary rites (Marcus 1992, 240). The most privileged of the elite, such as rulers, were buried within monumental pyramid-temples erected in their honor. Some royal ancestors came to be revered as divine.

These developments had a significant effect on the structuring of the built environment. Elizabeth DeMarrais, L. J. Castillo, and T. K. Earle (1996) argue that ideologies become important sources of power through their materialization. Once they are given concrete form, ideologies may be controlled, manipulated, and extended beyond the groups that originally subscribed to them. In the Maya area, an ideology that emphasized social differences—encompassing the myth of separate descent, divinely sanctioned kingship, and the role of the ruling elite in the maintenance of the cosmic order—was materialized in the built environment beginning in the Late Preclassic. Indeed, some of the largest religious architecture (temple pyramids, triadic platforms) and ceremonial spaces ever built in the Maya lowlands were constructed during this period (e.g., at El Mirador [Hansen 2001]).

As I have argued, the built environment may be used as a means of materially defining, institutionalizing, and reproducing social distinctions in society. Monumental architecture becomes a source of power by efficiently conveying the authority of the ruling elite to harness massive amounts of human energy and resources (Trigger 1990). Dominant elites control these socially valued spaces by restricting their access. Space within the emerging Late Preclassic/Early Classic Maya centers such as Lagartera became increasingly specialized and segregated. The creation of formal, restricted spaces associated with monumental architecture added a new dimension of social differentiation by reinforcing elite exclusivity (Joyce 2000, 71). As Michael Love (1999) has argued, such spatial "regionalization" (Giddens 1985) is vital in establishing and reinforcing social differences: "Exclusionary practices may seek to control when and where social interaction takes place between members of various social groups. The maintenance of dominance is in part dependent upon promoting social distance between elites and other groups" (Love 1999, 129). Commoners likely had access to these civic-ceremonial spaces during special occasions, such as public ceremonies, ritual events, and/or market days, but for the most part their everyday activities took place in the periphery. As regal-ritual spaces were segregated from the rest of the community, marked as distinct from the everyday experience of most people, social distinctions were reinforced and naturalized.

The emerging elites of the Late Preclassic and the ruling elites of Early Classic Lagartera imposed order in society by manipulating the scale, composition, and layout of the built environment. This strategy included the construction of massive and highly restricted sacred precincts such as the Ciudadela in the eastern part of the site, imposing temple pyramids (structures 18, 27, 48, 90), and triadic platforms with largely inaccessible courtyards (structures 73, 89, 92). Another intriguing characteristic of Lagartera's civic-ceremonial core is that it is, for the most part, vacant. The few residential patio groups at the center of the site that date to the Late Preclassic/Early Classic likely housed the royal elite and their retainers. It is interesting to note that the scale of these residential areas is still quite modest in comparison to the monumentality and elaboration of public architecture. Although royal residences do not appear to have been highly elaborate, their location within the monumental core—that is, spatially segregated from the rest of the population—may have been an equally effective means of emphasizing differentiation.

In sum, the built environment at Lagartera represents a strategy that emphasized and reinforced social difference. The preponderance of monumental civic-ceremonial architecture and spaces at Lagartera indicates that public display as well as governance were important functions of this center during the Late Preclassic and Early Classic. The grandiose plazas and buildings not only provided appropriate settings for public ceremonies but also reinforced the regal nature of Lagartera. Exclusivity and spatial segregation reinforced the special status of elites and helped to legitimize their rule during the formation of a regional state in central Quintana Roo.

The Late Classic Strategy: Inclusion and Diffusion of Power

The Early Classic to Late Classic transition was a period of sociopolitical restructuring throughout the Maya lowlands. Hieroglyphic inscriptions at various sites documented competition and conflict between major regional polities, including Tikal, Calakmul, and Caracol. This conflict resulted in the defeat of Tikal by Caracol, an event that led to decreased regional influence by the former center (the Hiatus from AD 562–692) and the rise of rival Calakmul (Martin and Grube 2000, 40).

By the end of the Early Classic, monumental construction at Lagartera appears to have halted. This decline may have been linked to the events described above. Lagartera's rise to prominence in central Quintana Roo may have been related to its ties with Tikal. During Tikal's temporary decline, Calakmul appears to have spread its influence northward. Indeed, references to the Calakmul polity on monuments at Dzibanché and as far north as Y'okop (or Okop), located approximately 100 kilometers north of Lagartera (Martin and Grube 2000, 103–4), suggest that the expansion of Calakmul's influence may have significantly affected the sociopolitical system in Quintana Roo. It may, in fact, have precipitated the decline of Lagartera as a primary regional center.

Throughout the Late Preclassic and Early Classic periods, Margarita had remained a minor center. Although its relationship to Lagartera is not yet well understood, Margarita's complexes A and B (and perhaps Complex D) experienced significant growth following Lagartera's decline at the end of the Early Classic. Complex C, whose monumental architecture and formal plazas suggest it was an important ceremonial locus during the Early Classic, was abandoned at this time. In the other Margarita complexes, considerable construction activity transformed the character of the built environment, signaling a reorganization of urban space.

Space within the civic-ceremonial cores at Margarita became more inclusive, more truly urban in nature during the Late Classic. Concurrent with a significant decrease in monumentality and reduced emphasis on ceremonial architecture, there was a dramatic increase in the construction of elaborate residential patio groups nucleated around civic-ceremonial plazas. I suggest that this new Late Classic urban pattern represents a shift in the political strategy of elites from one of exclusion and extreme concentration of power in the hands of royal elites to one that emphasized the incorporation of, and diffusion of, power among non-royal elite groups.

Throughout the Maya lowlands, the Late Classic was a period of overall population growth and prosperity as well as increasing inter-elite competition, factionalism, and conflict (Pohl and Pohl 1994; Webster 2002a, 442). Epigraphic and archaeological evidence indicates that along with these changing conditions, new political strategies emerged that incorporated greater numbers of non-royal nobles into the affairs of state. There is evidence of the creation of new political offices, including the appearance for the first time of non-royal elite titles in hieroglyphic inscriptions (W. Fash 1991, 160–65; Houston 1993, 130–34). Previously, such inscriptions had been concerned exclusively with documenting the life events, ceremonies, and political exploits of rulers. In conjunction with the appearance of new titles, non-royal elites began to commission monuments—hieroglyphic benches and stelae—to document their own genealogies, participation in important ceremonies, and political offices (W. Fash 1991, 162). At Copán, the construction of a *popol na* (mat house, or council house), a building in which lineage leaders or representatives of the polity's major subdivisions may have gathered to discuss the affairs of the kingdom, has been interpreted as a power-sharing strategy that differed significantly from an emphasis on the absolute power of a divine king (B. Fash et al., 1992).

This power-sharing strategy may have been materialized in the residential architecture as well. For instance, increasingly elaborate elite residential patio groups became more common at Copán during the Late Classic. David Webster (2001, 157) notes,

> Although we can detect impressive residences outside the Main Group before this time, around or shortly after AD 650 some of them began to include larger subplatforms and well-built masonry superstructures, often vaulted or enhanced with sculpture. . . . [T]he permanency of these constructions . . . tended to both differentiate them from the largely perishable structures of the common farmers who formed the bulk of the population and make them much more like the royal structures at the Main Group. If such permanency was formerly a royal household prerogative, it was eventually appropriated by others.

I suggest that a new ideology of incorporation and greater diffusion of power was also materialized in the built environment at Margarita during the Late Classic. The dense concentration of elaborate residential groups in complexes A, B, and D at this site suggests that a new sociopolitical strategy, in which a wider range of social groups were incorporated into the urban cores, was adopted. Indeed, the density of elaborate Late Classic residential groups at Margarita differed markedly from the earlier pattern found at Lagartera.

The Terminal Classic Strategy: Reoccupation and Rejection

In the central and southern Maya lowlands, the Terminal Classic was a period of radical social transformation marked by the collapse of the social and political order that had been sustained throughout the Classic Period. Although a review of the complexity of events and causes leading to the collapse is beyond the scope of this chapter (but see Demarest, Rice, and Rice, 2004; Webster 2002b), fragile sociopolitical systems, warfare, and environmental pressures have all been implicated. The material manifestation of this sociopolitical transformation included the end of the elite-focused high cultural complex of the Classic Period (for example, monuments, art, hieroglyphic inscriptions, architecture) as well as a sudden halt in construction at, and subsequent abandonment of, most Classic Maya centers.

Centers in central Quintana Roo suffered a similar fate. Our evidence indicates little monumental construction at Lagartera and Margarita after the Late Classic. Nevertheless, the widespread distribution of Terminal Classic ceramic material at both centers indicates that although new construction ceased, the sites were not completely abandoned. This final occupation was, however, radically different from what had come before. There is ample material evidence that for the first time commoners' houses (indicated by foundations for perishable structures or simple low platforms), lot walls, and other associated features were located *within* the monumental cores of Lagartera and Margarita. Rather than being evidence of a sequence of occupation continuing from the Late Classic, I interpret these architectural remains as evidence of a *reoccupation* following the collapse of the Classic Period sociopolitical structure and the abandonment of both centers by the elites, their retainers, and even well-positioned commoners who previously resided there. The new Terminal Classic residents were humble commoners—likely farmers—whose predecessors probably had inhabited the peripheries of the centers in earlier periods. This reoccupation was characterized by a drastic departure from, or even overt rejection of, the previous spatial order. Abandoned Classic-Period structures were modified to form modest household platforms; stone was indiscriminately quarried from the earlier buildings and reused for house foundations, lot walls, and other residential features; and ceremonial spaces that had been quite formal were completely transformed.

Similar reoccupations of abandoned cities during or immediately after this period of sociopolitical turmoil have been reported elsewhere in the Maya lowlands, such as at Copán (Fash, Andrews, and Manahan 2004, 283), Tikal, and Dos Pilas (Houston 1993, 47; Webster 2002b, 277). In the Dos Pilas example, villagers tore down the façades of monumental Classic-Period structures in order to obtain stone for the construction of house platforms and foundations as well as two concentric walls enclosing the center of the site (see Martin and Grube 2000, 66–67 for an excellent reconstruction). These constructions have been interpreted as defensive measures in a region that was characterized by endemic warfare (Demarest et al. 1997). Elsewhere, including at Lagartera, Margarita, and other sites in Quintana Roo, there is no evidence of warfare or an external threat that would explain the movement of people from the countryside into the cores of the abandoned cities. Although we identified an extensive system of walls in Margarita's Complex A, these most likely functioned as pathways, lot markers, and perhaps even boundaries between neighborhoods.

As I have argued, built environments may become identified with the social groups that created them, as well as with particular social orders reinforcing certain modes of social interaction. Because of this, the destruction of religious and elite architecture, the appropriation of previously formal spaces like plazas, and the transformation of formal civic-ceremonial spaces into squatter villages may be interpreted as an overt rejection of the previous social order. Thus, the final occupation at Lagartera and Margarita during the Terminal Classic represents a new strategy of appropriation and rejection that was materialized in the built environment.

One of the major difficulties in understanding the nature and role of ancient Maya centers derives from the fact that the material remains preserved at most major centers are the result of sequences of construction spanning long periods of time. Because the final form of an ancient Maya center often comprises many superimposed layers of construction, variability in the spatial strategies employed in the creation of a built environment may be extremely difficult to infer. Further, due to the relative permanence of architecture, once a spatial order has been established, subsequent construction often must be adapted to what is already present. Because of this, distinct spatial strategies may not be recognizable in the built environment of a single site. However, *comparative* investigations of divergent urban patterns that developed at different times within a single region—such as those documented at Lagartera and Margarita—may highlight dimensions of variability that provide us with additional insights into the nature, development, and role of ancient Maya centers. Understanding the source of this variability—the sociopolitical factors underlying the creation of distinct built environments—can illuminate various social processes that shaped society through its long-term development. Focusing on what Edward Soja (1989, 127) calls "the historical sequence of spatialities" will undoubtedly add a different dimension to our understanding of ancient Maya civilization.

Acknowledgments

I want to thank Norm Yoffee for the opportunity to contribute to this volume. I also wish to acknowledge the Consejo de Arqueología of INAH-México for permission to conduct the field research. Fieldwork was supported by grants from the National Science Foundation (BCS-0083571), the Ahau Foundation, and the University of Michigan. I also want to thank Peter Harrison for his interest in and support of this research; Joyce Marcus for her advice and encouragement; Adriana Velázquez Morlet, director of Centro INAH Quintana Roo for institutional support; and anonymous reviewers for their constructive criticism of an earlier version of this chapter.

Bibliography

Andrews, George F. 1975. *Maya Cities: Placemaking and Urbanization*. Norman: University of Oklahoma Press.

Ashmore, Wendy. 1986. Peten Cosmology in the Maya Southeast: An Analysis of Architecture and Settlement Patterns at Classic Quirigua. In *The Southeast Maya Periphery*, eds. Patricia A. Urban and Edward M. Shortman, 35–49. Austin: University of Texas Press.

—— 1989. Construction and Cosmology: Politics and Ideology in Lowland Maya Settlement Patterns. In *Word and Image in Maya Culture: Explorations in Language, Writing, and Representation*, eds. William F. Hanks and Don S. Rice, 272–86. Salt Lake City: University of Utah Press.

—— 1991. Site Planning Principles and Concepts of Directionality among the Ancient Maya. *Latin American Antiquity* 2:199–226.

—— 1992. Deciphering Maya Architectural Plans. In *New Theories on the Ancient Maya*, eds. Elin C. Danien and Robert J. Sharer, 173–84. Philadelphia: University of Pennsylvania.

Ashmore, Wendy, and A. Bernard Knapp, eds. 1999. *Archaeologies of Landscape: Contemporary Perspectives*. Malden, Mass.: Blackwell.

Ashmore, Wendy, and Jeremy A. Sabloff. 2000. El Orden del Espacio en los Planes Cívicos Mayas. In *Memoria de la Segunda Mesa Redonda de Palenque: Architectura e Ideología de los Antiguos Mayas*, ed. Silvia Trejo, 15–33. México, D. F.: Instituto Nacional de Antropología e Historia.

—— 2002. Spatial Orders in Maya Civic Plans. *Latin American Antiquity* 13:199–226.

Becker, Marshal J. 2003. Plaza Plans at Tikal: A Research Strategy for Inferring Social Organization and Processes of Culture Change at Lowland Maya Sites. In *Tikal: Dynasties, Foreigners, and Affairs of State*, ed. Jeremy A. Sabloff, 253–80. Santa Fe: School of American Research Press.

—— 2004. Maya Heterarchy as Inferred from Classic-Period Plaza Plans. *Ancient Mesoamerica* 15:127–38.

Blanton, Richard E. 1976. Anthropological Studies of Cities. *Annual Review of Anthropology* 5:249–64.

―― 1989. Continuity and Change in Public Architecture: Periods I through V of the Valley of Oaxaca, Mexico. In *Monte Alban's Hinterland Part II: Settlement Patterns in Tlacolula, Etla, and Ocotlán, Valley of Oaxaca, Mexico,* eds. Stephen Kowaleski, Gary M. Feinman, Richard Blanton, Laura Finsten, and Linda Nichols, 409–47. Ann Arbor: Museum of Anthropology, University of Michigan.

Castells, Manuel. 1983. *The City and the Grassroots: A Cross-cultural Theory of Urban Social Movements.* Berkeley: University of California Press.

Chase, Arlen F., and Diane Z. Chase. 2000. Sixth and Seventh Century Variability in the Southern Maya Lowlands: Centralization and Integration at Caracol. In *The Years without Summer: Tracing A.D. 536 and Its Aftermath,* ed. Joel D. Gunn, 55–65. Oxford: Archaeopress.

Childe, V. Gordon. 1950. The Urban Revolution. *Town Planning Review* 21:3–17.

―― 1957. Civilization, Cities, Towns. *Antiquity* 31:36–38.

Demarest, Arthur A., Matt O'Mansky, Claudia Wolley, Dirk Van Tuerenhout, Takeshi Inomata, Joel Palka, and Héctor Escobedo. 1997. Classic Maya Defensive Systems and Warfare in the Petexbatun Region. *Ancient Mesoamerica* 8:229–53.

Demarest, Arthur A., Prudence M. Rice, and Don S. Rice, eds. 2004. *The Terminal Classic in the Maya Lowlands: Collapse, Transition, and Transformation.* Boulder: University Press of Colorado.

DeMarrais, Elizabeth, Luis Jaime Castillo, and Timothy K. Earle. 1996. Ideology, Materialization, and Power Strategies. *Current Anthropology* 37:15–31.

de Montmollin, Oliver. 1988. Tenam Rosario: A Political Microcosm. *American Antiquity* 53:351–70.

Fash, Barbara, William L. Fash, Sheree Lane, Rudy Larios, Linda Schele, Jeffrey Stomper, and David Stuart. 1992. Investigations of a Classic Maya Council House at Copán, Honduras. *Journal of Field Archaeology* 19:419–42.

Fash, William L. 1991. *Scribes, Warriors, and Kings: The City of Copán and the Ancient Maya.* London: Thames and Hudson.

Fash, William L., E. Wyllys Andrews, and T. Kam Manahan. 2004. Political Decentralization, Dynastic Collapse, and the Early Postclassic in the Urban Center of Copán, Honduras. In *The Terminal Classic in the Maya Lowlands: Collapse, Transition, and Transformation,* eds. Arthur A. Demarest, Prudence M. Rice, and Don S. Rice, 260–87. Boulder: University Press of Colorado.

Foucault, Michel. 1977. *Discipline and Punish: The Birth of the Prison.* New York: Pantheon.

Fowles, Severin M. 2004. The Making of Made People: The Prehistoric Evolution of Hierocracy among the Northern Tiwa of New Mexico. Ph.D. diss., University of Michigan, Ann Arbor.

Freidel, David A., and Linda Schele. 1988. Kingship in the Late Preclassic Maya Lowlands: The Instruments and Places of Ritual Power. *American Anthropologist* 90 (3): 547–67.a

Fry, Robert E. 1973. The Archaeology of Southern Quintana Roo: Ceramics. In *XXL Congresso Internazionale degli Americanisti, Atti*, vol. 1, 487–93. Rome: The Congress.
——— 1987. The Ceramic Sequence of South Central Quintana Roo. In *Maya Ceramics: Papers from the 1985 Maya Ceramics Conference, Part 1*, eds. Prudence Rice and Robert Sharer, 111–22. Oxford: British Archaeological Reports.
Giddens, Anthony. 1985. Time, Space, and Regionalization. In *Social Relations and Spatial Structures*, eds. Derek Gregory and John Urry, 265–95. New York: St. Martin's Press.
Hansen, Richard D. 2001. The First Cities: The Beginnings of Urbanization and State Formation in the Maya Lowlands. In *Maya: Divine Kings of the Rainforest*, ed. Nikolai Grube, 50–65. Bonnerstrabe: Könemann.
Harrison, Peter D. 1979. The Lobil Postclassic Phase in the Southern Interior of the Yucatan Peninsula. In *Maya Archaeology and Ethnohistory*, eds. Norman Hammond and Gordon R. Willey, 189–207. Austin: University of New Mexico Press.
——— 1981. Some Aspects of Preconquest Settlement in Southern Quintana Roo, Mexico. In *Lowland Maya Settlement Patterns*, ed. Wendy Ashmore, 259–86. Albuquerque: University of New Mexico Press.
Houk, Brett A. 1996. The Archaeology of Site Planning: An Example from the Maya Site of Dos Hombres, Belize. Ph.D. diss., University of Texas, Austin.
——— 2003. The Ties That Bind: Site Planning in the Three Rivers Region. In *Heterarchy, Political Economy, and the Ancient Maya: The Three Rivers Region of the East-Central Yucatán Peninsula*, eds. Vernon L. Scarborough, Fred Valdez, and N. P. Dunning, 52–63. Tucson: University of Arizona Press.
Houston, Stephen D. 1993. *Hieroglyphs and History at Dos Pilas: Dynastic Politics of the Classic Maya*. Austin: University of Texas Press.
Houston, Stephen D., and David Stuart. 1996. Of Gods, Glyphs, and Kings: Divinity and Rulership among the Ancient Maya. *Antiquity* 70:289–312.
Joyce, Rosemary A. 2000. High Culture, Mesoamerican Civilization, and the Classic Maya Tradition. In *Order, Legitimacy, and Wealth in Ancient States*, eds. Janet Richards and Mary Van Buren, 64–76. Cambridge: Cambridge University Press.
Lawrence, Denise L., and Setha M. Low. 1990. The Built Environment and Spatial Form. *Annual Review of Anthropology* 19:453–505.
Love, Michael. 1999. Ideology, Material Culture, and Daily Practice in Pre-Classic Mesoamerica: A Pacific Coast Perspective. In *Social Patterns in Pre-Classic Mesoamerica*, eds. David C. Grove and Rosemary A. Joyce, 127–53. Washington, D.C.: Dumbarton Oaks.
Lucero, Lisa J. 2003. The Politics of Ritual: The Emergence of Classic Maya Rulers. *Current Anthropology* 44 (4): 523–54.
Marcus, Joyce. 1992. Royal Families, Royal Texts: Examples from the Zapotec and Maya. In *Mesoamerican Elites: An Archaeological Assessment*, eds. Arlen F. Chase and Diane Z. Chase, 221–41. Norman: University of Oklahoma Press.

Martin, Simon, and Nikolai Grube. 2000. *Chronicle of the Maya Kings and Queens: Deciphering the Dynasties of the Ancient Maya.* New York: Thames and Hudson.

McAnany, Patricia. 1995. *Living with the Ancestors: Kinship and Kingship in Ancient Maya Society.* Austin: University of Texas Press.

——— 1998. Ancestors and the Classic Maya Built Environment. In *Function and Meaning in Classic Maya Architecture,* ed. Stephen D. Houston, 271–98. Washington, D.C.: Dumbarton Oaks.

Moore, Jerry D. 1996. *Architecture and Power in the Ancient Andes: The Archaeology of Public Buildings.* New Studies in Archaeology. New York: Cambridge University Press.

Ortiz, Alfonso. 1969. *The Tewa World: Space, Time, Being and Becoming in a Pueblo Society.* Chicago: University of Chicago Press.

Pohl, Mary E. D., and John M. D. Pohl. 1994. Cycles of Conflict: Political Factionalism in the Maya Lowlands. In *Factional Competition and Political Development in the New World,* eds. Elizabeth M. Brumfiel and John W. Fox, 138–57. Cambridge, England: Cambridge University Press.

Rapoport, Amos. 1990. Systems of Activities and Systems of Settings. In *Domestic Architecture and the Use of Space: An Interdisciplinary Cross-Cultural Study,* ed. Susan Kent, 9–20. Cambridge: Cambridge University Press.

Robichaux, Hubert R. 2000. The Maya Hiatus and the A.D. 536 Atmospheric Event. In *The Years without Summer: Tracing A.D. 536 and Its Aftermath,* ed. Joel D. Gunn, 45–53. Oxford: Archaeopress.

Romero, María Eugenia. 2000. Chacchoben: un sitio del Clásico temprano en la Región de los Lagos. In *Guardianes del Tiempo,* ed. Adriana Velázquez Morlet, 73–87. Chetumal: Universidad de Quintana Roo-INAH.

Smith, Adam T. 2003. *The Political Landscape: Constellations of Authority in Early Complex Polities.* Berkeley: University of California Press.

Smith, Monica L., ed. 2003. *The Social Construction of Ancient Cities.* Washington, D.C.: Smithsonian.

Soja, Edward W. 1989. *Postmodern Geographies: The Reassertion of Space in Critical Social Theory.* New York: Verso.

——— 1996. *Thirdspace: Journeys to Los Angeles and Other Real and Imagined Places.* Cambridge, Mass.: Blackwell.

Swenson, Edward R. 2003. Cities of Violence: Sacrifice, Power and Urbanization in the Andes. *Journal of Social Archaeology* 3 (2): 256–96.

Tilley, Christopher. 1994. *A Phenomenology of Landscape.* Oxford: Berg.

Trigger, Bruce G. 1990. Monumental Architecture: A Thermodynamic Explanation of Symbolic Behavior. *World Archaeology* 22 (2): 119–32.

Van Buren, Mary, and Janet Richards. 2000. Introduction: Ideology, Wealth, and the Comparative Study of "Civilizations." In *Order, Legitimacy, and Wealth in Ancient States,* eds. Janet Richards and Mary Van Buren, 3–12. Cambridge: Cambridge University Press.

Villamil, Laura P. 1995. La Secuencia Constructiva del Edificio 16 de Dzibanché, Quintana Roo. Paper read at Tercer Congreso Internacional de Mayistas, Chetumal, Quintana Roo, México.

——— 2005. Divergent Cityscapes: Urban Patterns at Two Ancient Maya Centers in Central Quintana Roo, Mexico. Ph.D. diss., University of Michigan, Ann Arbor.

Villamil, Laura P., and Jason Sherman. 2005. Investigating Urban Diversity in South-Central Quintana Roo. In *Quintana Roo Archaeology*, eds. Justine M. Shaw and Jennifer P. Mathews, 197–213. Tucson: University of Arizona Press.

Webster, David. 2001. Spatial Dimensions of Maya Courtly Life: Problems and Issues. In *Royal Courts of the Ancient Maya, Vol. 1*, eds. Takeshi Inomata and Stephen Houston, 130–167. Colorado: Westview Press.

——— 2002a. *The Fall of the Ancient Maya: Solving the Mystery of the Maya Collapse*. New York: Thames and Hudson.

——— 2002b. Groundhogs and Kings: Issues of Divine Rulership among the Classic Maya. In *Incidents of Archaeology in Central America and Yucatan*, eds. Michael Love, Marion Popenoe de Hatch, and Héctor Escobedo, 433–58. Lanham, Md.: University Press of America.

Wheatley, Paul. 1972. The Concept of Urbanism. In *Man, Settlement and Urbanism*, eds. Peter J. Ucko, Ruth Tringham, and G. W. Dimbleby, 601–37. Cambridge: Shenkman Publishing Company.

Willey, Gordon R. 1974. The Classic Maya Hiatus: A Rehearsal for the Collapse. In *Mesoamerican Archaeology: New Approaches*, ed. Norman Hammond, 417–30. Austin: University of Texas Press.

9 Back to the Future

FROM THE PAST IN THE PRESENT TO THE PAST IN THE PAST

Lynn Meskell

At the time of writing I am engaged with archaeological and ethnographic issues surrounding heritage and identity within the borders of a newly crafted democratic nation of South Africa. Here the discourse of heritage is vital in reinstating the respective histories of the black majority who have been deprived of their pasts, who have had their sites and landscapes systematically erased in the brutal regimes of colonialism and later apartheid. These communities now identify as Zulu, Xhosa, Venda, Khoisan, Griqua, and so on. And yet their histories and connectivities are porous and overlapping since there was never a time when the indigenous inhabitants of what is now South Africa were not in contact. Colonial and apartheid forces created tribal homelands and Bantustans, thus inscribing landscapes with specific native identities although these were political constructions underpinned by fear and paranoia.

Dystopian landscapes have hardly been addressed in archaeology, since we have been so busy acknowledging the sensuous nature of connection and belonging that comes with an inherently positive notion of landscape. Here in South Africa identities were colonially ascribed, affiliations divided and reformed under the European rule of law (often around land issues) so as to create hostilities between once-homogenous groups. Destabilizing the rural populations by means of ethnic reformulation and competitiveness over land, colonial governments all over Africa created a system of indirect rule that served their strategic purposes. In the debate surrounding the most efficient means of native control the debate coalesced around the designations "race" and "tribe," with the latter deemed the most successful axis of political determination in the colonial arsenal. If "tribes" were warring against each other in this newly crafted sociopolitical landscape, they would not have the resources to fight against their European oppressors. For the "early settlers on the South African landscape, tribes were the defining feature of social reality. Tribalism, settlers generally agreed, was a source of danger." Because of its relative autonomy, "the tribal economy was a source of livelihood, tribal ideology a source of identity and common purpose, and tribal institutions a potential locus of peasant resistance" (Mamdani 1996, 91).

The legacy of colonial ethnic taxonomies and reconstituted landscapes still has devastating contemporary ramifications. In the poorest areas of the country and those of the old rural Bantustans, arable land is at a minimum, livelihoods are impossible to maintain, HIV/AIDS is rife, and so on. History has tangible effects on contemporary identities, and no amount of deconstruction could or should appropriately tell people today that, for example, "Venda" is a recent ethnic category and does not have long-term legitimacy and that, in fact, it is simply part of a deeper tradition from what is now Zimbabwe. The benefits of historical hindsight are not always adroit techniques from which to launch critiques of the constructedness of identity and memory. In my own work on the Iron Age site of Thulamela in the Pafuri region of Limpopo Province I have seen tensions flare over past ascriptions of the site to Venda communities and the deprivileging of Shangaan people who are constantly reminded that their ancestral land is in Mozambique (Meskell 2005). Of course, Pafuri lies at the northeastern extreme of South Africa and is directly abutted by Mozambique and Zimbabwe.

Modern nation-states have their own way of seeking to control ancient identities and landscapes. Moreover, in the current climate of xenophobia, migrants from both bordering countries are viewed as pariahs (called *kwerekwere*) on the emergent nation, taking jobs, bringing AIDS among other things (Comaroff and Comaroff 2001). Thus archaeological heritage and ancient identities are called upon to labor in the service of emergent identities in the present: hence the racial hierarchies of white and black have been supplanted by the split down ethnic and national lines. Archaeologists and anthropologists have been at the forefront of these processes for over a century, making baseless assertions about the racial identity of Great Zimbabwe's builders, the social complexity of elites at Mapungubwe (Hall 2005), the influences of Arab traders and importance of Indian Ocean trade routes for the rise and fall of black cultures, and so on. We are by no means exempt from dealing in identity categories, or in fact substantiating them, nor from giving cultural background to the states and governments who parsed out land, forcibly removed communities, and erased cultural memories of other times and places.

Linking Identity, Memory, and Landscape

Although this is the contemporary landscape of southern Africa, it is nonetheless linked to the preceding "Iron Age" of agropastoralists as well as hunter-gatherer traditions and the subsequent coming of European settlers who wrenched the peoples of southern Africa from their rich and divergent lifeways and propelled them on a horrific trajectory of repression and exploitation. Today those fractured pasts are being repackaged under the rhetoric of the Rainbow Nation and the national motto, *unity in diversity* (Meskell, 2006). As archaeologists have long been aware, past, present, and future are indelibly linked. This acknowledgment is reflected through the chapters presented in this volume as they attempt to chart how individuals, communities, and nations forged ever-changing identities, memories, and spaces of their own invention, foregrounded by expediency, desire, and political will. That we can observe those processes in the present is an important and potentially instructive endeavor. It is not that societies in the past were necessarily "other" and different in their desires, but rather that we have to be more sensitive and nuanced in reading the signs and interpreting them. Heavy-handed notions of control, domination, and resistance will never be adequate in toto. Archaeologists have to be sensitive to the forging of this triad of social institutions: identity, memory, and landscape as they intercalate with each other as well as a suite of other social factors.

Whereas the linkage between memory, identity, and landscape may seem quite innovative in a North American context, this constellation has had a long disciplinary history in British and European archaeologies, where interpretive, rather than positivist, approaches have held sway for more than two decades. It would not be possible to conduct an archaeology of British prehistory and its monumental landscapes without recourse to such theoretical framings. The list is long and impressive (e.g., Bender 1998; Bradley 1997, 1998a, 1998b, 2000; Edmonds 1999; Last 1998; Sognnes 1994; Thomas 1996; Tilley 1994, 1996). Even in the archaeology of Egypt it was possible to consider the performance of memory in everyday life (Meskell 1998, 1999), the reuse and recrafting of sacred landscapes under different rulers and periods that might lead to radical revisioning and reworking of memory (Montserrat and Meskell 1997). What were demonstrated in those studies, particularly those over the long term, are the fragility of memory and the subsequent fabrication of ancient landscapes.

The lesson often to be learned is that similar practices of commemoration may in fact lead to a scholarly conflation, whereby the diverse intentions of dedicatory practices during various periods may be read off as coherent memory making. In fact, if one were to look at New Kingdom practices and then Graeco-Roman ones, one would see that radically different understandings were at play, so much so that the domestic and funerary architecture of ordinary people was miscast as an ancient numinous place of local spirits (Meskell 2003; Montserrat and Meskell 1997). Disjunctures such as these are valuable lessons in the reading and misreading of the past and in reiterating the centrality of a contextual approach. The chapters that precede also aim for this sort of critical engagement with archaeological, iconographic, and textual sources and show the potential rewards of such an interpretive approach.

Memory Work

Western concepts of memory are inflected with the Aristotelian principle that memory is a physical imprinting. According to this classic view, material substitutes are thus necessary to compensate for the fragility of the human memory (Forty 1999, 2). Alternatively, anthropologists and historians over the past decades have imputed that collective memory does not necessarily dwell in ephemeral monuments, but in the performative elements of practice. Following Paul Connerton (1989), they argue that embodied acts and rituals, as Lori Khatchadourian has discussed, may be more successful in iterating memory than simply the forging of objects. Physical memorials designed to serve as perpetual reminders are imputed to be ignored and are considered less effective than commemorative performances. From an archaeological vantage, I have suggested (Meskell 2004) that studies of remembering must necessarily oscillate between the physicality of monuments, things, and representations and the often immaterial practices that locate subjects within new time/space understandings: trajectories that fuse past, present, and future.

Archaeologists must contextually explore the moments and tensions between material and immaterial memory work. We need to further tease apart discursive and non-discursive relationships to the past. Material instantiations of past individuals and epochs may serve as physical reminders—one need only think of temples, monuments, urban buildings, and so on mentioned in these chapters—but are the specificities of memory preserved? Does the monument serve to do the work of remembering for and within later communities, and thus form a non-discursive locus, a reservoir of *pastness*, that operates as a taken-for-granted in daily practice? This is very different from the forms of active commemoration that might coalesce around intentionally remembered individuals or events. All, however, entail a certain fabrication of memory, both literally and metaphorically.

Sanjaya Thakur explores these tensions in his study of Roman Athens in which he questions individual and shared memory and the ultimate success of the project of Romanization in Athens. Although it has been celebrated as a model of Rome's literary and oratorical self-fashioning, he questions the success of Augustan alterations to Athenian civic spaces, asking whether such strategic building was explicit or a secondary by-product of expansion. The visual impact of the new Temple of Roma and Augustus constructed upon the acropolis must have conveyed immense flexing of power. And yet Thakur allows for the possibility of viewers, specifically non-Roman viewers, imagining away the building, subjectively creating an historically prior landscape in their own minds. It is a nice example of people reinventing themselves through reinventing landscapes or alternatively, reworking the built landscape immaterially back to its previous modes.

The performative element of built space is powerful, what Edward Soja has referred to as a third perspective or third space. The spatial specificity of urbanism is investigated as fully *lived space*, a simultaneously real-and-imagined, actual-and-virtual locus of structured individual and collective experience and agency. Understanding lived space can be compared to writing a biography, an interpretation of the lived time of an individual; or more generally to historiography, the attempt to describe and understand the lived time of human collectivities or societies (Soja 2000, 11). One wonders how long such processes were at work in Roman Athens and how quickly the new spaces and places around the Parthenon became domesticated and even taken for granted by various constituencies? This fits nicely with Maurice Merleau-Ponty's notion that such intellectual forms of memory are mere descriptions of the past, a past as idea, from which it extracts characteristics or communicable meaning rather than discovering a structure. However, this would not constitute memory if the object that it constructs were not still held by a "few intentional threads to the horizon of the lived-through past" (1962, 85–86). Those threads are experientially woven, forming a rich, diverse, and subjective tapestry of memories. This meshes neatly with archaeology's disciplinary concern for materiality and the tangible residues of the past, as highlighted by Thakur.

Laura Villamil investigates similar processes that highlight the recursive constitution of spaces, places, and identities. In her chapter we see how the built environment shapes power and identity, yet within the same cultural milieu. Here the vectors of difference coalesce around class and status, rather than ethnicity, as in Thakur's example. Here, too, we see an inherent tension, common throughout the material record. Despite their seemingly concrete nature, even urban fabrics are malleable and subject to reinscription: an elite view may be tacitly challenged, possibly even ignored, by a non-elite one. Here I am reminded of the pyramid and temple complexes of dynastic Egypt and how the most sacred of spaces were reworked and reconstructed once they had fallen from use and thus memory. Ordinary domestic structures can supplant revered ones for reasons of expediency. As Villamil demonstrates with sites such as Margarita and Lagartera, the Terminal Classic phase saw the construction of ordinary houses around what was previously considered elite space. These farmers probably moved from the periphery of such centers, in her view, overtly rejecting the spatial order of things. Classic Period structures, often ceremonial ones, were modified to form the house platforms for the non-elite. This is a fine example of the rapidity of meaning change, the reworking of what constitutes the sacred in spatiotemporal terms, and the forms of resistance or challenge mounted by ordinary people to the status quo. Archaeologists have been more inclined to see elite and ritual centers more in terms of cultural stasis and revered memory than of creative and advantageous reworking, even subversive craftings.

The Archaeology of Amnesia

Many scholars would argue that material remembering requires spatiotemporal anchoring, since permanence and solidity are important in both the forging of memory and the healing processes of the living (Halbwachs 1992). Others have countered that memory is not localizable, and memory work must be performed to be significant and effective (Huyssen 1995, 2003). So what is the status of the object in the role of memory and forgetting? How do we accommodate the impossibility of memory? A dialectic position advocating that both physical manifestation and iterative performance are required for the instantiation of memory is surely preferable. Archaeologists should not assume a universal relationship between memory and the object. And this is complicated by the acknowledgment that in many cultural settings objects do not inhabit their object taxonomies. Materiality is intimately linked to doing and making, the sensuous process of human interactions with things. This might warrant investigating the deployment of memory in revisioning cultural and social processes of transformation, as outlined by Thakur and Villamil. Memory practices and experiences shift over time as perceptions of the past are reworked in the context of the present and also in anticipation of the future.

In Seth Button's and Hemanth Kadambi's chapters we are asked to remember the power of forgetting, specifically selective memory or willing amnesia. Hobbes once claimed that forgetting was the basis of a just state and that amnesia was the cornerstone of the social contract. Forgetting is an unavoidable strategy, since no individual or community can afford to retain everything. Iterating his theory of habitus, Pierre Bourdieu argued that the "unconscious" was a tactic of forgetting (1977, 79) and that amnesia allowed society to imbue myths, rites, law, and their attendant discordances with objective status. Memory can no longer be viewed as a set of ossified things or practices, which is the tendency of archaeologists, given the static nature of preserved archaeological traces. Button discusses what appears to be the purposeful forgetting of a symbolic vocabulary (that included the Linear B script and a suite of Late

Helladic IIIC iconographic motifs). In doing so, he argues, they paved the way for innovative developments in the Early Iron Age. As he makes clear in his study of grave circles in Mycenae, we must recognize the variability in the ways in which individuals and communities selectively chose to commemorate specific pasts and relegate others to a realm of the forgotten (Hallam and Hockey 2001, 3).

Susanne Küchler's long-term work in Melanesia (1993, 1999, 2002) forms a central text in the ethnography of forgetting and materiality. She sees that "the place of memory is not in objects, but in the space created by rendering absent the products of memorywork—a place that is substituted by objects." This is a subtle variation of the notion that objects embody memory: rather, that they come to signify the spaces in-between states of being, present and past. Her material base is the *malanggan*, a ritually elaborated wooden carving or vine weaving that invokes the ancestral body brought to life as it is placed upon the grave of the deceased. In her account, memory is an unmoored and mobile force and the malanggan is simply a receptacle for the soul of the deceased. Similar to the arguments laid out by Button, Küchler asserts that the dissolving of malanggan could be read as material for forgetting in an ongoing process of moving forward, as generative and reproductive sources for society (Küchler 1999, 68). Yet unlike Button, her study focuses upon a consistent taxonomy of material culture through time, and thus it depends entirely on the ethnographic moment one chooses to focus upon: the fabricating of a material entity or the final disintegration of the object. As I have previously argued (Meskell 2004), the malanggan still constitutes a site of memory, even if short-lived, as much as it represents an active erasure.

As Adrian Forty (1999, 13) has indicated, the modalities of separation, exclusion, and destruction, and the tension between memory and forgetfulness, are potent factors through which archaeologists and others might explore the manner in which any given object performs the art of forgetting. The purposeful erasure of memory is a theme also taken up by Catherine Lyon Crawford in her study of Near Eastern and Roman memory practices. She uncovers the object biography of Naram-Sin as it processed through the centuries that followed. Through these particular periodicities she underscores the fluidity of representation of past identities and the constructions of power that cohered in Naram-Sin's material form. Rather than cast these memory communities as having singular, strategic visions for the afterlife of the stele, Lyon Crawford correctly posits a more porous set of fabrications. This reiterates the tension previously outlined in this chapter: archaeological materials give the impression of lasting permanence and historical duration, whereas the significations woven around them are immaterial and impermanent. Of course all rituals and commemorations, "no matter how venerable the ancestry claimed for them, have to be invented at some point, and over the historical span in which they remain in existence they are susceptible to a change in their meaning" (Connerton 1989, 51). Our job as archaeologists is to excavate the specificities of their historical settings, especially as they transform through time. These are the afterlives of images, and Naram-Sin is a case in point. The potential transfer of the power of a deceased ruler to a living Elamite one may be one reason for the object's fetishization and collection. Marcel Mauss (1990) famously talked of this connection between materiality and magic, power and possession. And like memory and identity, we see the interplay between both physical and intangible dimensions.

Landscaping Power

Lindsay Ambridge takes the workings of past identities and attempts to link them to landscapes of power. In her account, the Napatan adoption of a suite of Egyptian emblems is depicted as purposive acts of identity negotiations and recraftings, rather than being read as reductive appropriations. Given an aesthetic choice, Napatan kings did not opt for a program of erasure or iconoclasm—so popular amongst their dynastic rivals. Instead they amalgamated the elite symbols of the pyramids into the Napatan landscape, thus leading to a duality of pasts. By incorporating these two distinct traditions in the Kurru pyramid field, these Nubian kings were negotiating between memories of pharaonic domination and the subsequent legacy of that colonial encounter. Ultimately this led to a form of cultural reconciliation, and we have seen similar efforts to combine various pasts, repressive and glorious, in a unified embrace of nation. This ties back to the start of this chapter, where I introduced the situation in post-apartheid South Africa.

Perhaps what is now needed in archaeology is an attention to the memory and identity practices of ordinary individuals, the bulk of ancient and contemporary populations, rather than an intensified consideration of elite monuments and structures, moments of stress and cultural transition. Another important focus for archaeologists is the recognition that memory is performed, and Lyon Crawford presents several examples of this. Linked to that premise is the centrality of bodily practices and discursive embodied regimes around material and immaterial worlds (Meskell and Joyce 2003). Practices of remembering and forgetting can only come about through repeated sets of actions and performance. We are beginning to see this worked through in prehistoric sites such as Çatalhöyük in Turkey, where sedimented practices over the long term created memory of specific individuals that continued to circulate materially and immaterially over the generations (Hodder 2006).

These practices concentrate specifically around the bodies of deceased persons and, in some cases, the crafting of specific images. Habitual bodily practice informs memory and serves to refashion and reiterate certain aspects of the past. For example, bodily memory is enhanced through ritual observances, funerals, ceremonies for the dead, festivals, and daily personal venerations. Though it is possible to observe this clearly in the rich seam of evidence from New Kingdom Egypt (Meskell 2002), it is now also possible to detect in the Neolithic of Central Anatolia through rigorous excavation and analyses, by looking anew at the physical and iconographic evidence and directing attention to microlevel practices. These residues represent the embodied actions that archaeologists might successfully apprehend at a material, textual, or representational level. Material objects reiterate these bodily practices; they tend to mediate the passage between worlds and act as a buttress against the terror of the forgettable self. Archaeologists are thus poised at the perfect intersection to examine both material and immaterial registers of culture's memory project, if we broaden our scope of analysis, as the chapters in this volume have done, and unravel the complexities of remembering and forgetting in diverse cultural landscapes.

Bibliography

Bender, Barbara. 1998. *Stonehenge: Making Space*. Oxford: Berg.
Bourdieu, Pierre. 1977. *Outline of a Theory of Practice*. Cambridge: Cambridge University Press.
Bradley, Richard. 1997. Death by Water: Boats and Footprints in the Rock Art of Western Sweden. *Oxford Journal of Archaeology* 16:315–24.

—— 1998a. Directions to the Dead. *KVHAA Konferenser* 40:123–35.
—— 1998b. Ruined Buildings, Ruined Stones: Enclosures, Tombs and Natural Places in the Neolithic of South-West England. *World Archaeology* 30:13–22.
—— 2000. *An Archaeology of Natural Places*. London: Routledge.
Comaroff, Jean, and John L. Comaroff. 2001. Naturing the Nation: Aliens, Apocalypse and the Postcolonial State. *Journal of Southern African Studies* 27:627–51.
Connerton, Paul. 1989. *How Societies Remember*. Cambridge: Cambridge University Press.
Edmonds, Mark R. 1999. *Ancestral Geographies of the Neolithic: Landscapes, Monuments and Memory*. New York: Routledge.
Forty, Adrian. 1999. Introduction. In *The Art of Forgetting*, eds. A. Forty and S. Küchler, 1–18. Oxford: Berg.
Halbwachs, Maurice. 1992. *On Collective Memory*. London and Chicago: University of Chicago Press.
Hall, Martin. 2005. Situational Ethics and Engaged Practice: The Case of Archaeology in Africa. In *Embedding Ethics: Shifting the Boundaries of the Anthropological Profession*, eds. Lynn M. Meskell and P. Pels, 169–94. Oxford: Berg.
Hallam, Elizabeth, and Jenny Hockey. 2001. *Death, Memory and Material Culture*. Oxford: Berg.
Hodder, Ian. 2006. *The Leopard's Tale: Revealing the Mysteries of Çatalhöyük*. London: Thames and Hudson.
Huyssen, Andreas. 1995. *Twilight Memories: Marking Time in a Culture*. New York: Routledge.
—— 2003. *Present Pasts: Urban Palimpsests and the Politics of Memory*. Stanford, Calif.: Stanford University Press.
Küchler, Susanne. 1993. Landscape as Memory: The Mapping of Process and Its Representation in a Melanesian Society. In *Landscape: Politics and Perspectives*, ed. B. Bender, 85–106. London: Berg.
—— 1999. The Place of Memory. In *The Art of Forgetting*, eds. A. Forty and S. Küchler, 53–72. Oxford: Berg.
—— 2002. *Malanggan: Art, Memory and Sacrifice*, Oxford: Berg.
Last, Jonathan. 1998. Books of Life: Biography and Memory in a Bronze Age Barrow. *Oxford Journal of Archaeology* 17:43–53.
Mamdani, Mahmood. 1996. *Citizen and Subject: Contemporary Africa and the Legacy of Late Colonialism*. Princeton, N.J.: Princeton University Press.
Mauss, Marcel. 1990. *The Gift: The Form and Reason for Exchange in Archaic Societies*. New York: W. W. Norton.
Merleau-Ponty, Maurice. 1962. *The Phenomenology of Perception*. London: Routledge and Kegan Paul.
Meskell, Lynn M. 1998. An Archaeology of Social Relations in an Egyptian Village. *Journal of Archaeological Method and Theory* 5:209–43.
—— 1999. *Archaeologies of Social Life: Age, Sex, Class etc. in Ancient Egypt*. Oxford: Blackwell.

——— 2002. *Private Life in New Kingdom Egypt*. Princeton, N.J.: Princeton University Press.
——— 2003. Memory's Materiality: Ancestral Presence, Commemorative Practice and Disjunctive Locales. In *Archaeologies of Memory*, eds. Ruth M. Van Dyke and Susan E. Alcock, 34–55. Malden, Mass.: Blackwell.
——— 2004. *Object Worlds in Ancient Egypt: Material Biographies Past and Present*. London: Berg.
——— 2005. Archaeological Ethnography: Conversations around Kruger National Park. *Archaeologies* 1:83–102.
——— 2006. Trauma Culture: Remembering and Forgetting in the New South Africa. In *Memory, Trauma, and World Politics*, ed. D. Bell, 157–75. New York: Palgrave.
Meskell, Lynn M., and Rosemary A. Joyce. 2003. *Embodied Lives: Figuring Ancient Maya and Egyptian Experience*. London: Routledge.
Montserrat, Dominic, and Lynn M. Meskell. 1997. Mortuary Archaeology and Religious Landscape at Graeco-Roman Deir el Medina. *Journal of Egyptian Archaeology* 84:179–98.
Sognnes, Kalle. 1994. Ritual Landscapes: Toward a Reinterpretation of Stone Age Rock Art in Trøndelag, Norway. *Norwegian Archaeological Review* 27:29–50.
Soja, Edward W. 2000. *Postmetropolis: Critical Studies of Cities and Regions*. Oxford: Blackwell.
Thomas, Julian. 1996. *Time, Culture, and Identity: An Interpretative Archaeology*. London: Routledge.
Tilley, Christopher. 1994. *A Phenomenology of Landscape: Places, Paths and Monuments*. Oxford: Berg.
——— 1996. *An Ethnography of the Neolithic: Early Prehistoric Societies in Southern Scandinavia*. Cambridge: Cambridge University Press.

10 Memory Groups and the State
ERASING THE PAST AND INSCRIBING THE PRESENT IN THE
LANDSCAPES OF THE MEDITERRANEAN AND NEAR EAST

Jack L. Davis

> These steps taken together denote a tone of assurance as regards the well-foundedness of the confidence placed in the capacity of historiography to enlarge, correct, and criticize memory, and thereby to compensate for its weaknesses on the cognitive, as much as on the pragmatic plane.... Memory can be divested of its function of being the birthplace of history to become one of its provinces, one of the objects it studies. (Ricoeur 2004, 147)

As a Mediterranean archaeologist who specializes in the past of classical lands, prehistoric and historic, and who conducts fieldwork in Albania and Greece, I have been asked to provide commentary on contributions concerned with the Greek and Roman worlds. The remarks that follow thus focus on chapters written by Catherine Lyon Crawford (chapter 2), Lori Khatchadourian (chapter 3), Seth Button (chapter 4), Sanjaya Thakur (chapter 5), and Lindsay Ambridge (chapter 6): these studies concern Greece, Armenia, Egypt, and Iran, in time periods as distant from each other as the third millennium–BC Near East and early Imperial Rome. But I have tried also to pay respect to the editor's admirable interdisciplinary program by considering briefly two other chapters, which draw their case studies from the archaeology of state-level societies in India and Mesoamerica.

The enormous debt that contributors owe to the lead of Susan Alcock, and to Richard Bradley, her former colleague at the University of Reading, is evident. No less relevant are the ideas of Maurice Halbwachs (1992) and Paul Ricoeur (2004). Chapters in this collection nicely complement essays recently edited by Ruth Van Dyke and Alcock (2003). The authors succeed in providing contributions that explore the workings of social memory within specific historical contexts—that is, a *mémoire collective,* as distinguished from that of the individual. For archaeologists who study complex societies it is of special interest that all chapters have considered how social memories are shaped through the intervention of the state.

We are treated to fascinating stories that add to what Alcock has called her "smorgasbord of memory tales" (Alcock 2002, 176). These are of no less value where they tramp over ground well trodden by classical and Near Eastern archaeologists. Alcock (2002, 31) notes,

> The types of data called for here—monuments, settlement patterns, tombs, urban centers, sanctuaries, and so on—involve standard, well-established categories for archaeological exploration, categories long investigated and mined for the answers to other types of scholarly questions. An archaeological approach to the investigation of social memory requires, it would seem, not so much fresh objectives for additional future fieldwork as the redeployment of evidence often already in hand.

But, as is the case with other profitable approaches to the analysis of archaeological data, thinking about familiar data through the lens of a new model, such as that of social memory, can encourage us to reconsider and also to refocus field procedures. Should attention be paid to features of landscapes or to locations of monuments that might otherwise be neglected? I return to this question at the end of my chapter.

Negotiating the Past in the Present

> Away with words!
> draw near,
> Admire, exult, despise, laugh, weep,—for here
> There is such matter for all feeling
> (Lord Byron, *Childe Harold's Pilgrimage,* canto 4)

In this section of my contribution, I review the substance of individual chapters, adding my own commentary. Later, I develop their common themes in several case studies of my own, all of which illustrate ways in which the ancient past has been negotiated and renegotiated since the fifteenth century in geographical areas now occupied by the modern Greek and Albanian states.

Lyon Crawford's contribution (chapter 2) concerns the third-millennium BC Stele of Naram-Sin and an assortment of other Mesopotamian objects that were collected a thousand years later at Susa in Iran by the Elamite king, Shutruk-Nahhunte. What is especially fruitful in her approach is an emphasis on the context in which these Mesopotamian relics were found in Iran and on their reception in Elam; she also deduces her conclusions in part from empirically observable physical characteristics of the artifacts themselves.

The relevant monuments were dedicated in Susa by Shutruk-Nahhunte to the god Inshushinak. In the case of the Stele of Naram-Sin, the original inscribed text had first been intentionally, but not completely, mutilated—an act that appears to have represented a magical capture of the king of Ur by the Elamites. Lyon Crawford suggests that "the reerection of this war booty acted as a 'memory transfer,' in which the memories, powers, and relationships associated with the former possessor became the property and prerogative of the new one, the Elamite king and the gods of Elam."

Such actions may show both a "marked subjugation" and a "marked admiration" for the past. But how exactly would the capture of foreign loot legitimize the authority of a local power? To address this question, Lyon Crawford turns to the concept of "memory communities," proposing that both collective and individual memory are "integral to this process of legitimization and assimilation."

In chapter 3, Khatchadourian draws extensively on Armenian scholarship that, both because of a language barrier and political obstacles, will have been inaccessible to most Western readers. Her remarks about how modern scholarly cartography of the Hellenistic Near East has privileged the Greek past over alternative pasts (see Alcock et al. 2001) are worth noting. There is room here for fruitful dialogue between classical archaeologists, Near Eastern archaeologists, and historians of other periods who have busied themselves with the deconstruction of early modern maps of the eastern Mediterranean and Near East (e.g., Salzmann's reading of a unique Ottoman map [2004, chapter 2]).

Khatchadourian shows how Hellenistic rulers borrowed titles from an earlier native Armenian (Yervanid) dynasty in order to make their rule appear legitimate. At the same time, she argues that Hellenistic Armenian culture was created with reference to that of Urartu, a predecessor state that had controlled the same area of the Near East: dead were buried in the ruins of its settlements, while Urartian-like patterns of settlement, consisting of citadels built in lowlands, were promoted. These are provocative suggestions, even if it is difficult to see how hypotheses such as these, which postulate specific motivations for particular human actions and their material consequences, can be objectively evaluated where documentary evidence is lacking.

Button, in chapter 4, turns our attention to the prehistory of Greece in a contribution that considers polity formation and reformation in the Bronze Age and Early Iron Age, and focuses on case studies such as the monumentalization of Grave Circle A at Mycenae and the significance of ritual practice at Bronze Age tombs during the Iron Age. Button here is talking about much more than the subsequent reinterpretation and recontextualization of an earlier artifact; he means the active and intentional employment of material culture, according to which those belonging to "some groups may have taken deliberate steps to homogenize the versions of the past available at tombs and sanctuaries."

Button argues that "the physical remains of the past and the questions of which ones were worth reusing, who could use them, and for what ends, had real importance in Early Iron Age Greece." (The concept of "importance" might in part be defined with reference to the effectiveness of a strategy in establishing claims of legitimacy or in the creation of regional identities.) The continued existence of Mycenaean ceramic types in the Dark Ages that followed the destruction of the Bronze Age palaces of Greece may provide additional concrete evidence in support of these claims (see Sherratt 2004, regarding Homeric feasting).

These are productive avenues for research, and it would be helpful to define the term *Mycenaean* more explicitly. *Mycenaean* was a social and political construct, an archaeological culture that took form in those geographical areas that fell within the orbit of the Late Bronze Age palaces of the Greek mainland. It was not, as is so often assumed, a monolithic ethnically Greek culture, coterminous in its extent with the borders of the modern Greek state or those of a prehistoric Greek "nation." Nor should the name *Mycenaean* be casually applied to all Late Bronze Age material remains in the southern Aegean (e.g., see Bennet and Davis 1999).

Thakur discusses in chapter 5 a building that is very familiar to most classical archaeologists—the Temple of Roma and Augustus, which he suggests was erected on the acropolis of Athens on the occasion of the Emperor Augustus's visit to the city in 22/21 BC. Thus it was that a monumental construction on the acropolis for the first time housed worship of a living person. Although he imagines that the monument was in part erected in an attempt to appease the emperor, to atone for Athens's erstwhile alliance with the forces of Antony, there appears also to have been Roman imperial involvement in its design.

The new temple was placed in front of the Parthenon, in reference to it and other significant ancestral sanctuaries of the Athenian state. It was not, however, intended to dominate older monuments on the acropolis or in the city below. Thakur suggests that, in this way, it effectively expressed the new political realities in which Athens was enmeshed without emphasizing the humiliating position in which Athens now found itself. His reading of the temple would seem to be constructed from the perspective of local Athenians, one "memory group" present in Athens of the early Roman Empire. But other interpretations of the monument are not only possible, but even probable, and this fact reflects the wonderful polysemic nature of responses to material culture to which Lord Byron referred in *Childe Harold's Pilgrimage:* "There is such matter for all feeling."

C. Brian Rose (2005) has recently argued, for example, that the significance of this monument should be understood in the context of contemporary Roman victories over the Parthian dynasty of Persia. Taking his paper side-by-side with Thakur's underlines the ambiguities necessarily involved in contextualizing interpretations of ancient monuments. Rose's reading would seem to reflect the perspective of a restricted memory group consisting of resident Romans, Roman visitors to Athens, and elite officials of the city. According to his interpretation, Athens, in erecting the Temple of Roma and Augustus, turned its back on the East, and reasserted its role as a representative of the West—in doubt at the time of its alliance with Antony. At least certain viewers would have understood the temple to be a victory monument: after all, it had been built in front of the Parthenon, a monument that celebrated an earlier conquest of Persia, and near statuary groups of dying Gauls perched on the wall of the acropolis to commemorate another victory of Greeks over Eastern barbarians.

Ambridge in chapter 6 has examined how kings of Nubia, who dominated Egypt from their capital at Napata after the end of the Egyptian New Kingdom and conquered both Upper and Lower Egypt in the eighth century BC, shaped their identity by acts of negotiation, rather than by a "passive inevitable imitation of a more sophisticated culture." The Nubians, like Khatchadourian's Hellenistic Armenians, drew elements from multiple pasts, including their experiences of colonial domination by Egypt during the Egyptian New Kingdom and memories of their own earlier Kerma culture that had flourished during the Second Intermediate Period of Egypt (1700–1550 BC).

Ambridge's analysis focuses on a reexamination of the royal cemetery at Kurru in the heart of the district of Napata. She emphasizes the significance of the decision of the Nubian kings to locate the royal cemetery near a rock formation at Gebel Barkal that was laden with symbolic significance when Egypt conquered and colonized Nubia. Tuthmoses III built Egyptian temples there on a hill imagined not only to be a southern extension of the cult of Amun at Karnak, but the original home of the god. The fact that in the cemetery were employed native forms of burial in tumuli as well as small pyramids of a type used for "private elite" burials by those Egyptians who had participated in the colonization of Nubia reinforced the legitimacy of the Napatan dynasty both in Egyptian and Nubian symbolic language.

The final two contributions of the volume explore the archaeology of geographical areas and time periods much less familiar to a Mediterranean archaeologist. Hemanth Kadambi in chapter 7 describes how the Chalukya dynasty of South India, in the sixth–eighth century AD, "drew upon local memories enshrined in the landscape to further their political agenda." Settled in their capital at Vatapi, in a landscape that was already sacred, they adopted the worship of preexisting cults and associated representational art, employed throne names for their rulers that reflected previous practice, and inscribed the area of their rule with hundreds of their own temples (using earlier buildings as models). In turn, subsequent dynasties encouraged deliberate architectural archaisms that reflected Chalukyan styles, modifying memories of the past in ways suitable to their own political strategies.

Chapter 8, by Laura Villamil, studies architecture and the use of space in urban centers of Mesoamerica. In particular she addresses "how ancient Maya elites used the built environment to *communicate* their power and authority, and thus how the elites manipulated the built environment as a political strategy at local and regional levels." Important is her attempt to suggest how an existing built environment can be a source of power for elites, as well as her emphasis on the role played by non-elites in negotiating the form of built environments.

With reference to the Late Preclassic through Terminal Classic Maya centers of Lagartera and Margarita in the state of Quintana Roo, in Mexico's eastern Yucatan peninsula, she clarifies how features of the built environment were rejected or selected by successive generations residing in the same urban areas. A dynamic interaction among all social groups at both a regional and local level resulted in their constant transformation.

Memory Tales of Modern Greece and Albania

Certain major thematic threads run through the essays just reviewed:

1. Most of the authors employ a liberal meaning of the word *memory* to refer to a shared knowledge of a past that for the subjects of the case studies has become "part of their shared experience, has ceased to be a set of facts and has become something that which involves them morally and emotionally" (Osborne 2003, 142). *Memory* seems a useful shorthand, even though we share Osborne's doubts whether any genuine recollection of remembered facts was in most cases involved. What seems of greater significance is the fact that, for the most part in their analyses, the authors view the construction of the past in the past as an active process that involved picking and choosing, "remembering" and "forgetting": in order to maintain control by emphasizing the legitimacy of their power and that of the state, elites often create or exploit particular images and notions of the past that they chose from various possible, competing views of their antiquities.

2. Material culture is particularly conducive to manipulation by elites, because its polysemic character permits ambiguous and flexible responses to it.

3. Elites can thus pick and choose which of multiple meanings attached to material cultural remains of the past it is to their advantage to emphasize. As Paul Connerton has emphasized (1989, 1), "control of a society's memory largely conditions the hierarchy of power."

4. Memories are not, however, simply attached to material remains top-down by an elite, but are the result of negotiations among all social classes.

5. The concept of "memory communities" recognizes variability in the response to the same monuments by different political and economic groups.

Memories can be difficult to control or erase, even when there is conscious effort by elites to do so (e.g., see Hopkins and Beard 2005, 35, regarding failures to disassociate the Emperor Nero with the district of Rome later occupied by the Colosseum). The acceptance of any ideological message must thus have depended as much on the willingness of the intended audience to receive it as on the political and social goals of those who promulgated it. There is, moreover, no reason to assume that elites were cynical regarding the message of their own ideology. It seems more likely that they will have promoted a version of the past that suited their ends and at the same time was in concord with their own personal and collective beliefs. The most successful strategies are likely to have been those that, in favoring one plausible version of the past over another, provided satisfying spiritual and emotional answers and solutions for both elites and non-elites.

In the remainder of my contribution I toss my own memory tales into the mix. These have, I think, something unique to contribute to the dialogue initiated by other contributors, who have for the most part drawn on prehistoric, para-, and protohistoric case studies. In such cases, the precise motivations of elites are difficult to demonstrate and usually can only be inferred where evidence for a particular social behavior is temporally correlated with particular patterns in material culture.

In contrast, my own stories about the control of memories attached to past remains in Greece and Albania are supported by historical and literary texts. These, like material culture, are multivalent, but because of them it is often possible to propose with greater confidence that actions of elite actors were intentional, and sometimes even to describe the roles played by non-elites in the creation of ethnic and national identities. Ground that is not familiar to most of us is explored, in part because Albania until recently was hidden behind an Iron Curtain erected by its Stalinist dictatorship, in part because the periods concerned are those of the more recent Balkan past. Modern material culture has until recently been of little interest to Mediterranean archaeologists.

All of my tales are interrelated, and concern ways in which Greek political, economic, and intellectual elites have drawn on material culture to fashion social memories in the present by remembering, forgetting, and commemorating the past. Such memories, although sometimes contested in and by neighboring states, have been powerful forces in determining the way in which the Greek nation has been viewed both by its citizens and by the world at large. My first story concerns the way in which investigations of ancient Greek ruins already in the fifteenth through eighteenth centuries served in southern Greece to heighten a consciousness that Greek-speaking Orthodox Christians belonged to a national group directly descended from the inhabitants of ancient Greece.

Ancient Geography, Venice, and the Morea

The Italian cities of Venice and Genoa both held possessions in the Aegean after the thirteenth century AD (Lock 1995, 135–60). There had already arisen in the later Byzantine Empire (by the twelfth century AD) considerable interest in ancient Greek civilization (e.g., Rhoby 2003) and its monuments (e.g., Papalexandrou 2003), and in the geography of antiquity (e.g., Avramea 2004), particularly as it could be reconstructed from the writings of Strabo (composed in the first century BC/AD). By the Renaissance, Western travelers to Greece had had considerable success in determining the locations of classical cities.

The isolated Aegean enclaves of Venice and Genoa served such efforts both as bases of exploration and as repositories for local knowledge. In the mid-fifteenth century, for example, the precocious Italian humanist, Cyriacus of Ancona, found two old Italian friends at the Venetian colony of Napoli di Romania (today Nauplion) in the Morea, that part of southern Greece now more commonly known as the Peloponnesus. With them he set out to find the site of ancient Mycenae (Bodnar 2003, 337).

At the time of Cyriacus's visit, the area of Mycenae was controlled by an autonomous Byzantine dynasty. By the end of the fifteenth century, it and most of what today constitutes modern Greece had been conquered by Ottoman Turks, in campaigns by Bayezid II, immediate successor of Sultan Mehmed, the Conqueror.

The Ottomans, like the Venetians, had not figured in the history or legends of ancient Greece and Rome. Like the Crusaders before him

(Shawcross 2003), Mehmed, who effectively ended the Byzantine Empire with his conquest of Constantinople (Istanbul) in 1453 and subsequently converted it into his own new capital city, was anxious to situate his ethnic group, the Turks, in the world of antiquity. Probably encouraged by Italians who resided in Constantinople, in 1462 he visited ruins that were said to be those of Troy. There he identified Turcs as Teucri, the ancient Trojans, praising these Homeric heroes and claiming that his conquest of Constantinople was just recompense for the outrages of the Greeks at Ilion (Babinger 1978, 210).

Italian humanists more aggressively pursued the rediscovery of ancient landscapes after AD 1685, when Venice captured the entirety of the Morea from the Turks. Until 1715, this part of southern Greece was administered for the benefit of the Serene Republic, and the intensity of antiquarian exploration by western Europeans in Greece appears to have increased dramatically.

In 1703, for example, Alessandro Pini, a Florentine doctor in the service of Venice, traveled throughout the Peloponnesus with the text of the ancient Roman traveler Pausanias as his principal guide; in his written record of his travels, he included extracts drawn from the works of a dozen other ancient and Byzantine authors (Malliaris 1997, 17). Pini, like Cyriacus, sought Mycenae. His contemporary, Francesco Vandeyk, a surveyor in Venetian service, even drew the walls of Mycenae (fig. 10.1) and recorded a detailed description of them and of the monumental Mycenaean "Tomb of Atreus" nearby (Liata 2003, 107–8; see also Lavery and French 2003, 1–3).

Immigrants were brought to the Morea by Venice from various parts of the Aegean, in order to replace large numbers of Turks who had fled in the wars of conquest that initiated Italian rule in 1685. They were settled and given land. Alexis Malliaris (2007) has commented that

> the blending of the population groups in the end imparted a cosmopolitan image to the cities of Nauplion and Patras that marked them as important administrative and commercial centers of the Peloponnese, and attracted others to them. People of Greek origin, from different parts of the wider Greek world, as well as those of Italian, Venetian, and Slavic origin who had been mercenaries in the Venetian army, blended and lived together in all possible combinations. Natives

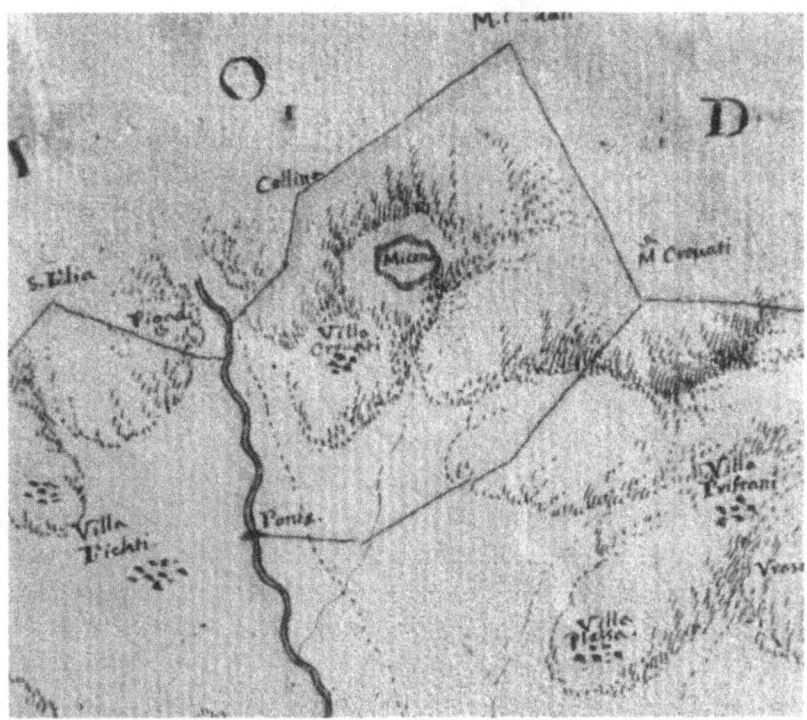

FIGURE 10.1 Citadel of Mycenae. Excerpt from a Venetian map of district of Argos, ca. 1700. (War Archive of the Austrian State Archive, cat. No. B.III.a.122. With permission.)

and foreigners, Greeks and Italians, Orthodox and Catholic, as well as christianized Muslims co-existed during the whole Venetian period.

He concludes that at this time the urban privileged increasingly developed a sense of identity that was based on exclusive membership in local communities of elites. A century later, these same oligarchies would play significant roles in supporting the movement for Greek national independence from the Ottoman Empire, and, after this was achieved, in establishing the new Greek state.

By identifying and documenting monuments of Greek antiquity, Italian travelers would have contributed significantly to shaping a landscape of Greece that resonated with memories of classical antiquity. Their discoveries must also have been a significant force in promoting unity among Christian elites of the Morea at the time of the Venetian occupation. A learned Italian like Pini could flatter himself that a Venetian Peloponnesus was having a civilizing influence on the local population (Malliaris 1997, 11; see Bellingeri 2005, but also Calotychos 2003, 39, who doubts that evidence is sufficient to prove that all elements in local populations shared such a consciousness of their past).

Barbarians and Place-Names in Modern Greece

Even after Greece won its independence from the Ottoman Empire in the course of the rebellion that erupted in 1821, the populations of those territories incorporated within the borders of the new state were ethnically diverse. Many of the inhabitants of the Morea, for example, spoke Albanian, rather than Greek, and some could have traced their ancestry to settlers who had immigrated there prior to the Ottoman conquest. A smaller Muslim population was slaughtered or had fled. Western European travelers documented the richness of the human tapestry that existed in the eighteenth century.

Greeks, Slavs, Albanians, and Turks, in turn, all left a mark on the toponymy of the Greek peninsula. Many place-names in the nineteenth century were consequently considered by the Greek government to be barbarian and thus inappropriate names for villages and towns. Prior to 1821, substantial progress had already been made in restoring ancient names to Greek landscapes on paper, as, for example, manifested in a detailed map drawn by Regas Velestinlis and published in Vienna in 1796–97 (Karamberopoulos 1998); the map was, in one sense, a plan for a Greek state that did not yet exist (see Calotychos 2003, chapter 1, especially page 54, note 5). One important project of the new nation was the obliteration of barbarian names in the landscape, part of a more general campaign that sought also to purify the Greek language of non-Greek vocabulary and grammar as well as to clear ancient Greek archaeological sites of medieval and early modern remains (e.g., Hamilakis 2001).

Greek names attested in the works of ancient Greek or Roman authors were restored. In other cases, appropriate Greek names were simply invented in a process that continued long into the twentieth century and that sometimes resulted from a dialectic between agencies of the central Greek government and local residents in the communities to be renamed (Alexandri 2002).

The goal of the Greek nation was to squeeze out memories of foreign occupations by building a sense of continuity between ancient Greece, Byzantium, and modern Greece. Petitions to the Ministry of Education of Greece from local communities describe foreign names as "painful reminders of a period of insupportable tyranny." Their authors asserted that "it is inappropriate for barbaric and dissonant names to exist within Hellas . . . [since these] give ground to our enemies and to every European who hates Hellas to fire a myriad of insults against us, the modern Hellenes, regarding our lineage" (cited in Alexandri 2002, 193).

To return to the case of Mycenae, once the ancient site had been identified, and had risen to international prominence because of excavations conducted by Heinrich Schliemann and Christos Tsountas, the nearby village, known as Harvati for centuries, assumed its official ancient name in 1916 as the result of an act of parliament, enacted in response to a petition from the town council. Justifications for the change presented by the latter are worth citing in full: "The name of Harvati preserves the memory of the establishment in the village either of Croatians or of a certain Croatian who owned it. This obscure and insignificant fact has caused the august name of Mycenae, the site of which lies nearby, to disappear" (Politis 1917, 227–28).

Toponymic cleansing in Greece, although never so systematic or successful in effacing past memories as in some other states such as Israel (e.g., Benvenisti 2000), has nevertheless swept non-Greek names from most prominent towns and cities of the country. Today, it has also created a kind of toponymic diglossia, where locals may preserve non-Greek names in everyday speech but will translate such "barbarisms" for outsiders and official purposes.

The Unknown Soldier, the Megali Idea, and Classical Greece

The ethnic homogenization of Balkan landscapes continued to be a concern of the modern Greek state in the late nineteenth and early twentieth centuries, when it pressed claims to "unredeemed" territories (that is, areas that had once belonged to the Byzantine Empire and where Orthodox, Greek-speaking populations still resided). In these instances elites drew heavily on memories of ancient Greece and Byzantium to legitimate their efforts. In a series of wars against Turkey and against its

Balkan neighbors, Greece followed a militaristic program of expansionism that came to be known as the Megali Idea, the Great Notion that a new Byzantine Empire would rise from the ashes of the Ottoman.

One striking architectural expression of this design is the Tomb of the Unknown Soldier in Athens, an imposing monument that stands in front of parliament, facing the central square of the city (Syntagma, or Constitution Square). The tomb itself is guarded by the familiar kilted Euzones, formerly the elite guard of the now abolished (1975) Greek monarchy. The monument itself reflects an ambitious scheme of landscaping initiated in 1925, when Greece followed the lead of Great Britain and other nations in erecting a monument to unnamed casualties of war. Much dissent and controversy ensued about its design, however, and the Tomb of the Unknown Soldier was not completed until 1932.

Unlike the British monument at Westminster Abbey or the French grave under the Arc de Triomphe, both of which honored the dead of World War I, the Greek tomb cast a broader net and had special resonances

FIGURE 10.2 General view of the Tomb of the Unknown Soldier, Syntagma (Constitution) Square, Athens, Greece (photo: J. L. Davis)

for a memory community that resided both inside and outside the borders of the state. Although it, too, represented the new wave of constructions reflecting the consequences of mass warfare and the "democratization of death" (Calder 2004, 16), the monument did not honor Greeks fallen in World War I: Greece had, in fact, played only a minimal role in that struggle. Instead, its focus was the commemoration of casualties suffered in wars of territorial expansion.

The Greek Tomb of the Unknown Soldier (fig. 10.2) consists of a rectangular paved pavilion. It is surrounded on three sides by low marble walls on which are carved names of major battles in which Hellenic troops fought in the Greco-Turkish War of 1897, in the Balkan Wars of 1912–13, and in the campaigns in western Turkey in 1921–22 (fig. 10.3). In this monument, a shared social memory marks the path to a collective national destiny rooted in the Megali Idea.

The tomb's stark anonymity contrasts with the message of many other war memorials, erected in the wake of World War I, that record individuals fallen in conflict (see Winter 1998; Calder 2004; and papers

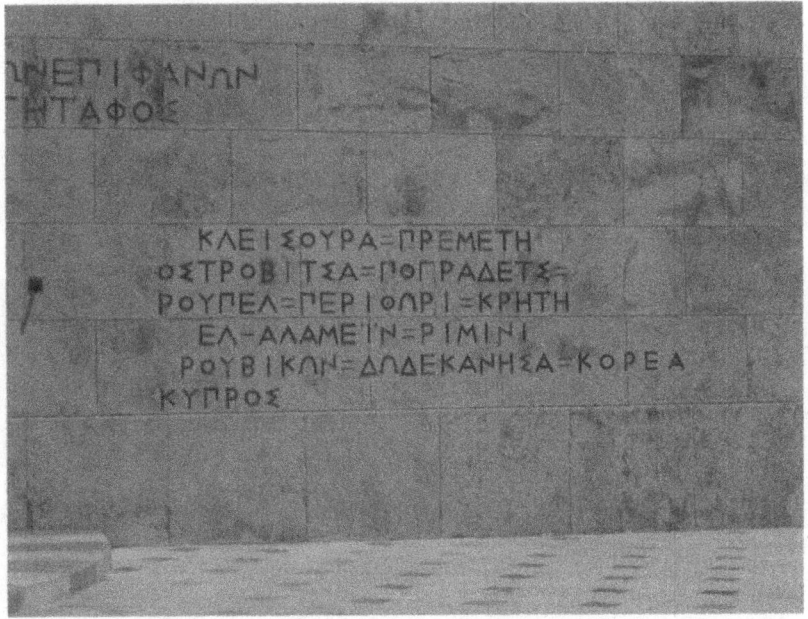

FIGURE 10.3 Names of battlegrounds on the retaining wall of the Tomb of the Unknown Soldier (photo: J. L. Davis)

in Saunders 2004). On the Greek monument only names of battlefields (for the most part barbarian) commemorate the sacrifices of the nameless dead, and personalities yield to an impersonalization defined by the state. But, whatever the case, memorials may be as much concerned with forgetting the past as remembering it. They may serve to allow "the living to forget the realities of the deaths" (Forty and Küchler 1999, 128; see also Rowlands 1999) and "the commemorative repetition of names may actually work against individuation over time" (Herzfeld 2004, 193).

Near the rear wall is a low, marble, box-shaped "tomb," set in front of a bas-relief (fig. 10.4) that depicts an ancient Greek armored warrior (a hoplite); the image is reminiscent of a work of sculpture erected on the island of Aigina in the fifth century BC. Engraved on either side of the warrior are quotations from a renowned funeral oration (as reported by Thucydides) that was delivered by the Athenian general Pericles early in the great Peloponnesian War between Athens and Sparta—a time when, ironically, Athens and Aigina were enemies.

FIGURE 10.4 Hoplite relief on the retaining wall of the Tomb of the Unknown Soldier (photo: J. L. Davis)

FIGURE 10.5 Hoplite shield on the retaining wall of the Tomb of the Unknown Soldier (photo: J. L. Davis)

The shield of the hoplite is repeated as a decorative motif on the walls of the monument: its devices (fig. 10.5) echo ancient (the Gorgon's head), Christian (the cross), Byzantine (double-headed eagles), and modern political themes (the phoenix risen from ashes). Into the rear wall of the pavilion are set modern sculptural re-creations of broken column drums that imitate those incorporated in antiquity into the northern wall of the acropolis of Athens as a memorial to the Persian destruction of the city in 480 BC. (figs. 10.6a and 10.6b).

The Tomb of the Unknown Soldier masterfully collapses both time and space. In so doing, it successfully enlists memories of ancient Greece in the service of the modern state: since "the past is still embedded in the present, it can therefore reawake and activate in the present processes which were thought to be over for good, because they belonged to a past which was over and done with" (Olivier 2004, 209).

FIGURE 10.6 (a) Column drums from destruction of Athens by Persia (480 BC) built into the northern wall of the ancient acropolis of Athens. (b) Replicas of column drums in the retaining wall of the Tomb of the Unknown Soldier (photos: J. L. Davis)

The fact that the lands now constituting Greece were in antiquity fragmented into the territories of dozens of warring city-states (such as Athens and Aigina) is ignored. Instead, the shared cultural achievements that are believed to unify Greeks are emphasized: it is these that have justified the wars commemorated in the pavilion. Ancient Greek culture has survived in the modern Christian state, a legacy of the Byzantine Empire. Easterners—first Persians, later Turks—are the common foe. The strangely barbarian names of many modern battlefields in the "unredeemed" lands, here awkwardly rendered in the Greek alphabet, recall earlier campaigns to purify the landscapes of the Greek state of such dissonant toponyms.

In the Tomb of the Unknown Soldier, Greece arrays itself in the front lines of the struggle with a barbarian East, as a defender of Western values, despite its reluctant efforts in World War I. Such an image of the nation has been reinforced by modifications to the monument in the years since its dedication. Names of battles in World War II have been added. There is reference to the abortive Cyprus campaign launched against Turkey in 1974. Finally, in 2001, two colossal statues were erected so as to overlook the monument at either side: one of Konstantinos Trikoupis, architect of the Greek constitution, the other of Eleftherios Venizelos, pilot of Greek expansionism in the early twentieth century and the prime minister who finally succeeded in bringing Greece into World War I on the side of the Allies.

A Contested Greek Past in Albania

Sole proprietorship over the ancient Greek past, as advanced by the modern Greek state, has not, however, always gone unchallenged. Scholarly attention has been focused in recent years on well-publicized disputes between Greece and FYROM, the Former Yugoslav Republic of Macedonia (as it is officially known in Greece), over rights to use the name Macedonia (e.g., Kotsakis 1998). But others in the Balkans, including Albanians and Turks, have also claimed to be heirs to an ancient Greek cultural legacy, one that has contributed to the formation of their own sense of social identity. I here briefly discuss a case in which Albanian, Turkish, and Greek ethnic groups all found meaning in the physical remains of the ancient Greek colony at Apollonia in central Albania.

The archaeological site of Apollonia is commonly viewed by Albanians as a significant part of their heritage. It is not generally construed to be a foreign intrusion but is rather seen as a significant node in the larger settlement system of ancient Illyria, a region where their ancestors developed an urban lifestyle in response to contacts with, and influences from, a larger Mediterranean world.[1] As such, the monuments of Apollonia evoke a strong sense of national pride and are widely known, even in popular culture (fig. 10.7).

The earliest account of the material remains of Apollonia was composed in AD 1436 by the same Cyriacus of Ancona who sought the location of Mycenae (Cyriacus of Ancona 1747, xxi. 143; Bodnar 1960, 43). Firsthand descriptions of visits to Apollonia begin to be plentiful, however, only in the nineteenth century.

FIGURE 10.7 The archaeological site of Apollonia in central Albania in modern Albanian life: (clockwise from top) a bridal party on the steps of the Roman prytaneion; the Agonothetes Monument as a corporate logo on napkins; advertisement for a bilingual (Greek-Albanian) theatrical production at the ancient site (photos: M. Russell; montage: R. J. Robertson)

Colonel William Martin Leake, the English traveler and spy, visited this area of Albania on September 22, 1805. As Leake approached the acropolis of Apollonia, in a nearby valley he noted scant remnants of a "temple," a structure that we now know was an elaborate Roman funerary monument of the second century AD. Seventy cartloads of stone had recently been carried away from there to build a new mansion (*saray*) for the Ottoman governor of the district capital of Berat, some forty miles away. And on a hill not far away he again witnessed the work of the governor of Berat, so recent "that the excavation made to carry away the foundations, of which not a single stone is left, affords a very tolerable measurement of the length and breadth of the building. One column standing in solitary grandeur is the only part of it which has been spared by the Pashá's masons" (Leake 1835, 373).

In these instances, the texts allow multiple interpretations. Surely one incentive for workmen to scavenge such large quantities of stone must have been the ease of its use for building material. Still, the round columns of a temple could hardly have been convenient for masons.[2] There can be little doubt that builders were making a conscious choice to draw on specific meanings attached to the antique remains they used.[3]

Leake also observed ancient building material that had been carted several kilometers from Apollonia for use in a village cemetery: "The burying ground of Radostín is full of pieces of fluted columns and other fragments of the good times of antiquity" (1835, 368). It is unlikely that such scattered remains of ancient buildings were brought here only because they were convenient grave markers. Wendy Shaw (2003, 43) has recently emphasized that in the Ottoman Empire the "acquisition of spolia [pieces of dilapidated ancient structures] . . . is not an accidental accumulation of excess objects or a convenient use of excess materials." She writes further (38),

> Much as hegemony in the Mediterranean had once been expressed through linguistic eclecticism, the practice of incorporating spolia into buildings, widespread in the Roman Empire and curtailed with the rise of medieval Christianity and its suspicion of Europe's pagan past, continued to be part of the local visual environment in the Ottoman Empire well into the nineteenth century.

In some cases meaning can only be surmised to have existed, and any precise significance is unclear, even in an historical context: it should not be assumed that those who chose to incorporate spolia in later structures had any knowledge of the historical context in which these artifacts were produced, or imagined that they themselves were descendants of the producers of those artifacts, that there was "a referential, historiographic understanding" of the past (Herzfeld 2004, 198). Yet it is evident throughout the Ottoman Empire, as well as in Istanbul itself, that those who reused buildings or incorporated spolia in new structures could draw on a wealth of shared memories of multiple pasts (see Papalexandrou 2003, regarding earlier, Byzantine, use of spolia; Brown 1996, with reference to Venetian exploitation of ancient remains).

In Istanbul, Alcock's concept of "memory groups" facilitates understanding of the significance of the conversion of the church of Ayia Irini into the Ottoman State Armory by emphasizing the multi-vocality of material culture. In this former Orthodox sanctuary resided an official collection of curiosities, including relics of Christian saints, displayed in a publicly visible location within the Imperial complex. Regarding the objects in the collection, Shaw (2003, 32) comments that "not only did they retain their religious significance in the eyes of Christian believers, their ownership by the new dynasty acted as a sign of hierarchical religious power within the empire. . . . The use of the former church to house them acted as a constant physical reminder of Ottoman dominion over the formerly Christian city."

In Albania, both the historical context and provenance of spolia also suggest that they were used in meaning-laden ways that could invoke significant and significantly different memories in social groups that sometimes were in political and economic competition with each other. Moreover, the precise meaning of the ancient buildings of Apollonia has varied through time and according to perceptions and agenda of particular memory groups, sometimes resulting in conflicting and contested interpretations. Greeks could view them in a manner entirely different from that of Turks or Albanians.

Already in the middle of the nineteenth century, the Greek Orthodox bishop of Berat collected inscriptions and other antiquities from Apollonia. Spolia from Apollonia were immured in his residence and in a nearby Greek school (Patsch 1904, 132, 177; Vlora 1911, 27, 50, 53, 55), while other remains had been transported to Istanbul with the support of the Greek community there. We know that the purpose was to strengthen Greek Orthodox identity within the Ottoman Empire.

The past could also be activated for more direct political ends. Indeed, by the turn of the twentieth century, the Greek character of Apollonia's antiquities was being used to argue that the administrative district in which it lay should be incorporated within the modern Greek state (Rikakis 1910, 3). One Greek historian compared the present inhabitants of the area to sharecroppers who no longer recognized the true owner of their property (Kougiteas 1905, 7).

Archaeologies of Memory: Rigor, Integration, and Heritage Management

> It was in the imagination of the Renaissance spectator who regarded collapsed remains at some remove of time and space that the irresistible decay of a ruin first became differentiated from dilapidation. Constituted by memory and distance, ruins are proxies for a past that is continually reinvented in the present. (Lyons 1997, 79)

As noted in the preceding section of this chapter, the modern Greek state has had its claims exclusively to control and interpret the Hellenic past challenged by its Balkan neighbors (see also Danforth 1995). Its official response most often has been to take steps to create and promulgate social memories that it thinks will promote an image of the Greek nation as heir to an ancient Greek civilization and as defender of Western civilization.

Greeks have long been supported in such efforts by western European scholars and intellectuals who have viewed the Greek nation as a forward bastion against non-Christian powers of the Middle East. Lord Byron, one of the most prominent early European travelers to the Balkans at the start of the nineteenth century, saw the Orthodox Greek community in this way and also understood the fragile nature of memory (1854, 1021): "It is singular how soon we lose the impression of what ceases to be constantly before us: a year impairs; a lustre obliterates. There is little distinct left without an effort of memory. Then, indeed, the lights are rekindled for a moment; but who can be sure that the Imagination is not the torch-bearer?"

It is this evanescent nature of memories that contributes to their very malleability and permits states to exploit them, but also makes them susceptible to contestation. Ricoeur (2004, 55), however, notes that "at the end of our investigation and in spite of the traps that imagination lays for memory, it can be affirmed that a specific search for truth is implied in the intending of the past 'thing,' of *what* was formerly seen, heard, experienced, learned."

The authors of the chapters in this volume have been able splendidly to show how past elites exploited the slipperiness of memory to achieve their own political and social objectives (see Low 2004). As in my case studies pertaining to the history of modern Greece, the mute material remains of the past to which memories are attached were extraordinarily useful tools in the hands of those who set about to organize and manage ancient complex societies.

A Partial Agenda for Archaeologies of Memory

What should come next? In conclusion, I outline three issues that might comprise a partial agenda for future archaeologies of memory.

The multivalent character of memories should itself challenge scholars to develop a more rigorous approach to memory studies. In the words of Claire Lyons, quoted earlier, "Constituted by memory and distance, ruins are proxies for a past that is continually reinvented in the present." The impetus that induced particular memory groups to choose to emphasize one past over others may thus be unclear, even in historical periods.

What evidentiary standards should be maintained when, in the absence of written documentation, a scholar leaps from recording patterns in material culture to making assumptions about the motivations of those responsible or about the emotional responses invoked in contemporary or subsequent populations? How, for example, can it be demonstrated that settlements were sited with reference to the locations of earlier sacred places? (In this regard, see also Alcock and Cherry [2006, 86], who emphasize the need for scholars to be open to "multiple, simultaneous interpretations" when considering meanings that monuments may assume.) Is it clear that such places were selected by elites in order to reinforce the legitimacy of their power? The preceding issues have been raised also by Herzfeld, who observes, in a review of recent archaeological studies of memory, that "methods often lack rigour and ideologically sensitive reflexivity; especially problematic are the frequent attributions of intentionality (2004, 191)."

The wide geographical and temporal range of the case studies explored by contributors to this volume is commendable: they manage at once to bridge gaps between Old and New World, Mediterranean and Near Eastern, and classical and Americanist anthropological archaeology. And as Van Dyke and Alcock (2003, 9) have emphasized, archaeological memory studies are jumping onto a "well-established bandwagon. Memory currently possesses a robust hold on the scholarly imagination." But the true potential of those memory studies that concern material culture seems as yet unrealized as an integrative force in the humanities and social sciences. The afterlives of objects are vitally important not only to archaeologists: there is a significant intersection between archaeological memory studies, the notion of "reception" in the history of art, and the anthropological concept of "object biographies." All such approaches necessarily emphasize the mutability and transience of the memories and meanings associated with particular objects and monuments.

Architects, architectural historians, and landscape architects might also be invited to the party, since they understand the important role that material remains have played in inscribing in landscapes monuments that will outlast the lifetimes of individuals. One thinks, for example, of the radical vision of Nazi Germany embedded in the architectural program advocated by Albert Speer. Planners in that instance cared not only for the monumentality and extravagance of their constructions, but also for their fate after the inevitable passing of the Third Reich: monuments that had "ruin-value" would "age and crumble with the grandeur of those constructed by the Greeks and the Romans" (Petropoulos 1996, 243–45).

Ian Morris has recently observed that a "new classical archaeology" that "speaks to central debates within archaeology as a whole" has become more "integrated into the intellectual currents within classics as a whole" (2004, 266–67). By grappling with issues of memory, classical archaeologists, in hand with their colleagues in the Near East and elsewhere, have gained additional common intellectual ground with scholars in a broad array of disciplines outside our fields. We should now take steps to share our practices and experiences with them through jointly organized workshops, symposia, conferences, and publications.

At the same time, we as archaeologists, students of material culture, should also tackle more general issues, concerning which we may offer unique insights. Forty (1999, 7) has written that we "cannot take it for granted that artefacts act as the agents of collective memory, nor can they be relied upon to prolong it." What exactly is the relationship between remembering, forgetting, and material culture? Is it true, as Forty writes, following Connerton (1989), "that as far as societies are concerned, material objects have less significance in perpetuating memory than embodied acts, rituals, and normative social behaviour" (1999, 2)? When is the material substance of artifacts sufficient "to evoke and awake the senses and create sensory memory in a synaesthetic manner, where one sense is stored in another" (Hamilakis 1998, 117)?

Finally, I return to a question posed earlier: Can there be a dialectical relationship between memory studies and archaeological field procedures? Here we are entering nearly uncharted ground. Alcock (*Archaeology*), in response to the question, why study how the Greeks remembered their ancestors? recently replied, "Because the more you think about it, the more you realize that the way people view their past affects how they treat its remains: what they preserve, what they destroy, what they cherish, what they trash. That filter can impact the way we see the archaeological record today."

It is no less the case that the way people imagine their past determines how contemporary archaeologists produce the archaeological record, particularly in the Mediterranean and Near East, where most archaeologists operate as agents of nation-states and have pursued archaeological agendas that closely reflect national agendas. I would follow Ricoeur in arguing that the task of those engaged in memory studies in archaeology, like that of historians writing history, is to support, correct, or refute the mémoire collective (Ricoeur 2004, 147). Archaeologists can empower themselves. Policies of cultural resource management need to be rethought. What time periods should be investigated? What types of sites and monuments should be studied and preserved? What is the temporal and spatial brief of archaeology and archaeologists? What constitutes an archaeological site? In many instances, current cultural resource management practices are still being determined by projects of nineteenth-century nationalism. It is time to reconsider the wisdom of such procedures and prejudices when they determine what aspects of past material culture we ourselves, as archaeologists, choose to remember or forget.

Acknowledgments

I am grateful to Sharon R. Stocker for thinking with me, as she always does. I also thank Yannis Hamilakis and John Bennet once again for helping me to appear better read than I am. Many issues here raised are discussed at length in Hamilakis's newest book (2007). Above all, I am indebted to the contributors to this volume for writing such thought-provoking chapters.

Notes

1. A noble Albanian family of the fifteenth century AD that controlled much of central Albania, including the site of Apollonia, could thus claim to be descended from the ancient Molossi, a tribe known to have occupied a part of the Balkan peninsula in antiquity (Elsie 2003, 39).

2. On the incorporation of spolia from Apollonia into specific buildings in Berat by Kurd Ahmed Pasha and others, see Vlora 1911, 27, 50, and 53. On the pasha's palace, see Vlora 1911, 55; also Kiel 1990, 26, 54, 57, 75, regarding his construction projects at Berat.

3. Quantin (1996, 229, n. 2) has suggested that the single column left standing in the temple at Apollonia was also not without meaning, and that the dismantling of the temple by the pasha's masons was deliberately incomplete.

Bibliography

Alcock, Susan E. 2002. *Archaeologies of the Greek Past: Landscape, Monuments, and Memories*. Cambridge: Cambridge University Press.
Alcock, Susan E., and John L. Cherry. 2006. "No Greater Marvel": A Bronze Age Classic at Orchomenos. In *Classical Pasts: The Classical Traditions of Greece and Rome*, ed. James I. Porter, 69–86. Princeton: Princeton University Press.
Alcock, Susan E., Henrick D. Dey, and Grant Parker. 2001. Sitting Down with the Barrington Atlas. *Journal of Roman Archaeology* 14:454–61.
Alexandri, Alexandra. 2002. Names and Emblems: Greek Archaeology, Regional Identities and National Narratives at the Turn of the 20th Century. *Antiquity* 76:191–99.
Archaeology 58, pt. 4 (July/August 2005): 16.
Avramea, Anna. 2004. Problèmes de la cartographie de l'Empire byzantin: l'évidence des textes. In *Eastern Mediterranean Cartographies*, ed. Giorgos Tolias and Dimitris Loupis, 25–34. Athens: National Hellenic Research Foundation.

Babinger, Franz. 1978. *Mehmed the Conqueror and His Time*. Princeton: Princeton University Press.

Bellingeri, G. 2005. Greco-romanità e Morea turco-veneta: in margine a un Regno d'equivoci. In *Venezia e la Guerra di Morea*, ed. M. Infelise and A. Stouraiti, 143–86. Milan: FrancoAngeli *Storia*.

Bennet, John, and Jack L. Davis. 1999. Making Mycenaeans: Warfare, Territorial Expansion, and Representations of the Other in the Pylian Kingdom. In *POLEMOS: Le contexte guerrier en Égée à l'âge du Bronze*, ed. Robert Laffineur, 105–20. Liège: Histoire de l'art et archéologie de la Grèce antique.

Benvenisti, Meron. 2000. *Sacred Landscape: The Buried History of the Holy Land since 1948*. Berkeley: University of California Press.

Bodnar, Edward W. 1960. *Cyriacus of Ancona and Athens*. Brussels: Latomus.

———, ed. 2003. *Cyriac of Ancona: Later Travels*. Cambridge: Harvard University Press.

Brown, Patricia F. 1996. *Venice and Antiquity: The Venetian Sense of the Past*. New Haven: Yale University Press.

Byron, George Gordon, Lord. 1854. *The Works of Lord Byron: Embracing His Suppressed Poems, and a Sketch of His Life*. Boston: Lee and Shepard.

Calder, Angus. 2004. *Disasters and Heroes: On War, Memory and Representation*. Cardiff: University of Wales Press.

Calotychos, Vangelis. 2003. *Modern Greece: A Cultural Poetics*. London: Berg.

Cassavetti, Demetrius J. 1914. *Hellas and the Balkan Wars*. London: T. F. Unwin.

Connerton, Paul. 1989. *How Societies Remember*. Cambridge: Cambridge University Press.

Cyriacus of Ancona. 1747. *Inscriptiones, seu Epigrammata Graeca, et Latina reperta per Illyricum a Cyriaco Anconitano apud Liburniam Designatis locis, ubi quaeque inventa sunt cum Descriptione Itineris*. Rome: G. Roiseccum.

Dakin, Douglas. 1966. *The Greek Struggle in Macedonia, 1897–1913*. Thessaloniki: Institute for Balkan Studies.

Danforth, Loring M. 1995. *The Macedonian Conflict: Ethnic Nationalism in a Transnational World*. Princeton: Princeton University Press.

Elsie, Robert. 2003. *Early Albania: A Reader of Historical Texts; 11th–17th Centuries*. Wiesbaden: Harrassowitz.

Forty, Adrian. 1999. Introduction. In *The Art of Forgetting*, eds. A. Forty and S. Küchler, 1–18. Oxford: Berg.

Forty, Adrian, and Susanne Küchler, eds. 1999. *The Art of Forgetting*. Oxford: Berg.

Halbwachs, Maurice. 1992. *On Collective Memory*. Chicago: University of Chicago Press.

Hamilakis, Yannis. 1998. "Eating the Dead: Mortuary Feasting and Politics of Memory in the Aegean Bronze Age." In *Cemetery and Society in the Aegean Bronze Age*, ed. K. Branigan, 115–32. Sheffield, U.K.: Sheffield Academic Press.

———. 2001. Monumental Visions: Bonfils, Classical Antiquity, and Nineteenth Century Athenian Society. *History of Photography* 25:5–12.

——— 2007. *The Nation and its Ruins: Antiquity, Archaeology, and National Imagination in Greece*. Oxford: Oxford University Press.
Herzfeld, Michael. 2004. Whatever Happened to Influence? The Anxieties of Memory. *Archaeological Dialogues* 10:191–203.
Hopkins, Keith, and Mary Beard. 2005. *The Colosseum*. London: Profile Books.
Karamberopoulos, Demetrios. 1998. *Harta tis Ellados tou Riga Velestinli*. Athens: Epistemoniki Hetaireia Meletes Pheron-Velestinou-Rega.
Kiel, Machiel. 1990. *Ottoman Architecture in Albania (1385–1912)*. Istanbul: Research Centre for Islamic History, Art, and Culture.
Kotsakis, Kostas. 1998. The Past Is Ours: Images of Greek Macedonia. In *Archaeology Under Fire: Nationalism, Politics, and Heritage in the Eastern Mediterranean and Middle East*, ed. Lynn Meskell, 44–67. London: Routledge.
Kougiteas, Panayiotis. 1905. *Pragmateia topografiki, istoriki, kai ethnologiki tis Ano Alvanias, Illyrias, Kato Alvanias i Makedonikis Illyrias kai Ipeirou*. Athens: Hestia.
Küchler, Susanne. 1999. The Place of Memory. In *The Art of Forgetting*, eds. A. Forty and S. Küchler, 53–72. Oxford: Berg.
Lavery, John, and Elizabeth French. 2003. Early Accounts of Mycenae. In *Archaeological Atlas of Mycenae*. The Archaeology Society at Athens Library 225. Ed. Electra Andreadi, 1–3. Athens: The Archaeological Society of Athens.
Leake, William M. 1835. *Travels in Northern Greece*. Vol. 1. London: J. Rodwell.
Liata, Evtychia. 2003. *Aryeia yi*. Athens: National Hellenic Research Foundation.
Llewellyn Smith, Michael. 1973. *Ionian Vision: Greece in Asia Minor, 1919–1922*. New York: St. Martin's Press.
Lock, Peter. 1995. *The Franks in the Aegean, 1204–1500*. London: Longman.
Low, Polly. 2004. Ancient Uses of the Past. *Antiquity* 78:930–34.
Lyons, Claire. 1997. Archives in Ruins. In *Irresistible Decay: Ruins Reclaimed*, ed. Michael S. Roth, Claire Lyons, and Charles Merewether, 79–99. Los Angeles: J. Paul Getty Research Institute for the History of Art and the Humanities.
Malliaris, Alexis. 1997. *Alessandro Pini: inedita descrizione del Peloponneso (1703)*. Venice: Greek Institute for Byzantine and Post-Byzantine Studies.
——— 2007. Population Exchange and Integration of Immigrant Communities in the Venetian Morea (1687–1715). In *Between Venice and Istanbul: Colonial Landscapes in Early Modern Greece*, eds. Siriol Davies and Jack L. Davis, 95–104. Princeton: American School of Classical Studies at Athens.
Morris, Ian. 2004. Classical Archaeology. In *A Companion to Archaeology*, ed. J. L. Bintliff, 253–71. Oxford: Blackwell.
Olivier, Laurent. 2004. The Past of the Present: Archaeological Memory and Time. *Archaeological Dialogues* 10:204–13.
Osborne, Robin. 2003. Are Memories Made of This? *Cambridge Archaeological Journal* 13:142–44.
Papalexandrou, Alexandra. 2003. Memory Tattered and Torn: Spolia from the Heartland of Byzantine Hellenism. In *Archaeologies of Memory*, eds. Ruth M. Van Dyke and Susan E. Alcock, 56–80. Malden, Mass.: Blackwell.

Patsch, Carl. 1904. *Das Sandschak Berat in Albanien*. Vienna: Balkankommission.

Petropoulos, Jonathan. 1996. *Art as Politics in the Third Reich*. Chapel Hill: University of North Carolina Press.

Politis, Nikolaos G. 1917. Toponymika. *Laografia* 6:221–36.

Quantin, François. 1996. Le santuaire de Shtyllas à Apollonia d'Illryie: Bilan et perspectives de recherche. In *L'Illyrie meridionale et l'Épire dans l'antiquité III: actes du IIIe colloque international de Chantilly (16–19 octobre 1996)*, ed. Pierre Cabanes, 229–37. Paris: de Boccard.

Rhoby, Andreas. 2003. *Reminiszenzen an antike Stätten in der mittel-und spätbyzantinischen Literatur: eine Untersuchung zur Antikenrezeption in Byzanz*. Göttingen: Peust and Gutschmidt.

Ricoeur, Paul. 2004. *Memory, History, Forgetting*. Chicago: University of Chicago Press.

Rikakis, Emmanuel. 1910. *Veration: Istoriki, Arhaiologiki, kai Laografiki Pragmateia*. Athens: Hestia.

Rose, C. Brian. 2005. The Parthians in Augustan Rome. *American Journal of Archaeology* 109:21–75.

Rowlands, M. 1999. Remembering to Forget: Sublimation as Sacrifice in War Memorials. In *The Art of Forgetting*, eds. A. Forty and S. Küchler, 129–46. Oxford: Berg.

Salzmann, Ariel. 2004. *Tocqueville in the Ottoman Empire: Rival Paths to the Modern State*. Boston: Brill.

Saunders, Nicholas J., ed. 2004. *Matters of Conflict: Material Culture, Memory and the First World War*. London: Routledge.

Shaw, Wendy M. K. 2003. *Possessors and Possessed: Museums, Archaeology, and the Visualization of History in the Late Ottoman Empire*. Berkeley: University of California Press.

Shawcross, Teresa. 2003. Re-inventing the Homeland in the Historiography of Frankish Greece: The Fourth Crusade and the Legend of the Trojan War. *Byzantine and Modern Greek Studies* 27:120–52.

Sherratt, Susan. 2004. Feasting in Homeric Epic. In *The Mycenaean Feast*, ed. James C. Wright, 181–217. Princeton: American School of Classical Studies at Athens.

Van Dyke, Ruth M., and Susan E. Alcock, eds. 2003. *Archaeologies of Memory*. Malden, Mass.: Blackwell.

Vlora, Ekrem Bei. 1911. *Aus Berat und vom Timor*. Sarajevo: Daniel A. Kajon.

Winter, Jay M. 1998. *Sites of Memory, Sites of Mourning: The Great War in European Cultural History*. New York: Cambridge University Press.

About the Editor

Norman Yoffee is professor in the Department of Near Eastern Studies and in the Department of Anthropology, University of Michigan. His latest book is *Myths of the Archaic State: Evolution of the Earliest Cities, States, and Civilizations* (2005). He is preparing a history and archaeology of the city of Kish, Mesopotamia.

About the Contributors

Lindsay Ambridge is a Ph.D. candidate in Egyptology in the Department of Near Eastern Studies, University of Michigan. Her research interests include settlement archaeology, landscape theory, and the social history of non-elites. She has excavated at the ancient Egyptian sites of Abydos, Amarna, and Mendes.

Seth Button is writing his dissertation in the Interdepartmental Program in Classical Art and Archaeology at the University of Michigan. His dissertation deals with environmental and social causes of change in settlement patterns in prehistoric Cyprus.

Jack L. Davis is Carl W. Blegen Professor of Greek Archaeology, University of Cincinnati. His books include *Papers in Cycladic Prehistory* (1979), *Landscape Archaeology as Long-Term History* (1991), *Sandy Pylos: An Archaeological History from Nestor to Navarino* (1998), and *An Historical and Economic Geography of Ottoman Greece* (2005). Currently he codirects regional studies and excavations in Albania and in the hinterlands of the ancient Greek colonies of Durrachium/Epidamnos and Apollonia and is preparing publications from excavations of the Bronze Age Palace of Nestor in southern Greece.

Hemanth Kadambi is a doctoral candidate in the Department of Anthropology, University of Michigan, and received his M.A. from the Center for Historical Studies, Jawaharlal Nehru University, New Delhi. He has excavated in India, Mexico, and the American Southwest. His research interests in studying Early Medieval South India combine historical sources with archaeological data.

Lori Khatchadourian is a Ph.D. candidate in the Interdepartmental Program in Classical Art and Archaeology, University of Michigan. Her research addresses the materiality of political and social life in Eurasia through spatial and ceramic analyses. Her dissertation is titled *Beyond Empire and Dynasty: Toward an Archaeology of Sociopolitics on the Armenian Highland (ca.* 600–200 B.C.*)*.

Catherine Lyon Crawford is writing her dissertation (*Embellished Space: Value and Display on Neopalatial Crete*) in the Interdepartmental Program in Classical Art and Archaeology, University of Michigan. Her research interests are on material culture in the Aegean Bronze Age and on exhibition archaeology in museums.

Lynn Meskell is professor in the Department of Cultural and Social Anthropology, Stanford University. She is founding editor of the *Journal of Social Archaeology*. Recent books include *Archaeologies of Materiality* (2005), *Object Worlds in Ancient Egypt* (2004), and *The Companion to Social Archaeology* (with R. Preucel, 2004). Her current research examines constructs of natural and cultural heritage and the related discourses of empowerment around the Kruger National Park, ten years after democracy in South Africa.

Sanjaya Thakur is a Ph.D. candidate in the Department of Classical Studies, University of Michigan. He is interested in the Latin literature and culture of the early Roman Empire. His dissertation examines the discourse on imperial succession as presented in the exile literature of the Roman poet Ovid.

Laura P. Villamil received her Ph.D. ("Divergent Cityscapes: Urban Patterns at Two Ancient Maya Centers in Central Quintana Roo, Mexico") in the Department of Anthropology, University of Michigan. She has taught in the Department of Sociology and Anthropology, Albion College, and she is now assistant professor in the Department of Anthropology, University of Wisconsin, Milwaukee. Her current research focuses on the development and transformation of ancient Maya urban landscapes and the relations between archaeology and the construction of national identities in modern Latin America.

Index

Achaemenid empire, 45, 49, 52, 55, 57
acropolis, 104–6, 108–12, 114–24, 126
Actium, 107–8
Aditi (mother of gods), 172; identified with Yellamma and Lajja-Gauri, 172
administration, 79–80
Aegina, 121
agora, 124
Agrippa, Marcus, 109
A-Group culture (Nubian), 130–31
Aihole, 156–78; Aihole group and dolmens, 160, 161f; Aihole temples, 164, 167, 174, 176; pillar inscription at, 178. *See also* Gauder-gudi
Akhenaten, 145
Albania: and incorporation of spolia, 248; negotiation of ancient past in, 228; and recent Balkan past, 234. *See also* Appollonia
Alcock, Susan, 2, 3, 38, 71, 105, 108, 155, 160, 173, 178, 181–82, 227–28, 251–52
Alexander the Great, 35, 38, 43–45; coins of, 67–69
Amarna, 146
Ambiger-gudi, 167
Amen, 138
ancestors, 62, 94, 203
Ancient Greek civilization: archaeological sites of, 238; and continuity with modern Greece, 237–39, 243, 245, 249; documenting monuments of, 237; Ottoman interest in, 235–36; and privileging over alternative pasts, 229

Ancient Maya time periods: Middle Preclassic, 192, 198; Late Preclassic, 192, 198–99, 202–6; Early Classic, 192, 199; Late Classic, 194; Middle Classic hiatus, 194, 205; Terminal Classic, 195, 199
Antikythera shipwreck, 20–22
Antiochus III, 45, 70
Antonaccio, Carla, 94
Antony, 106
Apelles, 35
Apollonia, 245–49, 253n1, 253n3
Appadurai, Arjun, 14, 15
Aramaic, 48, 53–54
Ararat, 47, 56–57, 60
archaeological data: and social memories, 250–53
Archaeological Dialogues, 2
archaeological record: effect of view of past, 252
archaeological theory, 1, 2, 6
archaic states, 25
architecture: and archaeology of memory, 251; manipulation of as political strategy, 232–33
Argishti I, 58
Argishtihinili, 55, 58, 63–64
Argolid (Argive plain), 94
Aristophanes, 69
Armavir, 47, 52, 58–59
Armenia: Hellenistic Armenian culture, 229–30, 232
Armenian plateau, 72
Artashat, 47, 60–62

Artaxata. *See* Artashat
Artaxiad dynasty, 45–47
Artaxiad stelae, 47–48, 55
Artaxias I, 45, 47, 49, 51–52, 70, 72
Asine, 83, 91
Assmann, Jan, 139
Assurbanipal, 16–18
Athena Promachos, 25
Athens, 80, 104–9, 112, 114–15, 117–24. *See also* Temple of Roma and Augustus; Tomb of Unknown Soldier
Augustus, 28, 35–36, 38, 104, 106–9, 111–12, 114–15, 118–25, 127, 231
Ayia Irini, 248

Badami, 156, 158, 164, 168, 169f, 171–72, 176, 180, 181–82. *See also* Vatapi; Yellamma, temple of
Bahrani, Zainab, 5
Balkans, 239, 245, 249
Bayezid II, 235
Bhutanatha: temples of, 169
Binder, Wolfgang, 111, 115
Bisitun, 55, 73
Bol, Peter, 20, 22
Bolon, Carol Radcliffe, 163, 170–72, 181
Bonnet, Charles, 134–35
Bourdieu, Pierre, 221
Bradley, Richard, 2, 45, 227
Brahmagiri, 162
Brahmanas, 158, 180; deities of, 172; Vedic, 173, 179
Bronze Age (Greece), 77
Brown, James, 93
Brutus, 106–7
built environment, 183–84, 187–89, 201–2, 203–7, 209
burials: multiple, 77, 85, 96; secondary, 76–77, 90–91
Byron, George Gordon, 228, 231, 249
Byzantine Empire, 235–36, 239–40, 245

Caesar, Julius, 107, 125
Cahokia, 93
Calakmul, 205
Caligula, 27
Caracalla, 28, 29
Caracol, 205
cartography and memory, 43; Greek past privileged by, 229
Caryatids, 109
Cassius, 106–7
Cassius dio, 121
Çatal Höyük, 224
Cato the Elder, 22
Cavanagh, William, 89
cemetery: Mycenaean prehistoric, 81, 82
C-Group culture (Nubian), 130–31, 147
Chacchoben, 193
Chaco Canyon, 7n1
Chalukyas, 155–79, 232; art of, 158–59, 170; of Kalyana, 158, 176; kings of, 157, 172–74, 176, 178; later Chalukyas, 159, 178; of Vatapi, 155–56, 158, 160, 170, 173–74, 178–79, 181; of Vengi, 158, 176. *See also* Jayasimha; Kirtivarman; Mangalesa; Polekesi; Pulakeshin; Vijayaditya; Vikramaditya I; Vinayaditya
chamber tomb, 90
Chichmuul, 193
Christianity, 30
Cicero, 22
cist graves, 82
classical archaeology: and issues of memory, 251–52
Claudius, 28, 35–36
Cleopatra, 108
Clytemnestra, 93
collapse: Classic Maya, 207
Connah, Graham, 133–34
Connerton, Paul, 218, 233, 252
Copán, 206, 207, 208
Corinthian capitals, 111, 115

cultural resource management policies, 252–53
Cyprus, 20
Cyriacus of Ancona, 235–36, 246
Czikszentmihalyi, 13

damnatio memoriae, 27
dedications, 95–97
Demos, 118
Denderah, 29–30
destruction, 76, 90
divine kingship, 202, 203–4
Domitian, 27
Dongola Reach, 136, 138, 140

Early Historic, 159, 169
Early Iron Age (in Greece), 94–95
Early Medieval, 155, 159, 179, 181
egalitarian, 83
Egypt, 218, 220, 224; identity of shaped by acts of negotiation, 231–32
Elam, Elamites, 5, 10, 12, 20, 25, 37–39, 223
Eleusinian Mysteries, 121
elites, 79, 89, 94; identity of, 237–38; and manipulation of material culture, 25–51, 232–33; and promotion of version of past, 234, 250; and social memories, 233, 235
environment: meaning of, 7
epic poetry: Grecian, 81, 91
equifinality, 96
Erebuni, 55, 57, 59
Erechteion, 105, 109, 111–12, 114–15, 117–18, 121
Erechtheus and Cecrops, 114
euergetai, 108
Euripides, 62, 81

Famidhana, 91–92
feasting, 83–84, 92
feudalism, 155, 181

field procedures: and analysis of archaeological data, 228; and dialectical relationship with memory studies, 252
forgetting. *See* memory
Forty, Adrian, 222, 252
Freedberg, David, 26, 37
Frend, Elizabeth, 82
Fritz, John, 7n1

Gauder-gudi, 164, 166f. *See also* Aihole
Gebel Barkal, 138–40, 145
genealogy, 77
Geta, 28, 29, 34
Getty Museum, 23
Giza pyramids, 148–50
globalization, 4
Goldstein, Lynn, 86
grave circle, 84; A (Mycenae), 84–89, 230; B (Mycenae), 84–86
grave markers (stelae), 85, 93
Graziadio, Giampaolo, 85–6, 92
Great Zimbabwe, 216
Greece: as defender of Western values, 245; material culture of, 234–45; modern continuity with ancient civilization, 237–39, 243, 245, 249; modern ethnic homogenization in, 239–43, 245; and Mycenaean culture, 230; and negotiation with ancient past, 228; toponymic cleansing in, 238–9, 245
Greek, 52; purification of language, 238
Greekness, 23
group membership, 91

Halbwachs, Maurice, 3, 227
Hammurabi's Code, 4, 19, 37
Harper, Prudence, 19
Hathor: temple of, 30
Haynes, Joyce, 140
Hellenism, Hellenistic, 43–44, 58–60, 62–63, 69, 72, 229–30, 232

Herculaneum, 23
hero cult, 95–96
Herzfeld, Michael, 251
Hire Benkal, 162
historiography: and social memories, 227–28
HIV-AIDS, 215
Hobbes, Thomas, 221
Horom, 56
Hussein, Saddam, 4

Iakovides, Spyros, 82
iconoclasm, 26–27, 29–31, 34
identity: Athenian and Roman, 112; and memory, 105, 138; royal, 141
ideology, 202–3
individuality, 91
inequality: material, 97
invention of tradition, 2
Iran: Mesopotamian relics in, 229
Iron Age, 159. *See also* Megalithic

Jayasimha, 173, 178
Julius Caesar, 107, 125

Kadambas, 167, 170, 173, 176
Kannada, 156; old, 158
Karnak, 138
Kashta, 139, 143, 145, 150
Kawerau, Georg, 111
Kemet, 129
Kerma: city of, 134–35, 137, 146; cultural group, 130–33; period, 128; and royal tumuli, 135–36; and tumuli of Western Deffufa, 134–45, 134f, 137
khatchkar, 55
kinship, 94
Kirtivarman, 173–74
Koortbojian, Michael, 25
Kramrisch, Stella, 172
Küchler, Susanne, 222

Kurru, 128, 139, 141–51
Kush, 137, 140

Lagartera (Quintana Roo, Mexico), 185, 191–96
Lajja-Gauri (fertility goddess), 170–72, 171f, 179, 181. *See also* Yellamma
Leake, William Martin, 247
legitimation, legitimacy, 12, 14, 77, 95
leveling mechanism, 93
life-event, 15
Linear B, 80
Lucian, 69
Lyons, Claire, 250

Macedonia: rights to name of, 245
Madagascar, 77, 91
Magnesia: battle of, 70
malanggan, 222
Malaprabha, 181; landscape of, 164, 174; river, 156, 158, 160, 162; valley, 155–56, 158–59, 171, 173, 176, 179
Malliaris, Alexis, 236–37
Mangalesa, 178
Marcus Agrippa, 109
Margarita (Quintana Roo, Mexico), 185, 196–99, 197f, 198f, 200f
mastaba, 143
material culture: elite manipulation of, 232–33, 250–51; and legitimacy claims, 229–30, 250–51; multivocality of, 248; and perpetuation of memory, 252–53; polysemic response to, 231, 233
materiality, 221
Maungubwe, 216
Mee, Christopher, 82
Megali Idea, 240–41
Megalithic, 159–60, 162–63; tombs, 168–69, 181
Mehmed the Conqueror, 235–36
mémoire collective, 228, 252

memory: and amnesia, 221; bodily, 224; communities and, 13, 105, 119, 229, 234, 240–41; and forgetting, 27–28, 31, 34, 90–97, 221; performance of, 15, 38, 218; social memories, 3–4, 6, 45, 55, 70–71, 217–19, 227, 233, 239, 249–53; transfer of, 229
Memphis, 145
Merleau-Ponty, Maurice, 220
Meskell, Lynn, 2, 14, 95
Mithridates, 106
Mithridatic wars, 22
Molossi tribe, 253n1
monumental architecture and memory, 187–88, 231, 234, 237, 250
Morea, 235–38
Morris, Ian, 95, 251
mortuary analysis, 76
mortuary variability, 76
Mycenae, Mycenaean, 77, 79, 83, 89–94, 96, 230, 235–39
Mylonas, George, 82, 84

Nabonidus, 5
Naram-Sin, 10–13, 18–20, 37–38, 229
nationalism, 252–53
Nero, 27
Nineveh, 16, 32, 34; library at, 16–18
non-elites, 233–34
North Karnataka, 155–56, 162, 168, 176, 180
Nubia, 128–51
Nylander, Carl, 31

object biography, 13–15, 251
O'Connor, David, 141–42, 150
Octavian, 107
Oshakan, 55, 57, 63–66
Ottoman Empire: and ancient Greek civilization, 235–38, 247–49, 253n3

palaces (Mycenaean), 79–80
Pallavas, 156, 158, 172, 176

Pammenes, 118
Panathenaia, 122
Pandion, 114
Pantheon, 109
Papademetriou, Ioannes, 82
paradigm, 3
Parpola, Simo, 17
Parthenon, 105, 109, 112–14, 116–18, 121–23, 231
Parthian campaign, 115
Parthians, 70
Pattadakal, 156, 157f, 160, 164, 165f, 167, 171–72, 180
Pausanias, 81, 236
Pearce, Susan, 16
Peleponnesus, 79
performance, 3
Pericles, 242
Persepolis, 57
Persian empires. See Achaemenid empire
Persians, 116
Philippi: battle of, 107
Pini, Alessandro, 236, 238
Piye, 139, 143, 145–46, 149
Pliny, 35–36
Plutarch, 60
Polekesi I, 158, 178
Polekesi II, 178
political centralization, 77
Pollitt, Jerome, 22, 36
Pompey, 70, 107
Propylaia, 109, 116–17
Pulakeshin, 172–73

Quantin, François, 253n3

race, 215
rank, 84–86
Rao, S. R., 164, 167, 180n3
Rapoport, Amos, 186
Rashtrakutras, 158, 174, 176; traits and style of, 174

Reid, Andrew, 141
Reisner, George, 133, 135, 152
Renaissance, 235, 249
Renfrew, Colin, 6
Ricouer, Paul, 227, 250, 252
Roma and Augustus. *See* Temple of Roma and Augustus
Roman: art collections, 22; copies, 22–26; empire, 70, 123; Greece, 141; republic, 106
Rome, 104, 106, 108–9, 114–15, 117–25
Rose, C. Brian, 231

Salzmann, Ariel, 229
Sanskrit, 158, 174, 181; sanskritized, 172
Saptamatrka, 168, 170
Saxe-Binford hypothesis number eight, 85–86
Schliemann, Heinrich, 81, 239
Schliemann, Sophie, 81
Seleucids, 44–45, 52, 70
Settar, 159
settlement patterns, 79, 83
Severus, Septimius, 28–29, 29f
shabti, 143
shaft grave, 84
Shaw, Wendy, 247–48
Shebitqo, 143, 147
Shiva, 169, 172
Shutruk-nahhunte, 10–11, 37, 229
Sinopoli, Carla, 141
Sippar, 10
site formation processes, 76
Smith, Adam T., 2, 69
social: classes, 233–34; complexity, 84, 183; persona, 91
Soja, Edward, 2, 185, 187, 218
Sontheimer, G. D., 168, 170, 180, 182
South Africa, 215, 223
space, 3, 185–86, 220
spatial strategies, 209
Speer, Albert, 251

Stamatakis, Panagiotis, 81
status, 85–86
Strabo, 22, 60, 69–70, 235
subjects, 47, 71
Sulla, 106–7
Sundara, 160, 161f, 162, 169, 180, 182
Susa, 10, 19–20, 26, 37

Taylor, William, 82
Teishebaini, 55, 63, 66–69
Telugu, 156; old, 158
Temple of Roma and Augustus, 104–5, 108–16, 118–24, 230–31
Thebes: Egypt, 138, 148; Greece, 80
Tholos tombs, 86, 89
Thucydides, 81, 242
Tigranes II (the Great), 61–62
Tiratsyan, G. A., 52
Tiryns, 81
Tomb of Unknown Soldier (Athens), 240–46, 242f, 243f
Török, László, 142, 150
tribe, 215–16
Trigger, Bruce, 1, 147, 188
Troy, 81
Tsaghkahovit plain, 56
Tsountas, Christos, 239
tumulus, tumuli, 82, 88
Tuthmose I, 137
Tuthmose III, 137, 232

Urartu, 44–45, 53–56
urbanism, 218

Vandeyk, Francesco, 236
Van Dyke, Ruth, 2, 71
Vatapi, 156, 158, 172; capital at, 178. *See also* Chalukyas
Velestinlis, Regas, 238
Venda, 216
Venice, 235–38

Vijayāditya, 173, 176
Vikramaditya I, 172–73
Villa dei Papiri, 23–26
Vinayaditya, 172–73

wealth, 93, 96
Wolf, Eric, 4
World War I, 240–45
World War II, 245

Yellamma (fertility goddess), 168, 168f, 169–70, 172; Ellama, 168; fertility cult, 169; identified with Lajja-Gauri, 179; temple of, 169–70; worshipped by Dhangars and Kurumbas, 170
Yervandid dynasty, 45, 52, 59, 72

Zeus, 67